Advance Praise for *Borders, Bandits, and Baby Wipes*

"A hilarious, tireless, and courageous look into what it is to be a modern-day explorer on the adventure of a lifetime. Bassam has an uncanny ability to put you right there in the moment with him, as if you were sitting shotgun." — Michael Kirtley, *National Geographic, Time, Newsweek*

"Bassam Tarazi's real-life adventure ignites the explorer in all of us by showing us parts of the world most of us haven't even dreamed of seeing, and parts of ourselves we're dying to discover." — Ben Polansky, co-founder of Matador Network

"Wow! I couldn't put it down. Bassam Tarazi has given us an incredible, riveting adventure with a unique human insight." — Derek Sivers, author of *Anything You Want*, founder of *CD Baby*

"What a ride! With entrepreneurial spirit, a philosopher's mind and the wit of a comic, Bassam Tarazi delivers a mighty jolt of global immersion and adventure." — Beri Meric, founder & CEO of IVY, The Social University

"A pure pleasure to read. Tarazi has written an ode to the explorer that reminds us why we travel in the first place. He illuminates all the beauty, frustration, wisdom and bonding that comes with trading our comfort zones for the inside of a rickety car in a foreign land." — Antonio Neves, author of *50 Ways to Excel in Your First Job (And in Life)*

"Bassam Tarazi takes the reader on a page-turning adventure few will ever get to experience in one lifetime, let alone many." — Matt Stabile, founder of *The Expeditioner*

"Bassam pushes the boundaries of what you think you know about our world, cultures and adventure — and leaves you wide-eyed and invigorated by his experiences." — Katie Quinn, video journalist, creator of *qkatie*

"Enthralling and inspiring. It's like Bill Bryson meets *Cannonball Run*. Tarazi's travel opus is a must-read because it reminds us why we choose to go into the great unknown in the first place."
— Ryan Van Duzer, Adventure Journalist

"It's a good old-fashioned quest through foreign lands mixed in with the self-discovery and immersion that only life on the open road can bring. This is a must-read for all those who love to explore, or those who wish they could." — Mario Schulzke, Founder of IdeaMensch

BORDERS, BANDITS AND BABY WIPES

A BIG ADVENTURE IN A TINY CAR

BASSAM TARAZI

Post Hill
PRESS

A POST HILL PRESS BOOK
ISBN: 978-1-68261-481-5
ISBN (eBook): 978-1-68261-482-2

Borders, Bandits, and Baby Wipes
A Big Adventure in a Tiny Car
© 2017 by Bassam Tarazi
All Rights Reserved

Cover art by Christian Bentulan

Map images provided by Google Maps. © Google, Inc.

Post Hill Press
New York • Nashville
posthillpress.com

Published in the United States of America

For Brooke and Greg

"Curiosity is the lust of the mind."

– Thomas Hobbes

Table of Contents

2:32 p.m., Kazakh–Russian Border near Shemonaika, Kazakhstan, August 11, 2014

"*Are* you a spy?" he repeated, without a crumb of sarcasm.

I looked down, pursed my lips, and snuck a laugh out of my nostrils. It wasn't that I didn't take him seriously; it was that I'd never been held to such international acclaim. I looked up at the 6-foot 2-inch, square-jawed Russian colonel flanked by two guards who, thankfully, had their machine guns pointed at the ground. The upper reaches of my unkempt beard crept far too high on my cheekbones for any modern sense of grooming, the mane on my head looked like a forgotten mangrove forest, and in between these oceans of hair was the patch of face I peered out from. The only weapon I toted was exhausted endurance.

If I were a secret agent, I had not been allocated the same wardrobe perks as James Bond. I wore Caribbean-blue, tattered flip-flops. A portion of my right big toenail was severed, and the rest of my nails were in dire need of a clipping. There were so many layers of dirt caked on my legs, insects could have fossilized in the fur. I had been wearing the same pair of hiking shorts for twenty-two days. My obnoxiously bright red shirt displayed an obscure illustration of a Mongolian warlord—perhaps Genghis Khan—with two Westerners in leather hats and the kind of goggles Chuck Yeager must have worn trying to break a land speed record, and the words "Mongol Rally" written in big letters.

I guess the colonel's question was a fair one since at that moment, my similarly attired cohorts Brooke and Greg were standing with us over an open silver box the size of a carry-on bag that could fit into a plane's overhead compartment. The box looked like a nuclear football, or something else a high-ranking cartel member might handcuff to his wrist while escorted by armed guards. Inside, cradled in black Styrofoam and surrounded by wires, giant batteries, a tiny camera, and a joystick, was a drone. This box had been confiscated from the back of our bumper sticker-plastered midget car—a 1997 Daihatsu Move. Its rear door remained open, displaying an assortment of duffels, packs, clothing, and goodness knows what else, looking more like a vagrant's overflowing shopping cart than a vehicle that had transported us from London to this inhospitable Russian border.

I might as well mention that the drone was indeed mine, and that, for reasons separate from that fact, Brooke and Greg were not on speaking terms with each other. They'd had a heated spat regarding driving tactics as we were leaving Kazakhstan two hours earlier. You know—the kind of drama that can erupt after 7,000 miles together, cooped up in a 42-horsepower coffin-on-wheels, with functional attributes so limited they didn't even include basic air conditioning.

I looked around at the scenery for a minute. If I hadn't known where I was, I would have guessed New England: soft rolling hills, lush green trees shadowing us on every side, and sunflowers earning their name in the summer splendor.

"Sir?"

The Russian-accented query reminded me of my actual whereabouts despite the visual similarities with the northeastern United States. Once again, we were going to need some border wizardry to slalom out of this mess.

Exactly how did we end up filthy, famished, frightened, and detained at the Russian border in the middle of a vehicular odyssey taking us one-third of the way around the planet?

I'll take responsibility for that.

Let's start from the beginning…

A License to Roam

As the youngest of three siblings and the only American-born child of a Palestinian father and a Dutch mother, I was never sheltered from the outside world because my family was *from* the outside world. During World War II, my mom's dad fought the Nazis barehanded and survived years in a worker's camp in Poland. In 1948, when my father was three years old, his family fled Palestine when it was partitioned to create Israel. My dad often reminisced about getting his PhD in Soviet-controlled Romania where "the walls had ears" during the late 1960s. There were more stories — about how my parents met in a Swiss mountain town, or how my brother and sister had to huddle under the dashboard of a car or in an empty bathtub to stay safe from gunfire in Beirut in the mid-1970s.

Ignorance and exclusion were not options for how my siblings and I were taught to process the realities of a complex world, even if we did grow up in idyllic Connecticut in the 1980s and '90s. And so, at a younger age than most, I had the tools and the support to climb the walls that limited most kids. My family experienced the world via maps and globes, through reading *National Geographic* and exchanging letters with our cousins in Europe, the Middle East, Australia, Atlanta, San Francisco, and Hong Kong. We sometimes celebrated weddings and holidays in Paris, Amsterdam, or Amman and we bonded through countless road trips up and down the Eastern Seaboard.

Our parents protected us from the puritanical myopia that grips much of the American psyche. I can remember vividly when I was seven years old and my dad, a theological scholar and Orthodox priest, took me to the movies and told the guy behind the counter, "One adult, one child for *Lethal Weapon*."

The man peered down to get a glimpse of me, then turned to my dad and asked, "Reverend, you know this is a R-rated movie, right?"

"I know," my dad replied, before turning to me and saying, "Bassam, you know what we're about to see is not real, right? It's a movie. You can't just go around shooting people."

"Yes, I know."

Perplexed, the attendant gave us the tickets and said, "Enjoy your movie."

My dad understood I could handle a little violence on the big screen because he had handled the realities of actual war when he was a boy, and he turned out just fine.

***

My mother, an oncology nurse, was raised in a country where breasts are seen on TV commercials and sex isn't the riotous taboo it was (and pretty much still is) in America, which is probably why on a Saturday morning when I was fourteen I walked into our kitchen and said, "Mom? I need to tell you something."

"What is it?" she replied, after putting the newspaper down and taking a sip of her tea.

"Melissa and I have decided that we are not going to have sex before we are married. We don't know why anyone would."

After a pause, she broke into body-convulsing laughter. I really didn't know what to make of it. After pulling herself together, she grabbed me by the hand and said, "Bassam, that is adorable, and I respect your decision, but you're going to change your mind, believe me."

She was right.

This didn't mean that we lived a libertarian free-for-all life. No, no, no...My father liked to remind me that the roof over my head was not "my home," it was his and my mother's and I was their guest until I had a home of my own. The rules of the house were not long nor especially strict, but they were absolute:

Don't raise your voice to your mother or father.
Don't ask Dad the same question that you just asked
Mom, hoping for a different answer.
Dinners will be eaten as a family and without television.
Eat what your mother cooked for you, including your
vegetables.
Use your brain.
Know the world.

These foundations were granite, immutable: respect, family dinners, think, read, and travel. That's pretty simple.

My parents were involved in all aspects of my childhood, from piano, to math, to soccer, to late-night diorama-making for science projects. Additionally, any minor rigidity in the household's already liberal law and order had been eased by my brother and sister, who had so graciously been raised before me. Perhaps because of this, I have a naturally defiant attitude towards the status quo. I wanted to play with my brother and his friends even though they were five years older. I wanted to be as smart as my sister. I wanted to know more. I wanted to do more. My parents supported my unending curiosity by providing a long leash. As a teenager, so long as I followed the basic canon of the house and did well in school, I was more or less able to do as I wished. Yeah, I partied, drank, and (finally) smoked some weed but I never went crazy with the privilege of unencumbered adolescence. The thought of disappointing my parents was always the silent (and sometimes maddening) voice of reason in my head.

I respect and cherish my folks greatly. Through their sacrifices, I saw the world and was entrusted with the freedom to choose the life I wanted. Regardless of what I was doing at any time—Boy Scouts, architecture camp, sports, filmmaking—they challenged me to be the best *me* that I could be. They taught me how a smile might save someone's life, that I'm no better than anyone else, that everyone is fighting their own battle, that the only option is to treat someone kindly, that I get out what I put in, and that I am always accountable for my actions. But most importantly, I was often reminded that the life I was given, the one "handed to me on a silver platter," was of no doing of my own, but one that was built with the sweat, toil, and luck of those who came before me. It was my duty to live a life worthy of that gift and those opportunities.

As if striking that same bell of wisdom, when I asked my aforementioned grandfather who had a little run-in with Hitler's SS during World War II what his best advice was, he responded, "Live an interesting life. No one wants to talk to an old man with no stories to tell."

Yes, sir.

As I grew older and made my own money, I continued to be much more interested in experiences over things, in stories over status. In my career, I took this inquisitiveness and became a scientist of the human experience. My first job out of college was as a nuclear engineer at Pearl Harbor. Then I wrote a few screenplays, took a detour in sunny California, spent half a decade helping build a hundred-million-dollar New York City construction company, got a "green" MBA (one focused on sustainable businesses), co-founded a film festival, and settled on a career as a business coach. The theme that remains constant no matter what I do is my monomania for travel. By my thirty-fourth birthday I had visited fifty countries. The stamps in my passport are from childhood travels, studies abroad, vacations, long weekends, the breaks between job changes, the free time of sometimes having my own business, and me throwing caution to the wind whenever the hell I could.

As a competitor and an athlete who no longer played organized sports, my trips started to become expeditions, a journey to be somewhere morphed into a quest to *get* there. I wanted to test my mental and physical capabilities. I hiked in Patagonia, scaled Mt. Kinabalu in Borneo, trekked to Everest Base Camp, navigated New Zealand's Grand Traverse, and climbed Mt. Kilimanjaro.

I like a little grit with my jaunts.

The more of the world I saw at its most primal and awesome, the more the Earth became my religion, the thing that grounded me and the truth that I needed to believe in, not just because of what it offered in that moment, but because it existed at all.

I love the Earth and the *idea* of the Earth.

I love the unpredictability of it; that no matter how well we're able to anticipate the seasons, the crops, and the tides, we can do very little to predict what the next year, month, or day of our lives will reveal.

I love the enormity of it. There's a sensation I get when I stand on an ocean's shore gazing out into the blue forever and think: *This is where a continent ends. Right here. I'm standing at the collision of two worlds — a collision whose existence we know intimately via maps we've traced with our fingers or globes we've spun. Land is only land because there is no sea, and it's here that my feet and ankles become part of their respective realms depending on the ebb and flow of the tides. For a few seconds, I am a tenant of a continent whose entire rocky story lies behind me, and in the next moment I am an occupant of the sea, at the mercy of the orchestra of currents playing their melody before me. The edge of two worlds, worlds that make up the entire surface of the moist mud ball we call Earth, ceding and gaining on each other in equal chunks, giving us the zero-sum boundary of a coastline. Isn't that amazing?*

I love the history of it; how the Earth displays the vast expanse of geologic time she's been through by giving us mountains, rivers, valleys, canyons, glaciers, lakes, and fossils.

I love the determination of it; how lives of all shapes and sizes clash and cohabit in billions of combinations and ecosystems, having arisen against inconceivable odds from one microscopic smudge that for a moment was the only living thing that ever existed. When this invisible blot looked at all the infinite nonexistence around it, it could have easily folded and said, "To hell with *this* nonsense," but instead said, "Nah. Not yet. In fact, I'm gonna cut myself in half so I have someone to share my story with."

I love the inevitability of time and its relentless surge forward, with or without me.

I love that for this ephemeral pulse, this sliver of chronological happenstance before my expiration date, I can look around and think, "I'm alive. *Holy shit*. I'm alive."

And what better way to combine terrestrial wonder, unpredictability, and gumption than the five-week Mongol Rally?

What Exactly Is It?

The Mongol Rally is the longest road trip you would ever want to take. It's a nearly 10,000-mile adventure from London to Ulaanbaatar, Mongolia, on an unspecified route, through terrain that would make a mountain goat's knees buckle, all in a vehicle inadequate for the task at hand. In other words, a machine that performs in the zone between a go-kart and a smart car. It's not a race, though. There is no award for finishing first. It's all about the journey *to* the destination and the experience of getting there, whether it takes weeks or months.

This fool's errand is the creation of a company called The Adventurists. They believe that travel has become too easy and that we have gotten soft as explorers. In their words, "Bollocks to that." Airplanes and all-inclusive packages have created a cultural teleport system that circumvents local customs, unplanned conversations, and developing-world complexities. Sidestepped are the millions of people whose identity can be corralled into a few syllables: Europeans, Midwesterners, or Uzbeks, refugees, or impoverished.

When you encounter the world one tire rotation at a time, you're forced to uncover the broad social brushstrokes of "they" to reveal the pointillism of "us." Up close, xenophobia loses its rigid borders of hostility through a kind gesture or a shared laugh. The Muslim becomes a Central Asian who becomes a Turkmen who becomes a hardworking father of three, who becomes Ahmed. Ahmed is no longer just a Muslim, but a man trying to provide for his kids by selling fruits and vegetables on the side of a desert road.

Stereotypes save time. Understanding takes effort.

The inaugural Mongol Rally was held in 2004. That year a mere six teams started in London and only four cars reached

Ulaanbaatar. The following year, forty-three teams started and eighteen finished. By 2006, the rally had gone beyond a novelty and 167 teams made the journey, with 117 reaching the ultimate goal.

It's not all about senseless spending and off-roading adventures. On top of the eight hundred and fifty-dollar entry fee, The Adventurists required each team to raise eight hundred and fifty dollars for a charity of their choice and another eight hundred and fifty dollars for Cool Earth, an organization that works alongside indigenous villages to halt rainforest destruction. Teams have raised more than six and a half million dollars for charity, to date.

Respect.

***

I first heard of the Mongol Rally in 2008 when I received an email newsletter from the travel website www.whereareyounow. com asking me to "Sort Out My Summer" via all kinds of trips and experiences. I was about to hit "Delete" when I read, "Mongol Rally…The 2008 adventure launches shortly, traveling a third of the way around the earth from London to Mongolia in cars with no more than 1 litre of power!" This seemed like it would be a decent chapter in an interesting life. There was a link. I clicked. And that, as they say, was that. I had to do this. Someday.

Year after year, timing and finances were never right. However, by the end of the summer of 2013, I had been running my own coaching and consulting firm, Colipera, for a year, helping business owners do the things they said they wanted to do (because let's face it, even successful people lack follow-through). I had self-published two books on accountability, created on online course called *Ready. Set. Finish.*, taught classes via General Assembly (a global education company), and spoken at various universities and companies, garnering a cool little following of people who liked my no-nonsense, you're-responsible-for-your-own-happiness, no-one-cares-more-about-your-goals-than-you-do delivery.

The 2014 rally didn't start until July 20. I could feasibly arrange my schedule and savings for a year in order to take off for a month or two. On August 11, 2013, eleven months before launch, I crawled into uncertainty's playpen and paid the entry fee for a team that didn't exist and a car I didn't have.

Who the Hell Would Do Something Like This with Me?

Anyone who has been lucky to travel knows that you can't just email an invitation to everyone in your address book willy-nilly. There are friends who stay friends because you *don't* travel with them. After carefully selecting the names of only the true travel veterans I had befriended during my exploratory past, I was confident that my initial dispatch would have tens of them scrambling to join me on the greatest motoring enterprise on earth.

I was mistaken.

Competitions like the Mongol Rally, Tough Mudders, Spartan Races, Ironman triathlons, and even *Survivor* are all a subset of events that may be fun, but not "water park" fun. Because of that, the Mongol Rally is one of those things that 100 percent of people say would be awesome to undertake, but when forced to commit, the vast majority will be smothered in a rubble of excuses like jobs, relationships, time commitments, and money.

"Dude, if you do it next summer, I'm in!"

Huh? You can't commit to something eleven months from now but you can twenty-three months from now? Right…that sounds like you're flakier than baklava.

Maybe my "Criteria for a Teammate" was too demanding:

- Be mechanically inclined
- Speak Kazakh
- Drive a stick shift
- Be able to ward off armed bandits

I wasn't going to make the trip by myself. I'm crazy, just not that crazy. Would I join some other team? No. I'm too much of a control freak to pass the decision-making mantle to someone else.

I tried again, this time via a Facebook post and thankfully, some of the spaghetti stuck. Enter:

Greg Johnson, thirty-four. Greg is a good friend of mine from college who, before reading my Facebook post, had been feeling the need for a life reset, or at least some extended time off. He hadn't been out of the country since studying abroad in Australia in 2002, and he hadn't had a proper vacation for over two years. He'd given up that luxury to work day and night for a tech startup that couldn't seem to "start up" enough to get out of the whitewater and the full-time treading of its staff that came with it. Greg was having a few existential, "What the hell am I working for?" moments when my Facebook post popped up in his feed. His response was simple: "I am so in. I need something like this more than ever." Serendipitously, he's a gear-head, and big enough (6-foot 2-inches, played football and lacrosse, does CrossFit—*take it easy, ladies*) to provide protection. Beyond the practical and physical attributes he brought to the team, Greg has lived in San Diego for so long that his walk had slowed to the speed a surfer needs to blend into his surroundings, and his stress receptors had numbed to stubs, giving him an air of equanimity no matter the situation.

Brooke Blackman, twenty-seven. I met Brooke on a Semester at Sea reunion cruise. I realize how bourgeois that may sound, so let me explain. Semester at Sea is a study-abroad program on a cruise ship that circumnavigates the globe. (Okay, that *still* sounds bourgeois.) She is an avid traveler and as a flight attendant for private jets, she's done her fair share of on-the-go problem-solving and please-sit-the-hell-down crisis management.

However, it was precisely this posh style of travel that Brooke was trying to get away from. She had seen plenty of the Earth from the pressurized air and filtered reality of the cabin of a G6 but she wanted an eye-level experience. While Brooke is beautiful, she isn't a girly-girl. She has the patience of a wolverine and the subtlety of a howitzer. When she was seven years old she worked at a hobby shop and got paid in jelly beans every two weeks. At twelve, she worked at a dinner theater so she could save enough money to buy her own bicycle. When she saw my post, her immediate reaction was unfettered excitement. A bonus was that Brooke knew way more about cars than I did, so she and Greg could tend to our vehicle while I navigated or ate a snack.

***

Our goals were similar but distinct, like three species from the same genus. Brooke wanted to prove to herself that she was strong enough to do something like the Mongol Rally. Greg needed a life reboot. I wanted to travel in new ways to new places and I was determined to make it to Ulaanbaatar. After all, my whole coaching shtick was "Ready. Set. Finish." I needed an accomplishment I could point at.

Greg and Brooke wouldn't meet until a week before the rally, when we flew to London from New York. Then again, I didn't even know Brooke that well. Before this trip, we had probably spent no more than twenty-four hours together in the same room. I was a little concerned about going with someone who wasn't much more than an acquaintance, but this entire trip was going to be an expedition of firsts, so why get picky now? Plus, a team of three was safer (and cheaper) than a team of two.

Earning the Right to Launch

Saying The Adventurists organized the rally is like saying a school organized a cafeteria food fight. They provided the playing field but we were on our own when it came to making it through unscathed.

The eight hundred and fifty-dollar entry fee covered some launch day and arrival coordination (assuming we reached Mongolia). This, of course, didn't include the purchase of the car, the visas, the plane tickets, the food, the gear, or anything else the three of us would forget right up until the day we left London, not to mention the fundraising efforts we had to undertake.

Since putting this team together was my idea and I had traveled the most, I became the de facto leader when it came to route selection and overall logistics. Brooke would handle the car search, and Greg, being the most tech savvy, spearheaded our logo, team webpage, and fundraising page.

The Route

All we had to do was drive a tiny car from London to Ulaanbaatar — cities separated by 4,338 miles as-the-crow-flies (about the distance from Portland, Oregon, to Lima, Peru), but on roads that do not follow the crow. Although there are an infinite number of tarmac tendrils and dirt divots between London and Mongolia, the geographic obstacle influencing our most important decision was the Caspian Sea. The Caspian was the heart of our journey and the hellacious routes that went north, south, and across it were the major arteries. The northern passage called for a dual entry Russian visa and travel via Ukraine; the southern course meant navigating through Iran; and the central track demanded we cross the Caspian Sea on a ship. (There was also a fourth way, but it should barely be mentioned in a whisper. We could be complete lame-asses by driving 5,500 miles from England through France, Belgium, Germany, Poland, Belarus, Russia, and Mongolia, but that would be like doing the Tour de France on a motorcycle and patting yourself on the back.)

I chose the roughly 10,000-mile central route (about the distance from Juneau, Alaska, to Cape Town, South Africa) because bopping around war-torn Ukraine (which Russia had just invaded) seemed ill-advised, and three Americans motoring through Iran wasn't a diplomatic situation I wanted to test, as much as I would have liked to visit. Sailing out of Baku, Azerbaijan, couldn't be that hard, right?

In addition, I had three nonnegotiable must-sees in Europe: Berlin, Budapest, and Istanbul. Other than that, I was open to any suggestions or desires Greg and Brooke had. Their requests were to avoid places where we could be kidnapped (Brooke) or detained (Greg). While I couldn't make promises on either of those petitions, everyone seemed pretty happy with my twenty-country route that included all the 'Stans except for Afghani(stan) and Paki(stan).

In order to run the gauntlet lawfully, we needed to procure visas for Turkey, Azerbaijan, Turkmenistan, Uzbekistan, Tajikistan, Kazakhstan, and Russia, some of which had applications rivaling those of Ivy League colleges.

You getting all this?

It ended up being a bureaucratic collage of wallet-sized pictures, digital photos on a white (not cream) background, proof of hotel bookings (which we later canceled), international drivers' licenses, travel insurance, scans, re-scans, originals in black pen with no corrections, bank statements, notarized letters, notarized letters on *letterhead*, international UPS fees, and a partridge in a pear tree. It never seemed to end. The Russians wanted to know every country we'd been to in the last *ten years* and the contact information for each of our last three bosses. That third boss of mine was a drunken restaurant owner in South Carolina with whom I hadn't been in touch for nine years.

*Ah...*nation states and their borders.

The Car

This wasn't just about purchasing a car that fit the requirements of the rally; it was about procuring it, about three Americans getting it registered to an address in the UK, and about an insurance broker granting us a rare short-term policy. The criteria for our chariot:

- Budget: one thousand, five hundred dollars. Anything more would be sinful.
- Vehicle size: At least four doors and a roof rack. We are all quite tall and weren't interested in developing scoliosis.
- Wheels: Preferably four.
- Engine size (max): 1,000 ccs (1.0L); this is the only requirement The Adventurists make. How small is a 1,000-cc engine? Vespas have 850 cc. Some golf carts have 500 cc.
- Transmission: Standard; in a standard car, the driver chooses how much power is exerted to get over a hill or out of a ditch, and it's a car that can be started with a push and a roll in case of a dead battery.

From her home in Miami, Brooke scoured European car sites online, but she had serious problems finding a car crappy enough for our needs.

This piece of shit will work perfectly! Oh — it has a 1.3-liter engine and is therefore a tank. Next!

Putting into the search bar things like: "Weed-whacker engine, uncool, unfit, marginally safe, wait, don't send that to the scrapyard yet," wasn't a magnet for results.

Initially, we tried to purchase our car in Holland since I have family there, but it was far too difficult without being a Dutch citizen. We conceded and eventually moved our search to England, where steering wheels are on the right-hand side of the car. Throughout the 10,000-mile trip ahead of us, only the first hundred miles had traffic laws benefiting a car with this setup.

Splendid.

Adding insult to idiocy, when sitting on the right-hand side of a standard car, first and second gear were no longer being "pulled" towards the body with the right hand; the shift was "pushed" away from the body with the left. I couldn't imagine that being a problem navigating a roundabout during a sandstorm.

After months and months of searching, Brooke found a 1997 Daihatsu Move SE — the Japanese van-car midget lovechild.

Steel wheels, stick shift, a roof rack, headroom for a giraffe, *and* a spoiler. It had 847 cc. and 42 horsepower. *Forty-two!* A Toyota Corolla has 140 HP. A Nissan Leaf has 107 HP. Riding lawnmowers are around 20 HP. We had 42 to transverse a third of the earth. Brand-new, this puppy would do 0–60 in 19.4 seconds. A Porsche 911 Turbo could do 0-60-0 (that's zero to sixty to zero) *three times* before we did 0–60 once. Think about that.

We were outrunning nothing.

Have I mentioned it didn't have power steering?

The dealership offering the car, Webbs of Ealing, was surprised at how excited we were to take scrap metal off their lot and their books. Brooke worked with Phil, the saint of sales, who was incredibly accommodating. My cousin lived in London and agreed to take the car for a test drive. He noticed the clutch was a bit worn and the emergency brake light was on, but the car did exist and it did operate. Luckily, the previous owner had new front shocks installed and kept good maintenance records. We agreed on a sale at the end of April for one thousand, four hundred and thirty-six dollars. The dealership was kind enough to store it free of charge until our arrival in London in two months' time.

We had a car. Now we had to get her repaired, registered, insured, and packed before we could launch on July 20.

I had suggested we call our team either *Trans-Siberian Fail Road* or *Parco Molo*. On hearing those, Brooke's grandmother suggested *Marco Polover*. It was brilliant. We loved it. Brooke christened our car *Donata*—Marco Polo's wife's name. Maybe her name should be: Do-*nada*. We would find out soon enough.

Future ralliers should check out Webbs of Ealing and ask for Phil. He was amazing!

Webbs of Ealing
Hanger Lane
Ealing
London W5 2ED

The Charity

I had done some work with and knew the executive team at Global Glimpse, a nonprofit that provides short-term, life-changing international education for high school students from all socioeconomic backgrounds. This was a cause very dear to my heart because from a young age I had been fortunate to have international adventures simply because my parents had the means to provide them to me and my siblings. Many children don't get that chance.

Greg and Brooke were fully on board with the cause as our beneficiary.

We didn't want just to raise money for Global Glimpse, though; we wanted to raise money for ourselves to help offset the roughly twenty thousand dollars the rally would collectively cost us. We came up with the idea of a one-for-you and one-for-me campaign. For every dollar we raised, fifty cents would go to Global Glimpse and fifty cents to us. The better our sell was and the cooler our webpage looked, the more money we'd bring in. We skirted embezzlement charges by actually communicating this ratio to our would-be donors.

While I put together our intro video, Greg designed our logo and created our website explaining who we were, what the rally was, who we were raising money for, and what the benefits of contributing were (other than the obvious). We came up with six donation tiers that yielded different perks: from a personalized video thank-you from the three of us, to a photo book we'd mail you at the end of the rally, to a two-foot wide sticker of your logo or whatever photo you wanted that would be plastered on our car for the entire journey.

On May 8, 2015, with the website www.marcopolover.com up and running, we launched our sixty-day fundraising campaign on www.indiegogo.com, channeled our inner salespeople, and hit up friends and loved ones for cash in all denominations. Our efforts brought in thirteen thousand, one hundred dollars from fifty-four supporters. Half of that (six thousand, five hundred and fifty dollars) went to Global Glimpse, eight hundred and fifty dollars went to Cool Earth, and the rest went to us.

The British Invasion

When Greg, Brooke, and I clinked glasses of whiskey outside our departure gate at JFK, the excitement of finally heading to London emanated from our phosphorescent smiles like we were fifteen-year-olds celebrating the inaugural ransack of our parents' liquor cabinet.

We spent every day and night during the week before launch at my cousin's house in London prepping Donata and ourselves. Getting a car registered and insured in the UK as a nonresident was not a cheap, tidy process done over tea and crumpets. Servicing our street-legal turtle shell was also a hit on the wits and the wallet. We paid 120 percent more for the repairs on the car (new clutch kit, emergency brake, sump guard, air filters) than we did for the car in the first place. And still, she stuttered at startup and the AC stood for "Ain't a Comin'." Yeah, our baby was the runt of the litter but we loved her because she was *our* runt.

We were in the parking lot at Halfords, a company that sells car and bike parts, jerry-rigging our cargo carrier to the roof with *straps*—because we were unable to find anything that screwed securely into the rack—when an old man and woman pulled up. The gentleman inquired in his British accent, "Wot ya dooin?"

Brooke announced, "We're on an adventure! We're driving from London to Mongolia to raise money for charity."

The man looked at us with concern, and pointed insultingly at Donata. "In *that*?"

Our unbridled confidence in the face of constant befuddlement from others was a real-life lesson in the yin and yang of faith and disbelief. Possibility and stupidity might be the same truth—your stance is not a universal surety, but simply dependent on the angle of your perspective. If we overthought how preposterous a task we were trying to undertake, we would cast ourselves in the leaden boots of doubt.

***

There were conversation threads on the private Facebook message board that synced all the Mongol Rally teams together so that we could see what certain groups were bringing on the trip and what we might be forgetting. Realizing and deciding what we needed to buy had been a Sisyphean surprise. Five pounds of baby wipes, a plastic toilet seat, racing goggles, and a wind-up radio? *Check!* The upside-down exchange rate from USD to British Sterling was like having to pay a loan shark 55 percent on top of whatever number we saw on price tags. We spent money like Babylonian kings and we hadn't even begun the rally yet, but we'd rather have a trip fail because of an unknown that we couldn't prepare for, than a kind-of-known that we just didn't want to prepare for. When we needed that tool, bug spray, map, zip tie, or metal jerry can filled with extra gasoline, we'd be ready. Of course, had we consulted an oracle, we would have also been told to bring a Breathalyzer, a bucket, walkie-talkies, fog lights, and tons more snacks, but those are stories for later.

We packed Donata, inexorably tied to the volumetric storage limits that the Daihatsu engineers had delineated for us—11 cubic feet (or 80 gallons). In comparison, a Volkswagen Golf has 25 cubic feet, two and a half times what we had. We figured out what couldn't fit by Tetrisian trial and error. Speaking of geometric shapes, one of the largest items in our car was the approximately 30-inches x 18-inches x 8-inches rectangular metal box that housed my DJI Phantom drone. As if three Americans trying to cross Central Asian borders by way of a sticker-plastered crap-mobile wouldn't draw us enough attention, I had decided to bring a drone and GoPro camera to really spit in the face of "blending in."

I'm a documentarian of bold desires.

We had so much stuff that we were forced to remove the back right seat so that a wall of luggage filled the floor-to-ceiling space behind the driver. Not much wiggle room. Also, the back window on the left was broken, and descended only four inches or so, turning our backseat into ground zero for automotive claustrophobia, only a marginal improvement to being bound, tied, and held in the trunk of a sedan.

Oh…and all necessary apologies and condolences to our axles. We were going to be exceeding the maximum weight limit of the car by three or four hundred pounds.

July 19, 2014—All Roads Lead to This

It was Launch Day Eve. In the eleven months of preparation, 2,421 emails went back and forth between me and many other human beings regarding the trip. That's more than seven emails per day, every day. Emails not just to Greg and Brooke, but also to The Adventurists, visa services, embassies, consulates, prospective donors, possible dealerships, shady mechanics, and transatlantic airlines.

Finally, there was no more paperwork, no more fundraising, no more lists, no more deliveries, and no more trips to the supermarket or hardware stores. Forget about *getting* to Mongolia, the logistics involved in legally operating, owning, and moving a car, with us in it, across twenty countries, was a feat unto itself. Three hundred and thirty days of prep for thirty days of travel had sapped us mentally and economically, but we were also giddy, having now truly earned the right to launch.

For almost a year, the entire rally and all its preparation and unknowns had been ahead of us, but the first part of the rally was about to be *behind* us. On our last night in London, I lay in bed wondering, *What would we do if we needed a new transmission in Serbia? How would we find a doctor if we got into a car accident in Kyrgyzstan? What would happen if we were arrested in Turkmenistan? When and where was I going to be able to masturbate over the next month?* (Priorities!)

I was dealing with the inescapable weariness we all feel towards things that have not yet started. I was manifesting and magnifying fear because my brain knew that the next day would bring change, and it didn't know if it wanted to cling to the existing conditions of my life or if the risk of the journey was worth the emotional reward. I seesawed between exploration and status quo, between stupidity and common sense, between, "Live a little!" and "Are you insane?" Between, "Go see the world" and "I just want to go home," between, "We probably shouldn't do this" and "We're never going to forget this."

On top of these Mongol Rally fears, I was also wrestling with thoughts about my professional future. Over the previous year things had gone great for me as a coach, speaker, and writer but the constant "always on" world of a solopreneur was not allowing me to totally let go on this trip.

One of the main catalysts to becoming a coach was the work-from-anywhere, live-anywhere geographic freedom that it would provide me, but in order to be anyone in the coaching business I had to connect with the outside world and build their trust. I had to give, I had to blog, I had to tweet, I had to share…constantly. The irony was that in my quest for freedom, I was becoming a slave to my online persona. I worried how people I didn't know perceived me, because I needed them. "They" would fund my freedom. I was always plotting and creating ways to make more money helping people, even if I secretly thought that a particular person had no chance at succeeding at what they were doing. Advising became transactional. Monthly coaching agreements paid monthly rent. Speaking engagements bankrolled future travel arrangements. I was never the paragon of selflessness in life, but there now seemed to be a contract to my kindness and I didn't know if I was starting to lose the ability to be deeply empathetic. The cherry on top of this conflict cupcake was that I constantly wondered whether I was really good at what I was doing as a coach or if I was good at acting the part.

Real confidence boosting stuff…

If this wasn't enough for me to make sense of, a few weeks before the rally, Omnibuild—the construction management company where I previously worked full-time and was now consulting for—had asked me what it would take to get me back working full-time. I really loved the team at this company—they supported my push to having my own coaching business in 2012 and were even the biggest financial sponsors of Marco Polover. Now they were growing tremendously and they wanted me to do for them and their staff what I did for other entrepreneurs and companies. They told me I could name my title and salary. Not a bad proposition. But I had my own business. Wasn't that supposed to be everyone's dream? Would I be selling out if I went back to work for The Man? Omnibuild told me to enjoy my trip, think about their proposal, and we could discuss when I was back.

The decisions swirling through my brain that night triggered so much illogical anxiety of the upcoming expedition and my professional future that part of me tried to think up a reason why I *couldn't* go on the rally tomorrow. Thankfully, I didn't bolt. I took some deep breaths and reminded myself that I had prepped almost a year for this. I had teammates counting on me to be the leader of the squad. Friends, family, and colleagues had donated more than thirteen thousand dollars in support of Global Glimpse and our Mongolian quest.

Even more powerful than all that, I had to go because that's what adventurers do. From Nellie Bly to Neil Armstrong. From Amelia Earhart to Edmund Hillary. From Gertrude Bell to Ernest Shackleton, we've always been infatuated with the explorer. Travel is the common denominator in the language of "cool." It elicits interest. It signifies status. It's the opportunities it beckons, the freedom it implies, and the feelings it evokes. It's about doing your life, your way, in that moment.

Travel is everyone's chance at fame. Stories are our currency.

Day 1

Brooke, Greg, and I wheeled out of northwest London at 5 a.m.

Brooke, Greg, and I wheeled out of northwest London at 5 a.m. dressed like we were going to the gym. Comfort above all else. Wherever there wasn't a sticker covering the maroon paint of her body, Donata glimmered in the early morning sun. On her roof, the jerry can and spare tire had been snared into the strap assembly system that corralled the cargo carrier. We'd gorged on a sublime breakfast my cousin had prepared — eggs, pancakes, fruit, yogurt, granola, bread, jam, and Austrian honey. We'd talk about that breakfast for weeks.

Assuming the launch proceedings went as planned, later that evening we'd reach Emmen, a small town in northeast Holland. Cousins from my mother's side of the family would be waiting for us.

We drove across The River Thames, turned into Battersea Park on Carriage Drive, and followed signs for the Mongol Rally staging area. We couldn't miss it! More than two hundred cars were positioned side by side in four orderly columns in a parking lot south of the Children's Zoo. Most of these teams had camped there overnight. Some people were disheveled, hungover messes, stumbling around like they had awoken in a cornfield on the third day of Woodstock. It didn't take us long to hear the story about a guy who'd punctured his testicle trying to scale one of the wrought-iron fences that surrounded the park. He was now in the hospital getting his speared nut put back together and hoped to meet his team in Uzbekistan.

At the other end of the spectrum were the teams dressed in suits and tuxedos, making the final cosmetic additions to their cars, embracing the unwritten rule (unwritten because Marco Polover sure as hell did not know about it) that launch day is best experienced as half costume party and half Westminster Dog

Show. One car had a whiskey barrel on top, one had a foosball table, one had a *sailboat*. Five guys in a pink Toyota Previa were securing a ten-foot-high inflatable giraffe to their roof. Another team was attaching a *welded* cage and stripper pole to theirs.

Then there was Marcus. He was driving an incandescent blood red Ferrari. The Adventurists let him in as a comedic exception, because driving to Mongolia in a high-priced sports car with the ground clearance of a vacuum cleaner was as impractical as driving there in Donata. The most amazing part about Marcus was his attitude. It was a brew of complete and utter lack of preparation (his car looked like it was packed with enough provisions to comfortably make it back and forth to a family picnic down the road) mixed with an excessive dose of optimism somehow bereft of all arrogance. I was fascinated by Marcus's unthreatening, buoyant mind-set. It was a vintage of *joie de vivre* that I had never tasted.

This was the human fabric of the Mongol Rally.

Walking among the teams and around the cars, there was a sense of camaraderie, but it was protective, like allies in a war. We were united by the expedition but solo in the pursuit. Our amazing trip was just part of a larger overlapping quilt sewn from the cloth of curiosity. There were people who were planning to zip through Russia and get to Mongolia in two weeks, and there were others who would drive through Italy, Greece, and Iran. There were those who were going to hit up the Pamir Highway in Tajikistan. We wouldn't see the majority of these people again so it didn't pay to build a strong bond with random teams in London. It was "us dot com," for better or worse.

I smashed the proverbial champagne bottle on my drone and took it out for its maiden voyage. From high above the parking lot, these variegated automobiles were laid proud, in perfect symmetrical order, like a psychedelic battleship fleet. It was one of the most iconic shots I got from the drone all trip.

Finally, we were told to get into our vehicles and start our engines. A mix of *whirrs*, backfire, and staccato stuttering emanated from the exhausts and hoods of this Legion of Vroom.

Whoever could start their engines joined in with what groups of motorcyclists know all too well: the dickhead tendency to rev your engines while stopped and in neutral at an intersection. It was like hearing an amplified beehive on a construction site in a fully operational manufacturing plant. But could you blame us? This was it. It was H-hour, D-day. I am Donata, hear me roar.

Behind the wheel, Greg steered our car into the longest conga line ever, eventually taking us up and over the starting ramp. Before leaving London, The Adventurists had suggested that all teams take a scenic drive out of the city by way of Big Ben, Parliament, Buckingham Palace, and the like. On the Tower Bridge, hundreds of friends and family members of rally teams showered us with cheers and well wishes. They shared our euphoria and splendor in what we were about to experience. We felt royal and humbled all at once.

Originally, we had planned to take the ferry across the English Channel but my cousin reminded us that the Chunnel would save us almost two hours even though it was thirty-seven dollars more per person. This was the first lesson on the road less traveled: Figure out the monetary value of your time and be happy to pay anything that fits into that equation. For us, two hours was worth far more than thirty-seven dollars apiece.

On our way to the coast of England on the M20 highway, we saw, passed, and were passed by plenty of other rally teams with passengers hanging out of windows, riding on roofs, or standing next to cars that had already broken down. The normal people on the highway must have thought that they were on the set of some Kubrickian version of *Mad Max*.

When the road split between Dover and Folkestone, I was happy to see about 90 percent of the cars go to the ferry (at Dover) and only 10 percent go to the Chunnel (at Folkestone). Not only were we saving time on the crossing, we were avoiding the sure-to-be shit show of far too many rally cars trying to get onto the same ferry.

***

At 31.4 miles in length, the Chunnel is an engineering marvel. The actual train has no windows, no glitz, and no glam—just mechanical readiness. We loaded our cars single file, with a Mongol Rally team from Ireland behind us. There were no seats on the train but we were allowed to get out of our cars and mingle for the thirty-five-minute trip.

Since the United Kingdom (for now) and France are both part of the European Union, there are no border checkpoints between them. However, leave it to the French to throw a wrench in the travel wheel. I noticed the Irish team studying a diagram so large and comprehensive, I thought it must be blueprints for a nuclear device. Instead, it was a description of how we were to place glare-reducing stickers onto our headlights. A lack of glare-reducing stickers equals a ticket in France. This diagram had the placement locations for pretty much every make and model of car that could be on the road in 2014. Unsurprisingly, it did *not* include a 1997 Daihatsu Move SE, so we'd have to improvise. Brooke channeled her inner arts-and-crafts, cut out a few shapes from our peacock-patterned duct tape, and put them on our light bulbs to show that an effort was made to be somewhat lawful.

The Irish team also had a Euro Travel Kit—something else we lacked. Apparently, if you put your hazard lights on in Europe, you have to place reflective warning triangles behind your car and wear a high visibility vest while doing so. How we missed buying a mandatory travel kit for one of the two continents we'd be driving in was a bit baffling but—no problem—we didn't plan on breaking down.

What else?

In France, the law was that every car on the road needed to carry a Breathalyzer. *Jesus.* How prevalent was drinking and driving in France that the cops were churning through Breathalyzers faster than toupees in a monsoon?

Under low-hanging, undulating gray skies we entered France via Coquelles on the A16 highway. We scanned for cops or police checkpoints. The hilarity of our plight was put into context when a sign for "Dunkirk" whizzed by. Here we were sprinting twenty miles to the Belgian border on perfect roads during peacetime while sweating the consequences of a slice of tape on our headlights, in a place where in 1940 the Nazis dumped the Allies into the sea, forcing them to retreat to England.

Hey, champagne problems are still problems. Thankfully, we made it out of France unscathed.

Belgium sped by—*Look! Antwerp!* Before we knew it, we were in The Netherlands, land of my mother, where the roads were efficient, beautiful, and economical, like Dutch architecture. Curves were cleaner, angles were crisper, colors were richer, signs were clearer. It was like the Department of Transportation designed everything as if a guest were still sleeping in their house: considerate, tiptoeing softly, not an extra noise made, but breakfast was warm and ready.

Holland's extraordinarily smooth terrain (26 percent of the country is below sea level—hence the importance and lore of little Dutch boys plugging dikes) provides unobstructed views of fields, farms, and cows for miles on end. Inevitably, during our drive through the lush countryside the blended aroma of budding flowers, cut grass, and fresh manure filled the car. There is something weirdly charming about the scent of preindustrial effort.

"Oooh, what's that smell, Bassam?"

"That, Brooke, is Holland."

"It's kind of gross but…I kind of like it."

"Me too," said Greg.

This is probably a good time to mention one of our most important rules: No Driving at Night. I had spent months researching routes, distances, and average time of stops to figure out how we could always move during the long summer days. Donata was barely fit for daytime travel in an empty parking lot, let alone foreign roads in the pitch dark. Unfortunately, traffic, detours, and the fact that we were driving a seventeen-year-old buggy meant we were now staring at looming nightfall under swollen gunmetal skies, tens of miles away from Emmen.

And then...the heavens opened.

I can't remember the last time I had seen a storm like this but it was surely in a hurricane.

It was terrifying.

Our headlights pierced through the rain about as well as honey flung at a screen door. Our windshield wipers moved like a man in a straightjacket trying to chase away a swarm of wasps. The excitement of being on the rally was replaced with the realization that we might die on the first day.

Remember, our cargo carrier was *strapped* to our roof—not bolted into the rack—so the bands went *over* the cargo carrier, *through* a door, across the inside ceiling of our car until it connected to the other side. This did not make for a tight seal at the windows. Water accumulated on and dripped off the two horizontal straps that were ingeniously placed over the front and back seats, leaving us wet and in need of a bucket for bailing.

With towels draped all over our interior, we hydroplaned into Emmen around 9 o'clock, three hours after our initial ETA. My dashing, retired uncle and his three beautiful, blonde-haired, fair-skinned daughters, each a mother in her own right, came out of the house to greet us. I could see conflicting feelings dueling it out in their minds: *I'm so excited to see Bassam; I can't believe he's actually trying to drive to Mongolia in that thing.*

Over dinner, my relatives all but gave us the obligatory pat on the back for the sure-to-be failed effort. Maybe they would be proven right, but for now, Belgian beer filled our stomachs and muffled the doubting voices inside our heads. Day 1 was complete. That was to be celebrated.

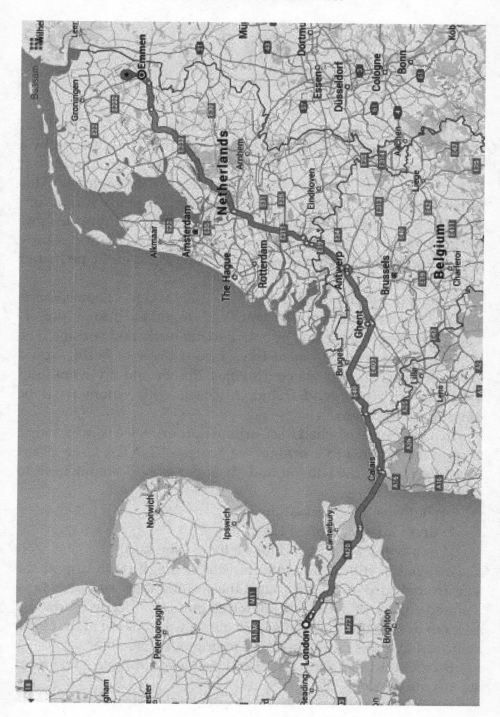

Day 2

Brooke checked the Mongol Rally Facebook page and learned that in Belgium one of the rally cars had been flipped and totaled by a truck. It was not as if the trucker hit a raccoon scurrying in front of him—he didn't see a *car* he'd rear-ended on the highway. This is how small and non-formidable our vehicles were. If our run-in with the Dutch typhoon hadn't drawn our attention to how dangerous this trip could be, the news of this accident certainly did. We emphatically renewed our "No driving at night, no matter what" vow.

Fattened up on breakfast and with packets of *stroopwafels* (think: waffles and caramel mushed together into a perfect cookie) for snacks, we said goodbye to my uncle and cousins. The clouds parted and we hoped the six-hour drive to Berlin would be uneventful so that we could enjoy dinner and an evening of partying with my good friend, Michael, with whom we'd be staying for the night.

Just before we reached the German border, as we went through a roundabout next to a bridge, we heard a *CLING-CLI-ng-Cling-cling-cli-cl*…and then the sound disappeared off somewhere to our right.

"What was that?" asked Brooke.

"I don't know," replied Greg.

"Let's swing around and take a look," she said.

In what is still a complete miracle to me, Brooke turned the car around, drove back through the roundabout, and somehow spotted a piece of metal in a stretch of grass that needed mowing. She ran over to the spot while I, of course, was looking at the clock, annoyed that this detour was tightening our timetable.

Brooke returned with a bolt so large it could have come from an aircraft carrier.

"Greg, is this ours?" she asked.

"If it is, it isn't good. A bolt this big is only one of two things: a suspension bolt or an engine mount bolt."

I wasn't buying it. I ate the rest of my salami and cheese sandwich, convinced we'd heard Santa Claus and reindeer bells. Even if that was a bolt to a vehicle, there was no way Donata was shedding off integral parts of her frame on the velvety Dutch roads.

Greg said, "There's nothing we can do about it now, but maybe we can stop at a garage one day and have them take a look."

On we went...kind of. After entering German woodlands, we were supposed to take the A31 highway south. It was as simple a navigating task as Vasco de Gama sailing from Lisbon to Gibraltar, but we somehow missed the turn and proceeded to trace the sign of the cross on the roads as we went east, west, east, north, south, north before we headed back east to Berlin. One hour and ten minutes into our drive, we were already one hour behind schedule. *Wonderful.*

A few hours later, we stopped for a McDonald's lunch about sixty miles west of Hannover. Back in the car, Brooke put it in reverse and Greg said, "I just felt the chassis shift."

Even a Luddite could tell you that couldn't mean anything good. Greg and Brooke opened the hood and assessed the miniature engine. Greg asked me to put the car in reverse and release the clutch. I did and they yelled in unison: "Stop, stop, stop!"

No, no, guys, it's fine. Let's get to Berlin.

Luckily for us, there was a mechanic that shared the parking lot with the McDonalds. Unluckily for us, they did not service Daihatsus. They gave us the address of a place that did in a town called Herford, twenty minutes south.

We located the garage after a little bit of orienteering fanfare. The lovely Annette, a co-owner of the dealership/garage, met us when we pulled in. She was in her early forties and had her inquisitive, ten-year-old daughter with her. Thank God Annette was bilingual, because we were not. Forget about the car trouble, she wanted to know what we were doing in a car like ours in the first place. We told her about the rally and she pointed at Donata, asking, "In *zaat?*"

"Yup!"

"How far iz it?"

"Ten thousand miles...Sixteen thousand kilmote—"

"*Sechzehntausend kilometer? Sheize.*" The concern in her eyes was that of a mother.

As Greg had guessed, our engine mount bolt had sheared off. It must have been a long time coming. The mechanics assured us that they could replace it and Annette and her daughter offered us Cokes and coffee while we waited. The repair took about thirty minutes. The charge? *Nothing.* The kindness? *Immeasurable.*

When Annette found out that we had a quarter tank of gas, she gave us fifty euros and told us to fill up at the next corner. She doubted our chances of making it to Ulaanbaatar, let alone Berlin, since we sheared an engine mount bolt two days into the journey on the best-maintained roads on earth. It was the nicest thing she could do for a bunch of buffoons who probably stood a better chance of climbing an ice wall with their hands covered in coconut oil than reaching Mongolia in a 1997 Daihatsu Move.

If you're going to have an automobile break down, do it in Germany. We came to town with an engine rattling around like a lottery ball, and we left town in tip-top shape and on a full tank of gas. The kindness of strangers is vaster than anything you can anticipate.

We rolled on, witnesses to an expanding sunset—its colors stretching farther east the more it sank to the west, like some sort of celestial seesaw where angels had the freedom to finger-paint clouds with pastels. In this dance of light and shadow, the mighty industrial Germany appeared as you would imagine it in a children's book. The pines reached to the sky, the grass was an impossible green, and the modern windmills spun and spun, having no interest in resting in the darkness.

After another missed turn on the highway, we abandoned our "No Driving at Night" rule, and rolled into Berlin around 10 o'clock, seven hours behind schedule. No grand dinner, no big party—but grateful for a friendly face.

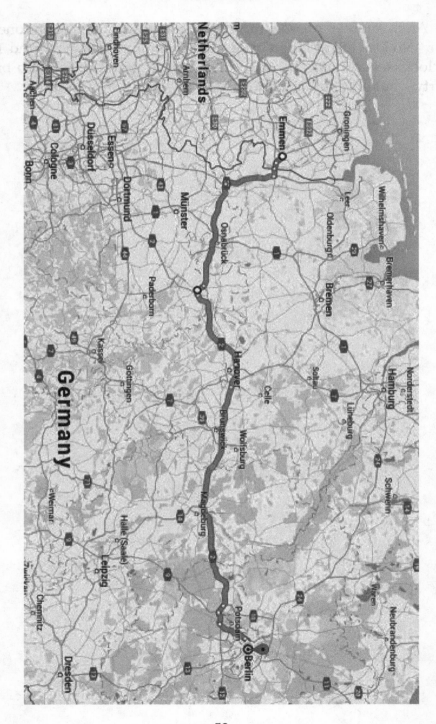

Day 3

Germany had won the FIFA World Cup the previous week, so maybe Berlin was still on an adrenaline high, because everyone treated us like royalty and, Donata like a diplomatic vehicle. I zipped her around the city, throwing the hazard lights on wherever we wanted to stop and take photos: Checkpoint Charlie, the square right next to Brandenburg Gate, and remnants of the Berlin Wall. No one gave us any trouble; in fact, they seemed to admire us

We only had time for a morning read of the Berlin CliffsNotes, but among the trams, the outdoor eateries, and the graffiti we were utterly addicted. Before ending this brief love affair, Brooke, Greg, and I bought snacks for the road. Car grub always included Snickers bars. Not only is it the heartiest candy bar around, there is no bodega or market on the planet where a Snickers bar does not wait to be plucked.

Our goal for the day was Klenová Castle, tucked away in the southwestern part of the Czech Republic in a town called Klatovy. This would be the only time on the rally that our driving would have any bit of a westerly tract. We aimed for this obscure town because The Adventurists were throwing a castle party as the central European launch to the rally. We could have chosen to skip it but none of us had a story to tell about a central European castle party yet, so we decided to invest in some memories.

The German Autobahn is a master class of engineering. Even when there was a lane closure or roadwork approaching, we weren't mad because we'd been duly informed as to what was coming. Not a cone was out of place, not a lane had been mislabeled. It was perfection in minimal delay, so instead I focused on my rearview and prepared for the incoming missiles.

"Five...four...three...two...one!" I counted down. Greg and Brooke had no idea what I was talking about and then *nnnnneeeee- yunggggggggg*. The Doppler effect of a speeding Audi, BMW, Mercedes, Porsche, or Volkswagen was more akin to a passing train than it was to an automobile. Simultaneous with the audible *zings*, we were physically reminded that air is indeed a fluid as the wake displaced by these land rockets going 130, 140, 150 mph wobbled our car, forcing me to steer it back away from the shoulder. At our average speed of 60 to 70 mph, it was as if we were standing still.

Our automotive inferiority was on constant display.

We hoped to stop in Prague on the way through and still get to the castle with plenty of sunlight, but as was becoming the norm, we misjudged our time, skipped Prague, got a little lost in the Czech countryside, and had to scurry to the castle after the sun had already bid the day adieu.

Klatovy, a tiny, rustic town was settled in 1260 AD. For those who didn't pay much attention to history class in high school, 1260 AD was that time during the Middle Ages when barons and dukes ate grapes in the castles while serfs tended to the fields in the foothills below, hoping not to be lanced by some strange fellas storming in on horseback. For whatever reason, Klatovy's twenty- two thousand twenty-first century residents had completely deserted the city. Current missing populace aside, where were all the lights, music, and noise from the Mongol Rally party?

A Spanish rally team was at the base of the castle, their headlights swinging around the vacant town, ostensibly as lost as we were. We joined forces and realized that we had no one to call and no resources to double check. The Adventurists were great at giving us just enough information not to go ape shit about the lack of information provided.

When we reached the top of a hill at the side of the castle, we still hadn't found the party. We were about to head back down the road we came up when on a whim, we chose a different path. It was there in the dying light of dusk that we saw a posterboard taped crookedly to a partially hidden tree, fifteen feet from the road announcing that we had — finally and miraculously — reached our destination in the suburban hills of the Czech Republic.

There was life here.

On a small, grassy plateau, about a hundred cars were parked in somewhat concentric circles. For every car, there was a tent surrounded by revelers drinking or relaxing in camping chairs. Bordering this outpost were forests on all sides except for the one abutting the castle. The Adventurists' representatives at the check-in desk informed us that we could buy food and drinks down by the castle, where the techno music was blaring. We were told to find whatever flat ground we wanted to camp on but we should be wary of going too far away from the outer edge of the group.

"Why?"

"Gypsies. They'll rob you clean."

We wanted to park far enough away from the teams who would stay up all night partying, but close enough so that whatever bandits lurked in the hills didn't steal all our shit. We found a spot dangerously close to breaching the latter rule, but made sure we had a two-car buffer between the wildlings and us. We couldn't fret for long because darkness was extinguishing the last western tint and we needed to set up our tent for the first time.

On its tag, the tent was described as "palatial." We thought that was a ridiculous marketing ploy until we put the thing up and realized we, by far, had the biggest tent of everyone there. There was a reason for this. A friend of mine who had gone on the rally a few years back had given me the advice, "Get a tent that you can stand up in because when you're hunched over in your car for twelve hours a day you don't want to be hunched over in a tent."

"Why can't I just stand outside?" I'd asked her.

"Because it will be hotter than a frying pan, the mosquitoes will eat you alive, or it will be pouring rain."

Righto.

***

As soon as our Battalion HQ was set up, we meandered to where the ralliers were indulging in a lavish buffet of kebabs, beer, and music. The initial thing a sober person notices when confronted with an intoxicated mob is that everyone is screaming at the top of their lungs.

It was one of the first times I realized I was middle-aged. Instead of being in the moment and partying like there was no tomorrow, I was wondering how much sleep I would get if I feigned stomach pain and snuck back to the tent. I far too logically explained how unnecessary another beer would be. Instead of celebrating an early twenty-something's freedom to party, I felt sorry for how bad he was going to be hurting the next day.

The hellcat in me had clearly died.

Greg was in the same boat.

After showing enough face time not to be labeled "lame old guys," he and I headed to the tent for some shut-eye. On our way, we ran into Brooke and her new friend, Ida. Ida was beautiful, sassy, quick-witted, and the lone female member of another three-person, American-based team who happened also to be driving a Daihatsu Move. This blonde and brunette pair had been scrounging around for more wine when they heard the most upsetting news spreading faster than the clap through a nineteenth-century brothel—one of the rally teams just had all their stuff stolen. Clothes, food, electronics. *Everything.*

Fuck. This was our first experience with the audacity of gypsies.

It happened to two forty-something New Zealanders, Darren and Myles, who were parked right next to us, on the edge of the outer circle towards the woods. Yes, we had been warned to stay close, but like king penguins trying to keep warm, *someone* had to occupy the perimeter.

Darren and Myles were quietly giving their accounts to the local police who were now on-site, but I half expected those two

Kiwis to start whipping through the forest like enraged Tasmanian devils. No one knows what he or she would do in a situation like that, but how I reacted as an innocent bystander was quite shocking.

First, I pronounced, "Oh my God, that *suuucks*," to echo the sentiments of the fifteen people around us and to prove that I was not a sociopath. Almost immediately after that, I couldn't ignore the euphoria coursing through my blood knowing that our car hadn't endured the same fate. I felt badly that it was Darren and Myles, but I was way more thankful that it wasn't us.

Then, strangely, and what felt unintendedly, I judged them for parking so far away from the rest of the group, as if they got what they deserved or something, and now their negligent decision forced me to choose how good of a person I was supposed to be. I wasn't alone. All of us were sliding beads on our mental abacuses, weighing how much to care, and how much that care would cost.

Are we going to give up our food/tent/clothes/tools to these strangers? I didn't choose to be next to them.

It's only the second day. I spent months preparing and thousands of dollars. I need to think of what's best for my team in the long run.

Maybe someone else will help.

There are people from The Adventurists here, I'm sure they'll help.

The cops are here. I'm sure they're taking care of it.

Levels of empathy are directly proportional to the proximity to an incident's epicenter, and right then, we fifteen controlled the reaction that would ripple out to the rest of the ralliers. We ultimately stuck with a collective, "Oh my God, that *sucks*," level of concern — right in the wheelhouse of what I had given so far.

If the situation and circumstances had been different (no cops, fewer teams, earlier in the day, or on our home turf...) perhaps we all would have acted differently, maybe even valiantly and selflessly. But that night in the Czech hills, a small group of us silently rationalized grand inaction, and in doing so, morphed the Kiwis from group members to outsiders, the exact opposite reaction the rally was supposed to bring out in us. It wasn't that we were bad people, it was that we had our own vulnerabilities to deal with, and in crowds of strangers, most of us tend to be more interested with fitting in than doing what's right.

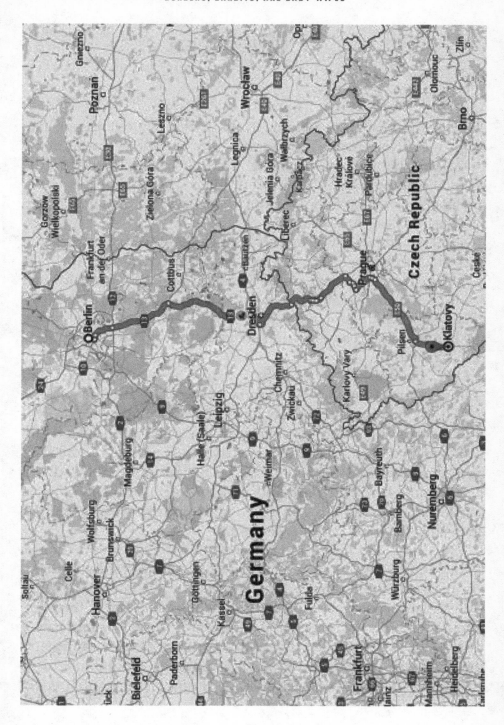

Day 4

Tents have near-impenetrable walls that keep out things like bugs, water, and me trying to crawl back in after I've peed in the middle of the night. Courteously, I didn't completely unzip the screeching zipper upon reentry but I inevitably scraped my back against the small opening, shaking the whole tent, and waking up Brooke and Greg anyway.

When it comes to noise, tents are like satellite dishes amassing and magnifying every decibel, causing conversations nearby to be never less than deafening. These "walls" attracted not just sound but also, heat. There was no "sleeping in," there was only "sleeping until the sun interrogates you." And in northern Europe the summer sun rose early and set late, turning our resting place into an inferno.

We bought some breakfast that The Adventurists had coordinated onsite and then hit the road fairly early. We found Wi-Fi at a gas station and Google Maps told us that we'd be in Budapest by late afternoon, but just like when we left Holland, we got turned around on the country roads and were forced to navigate by compass for a while. It was a beautiful rural woodland drive through rolling farmland and thickets of timber, albeit a serious workout for Greg as he propelled our no-power-steering stick-shift-having car on the serpentine roads.

One thousand miles into the rally and Donata was a champ. Don't judge her sagging axle and knock-kneed tires; she was doing the best she could. She was systematically ten or twenty mph slower than what Google Maps assumed is a fair rate of travel on international highways, leaving us constantly late. We kept trying to add time to Google's estimates to account for speed, stops, and the unforeseen. What started as a 1.1 multiple, crept up to a 1.2 or 1.3 during these few first days while driving in generally perfect conditions. Lord knows what would happen when we were confronted with crappy roads and border crossings.

We elicited curiosity from passersby because we were as incongruous in the general traffic as a pterodactyl would be on a bird feeder. You have to remember the visually amusing state of our car. We had a spare tire, jerry can, and cargo carrier strapped asymmetrically to our roof. We had photos, company logos, and Mongol Rally banners covering every inch of our hull, including one eighteen-inch-wide image of a guy spraying beer in his friend's face.

Typically pinned in the right lane on any highway due to our embarrassingly low maximum velocity, it was the person riding shotgun (remember, the steering wheel was on the right side of the car) who had to wave to everyone who honked their horn, took photos of us, or gave a thumbs-up in support. Diplomatic relations with our fans was a full-time job. Every now and then, they'd want to ask us a question. We'd scream our answers out the front passenger window: "America! Mongolia! Charity! Thanks!"

Speaking of screaming, ordinary conversations among the three of us were always just short of a yell. As you recall, and I'll never forget, Donata had no air conditioning so our antidote to the summer heat was to roll down the windows. When you combine that gusty ripple with the howl of a disagreeing engine, the bellow of an exasperated muffler, and our karaoke leads coming out of the car speakers, civilized banter with inside voices was out of the question. It was like trying to chitchat directly below a helicopter. During highway travel, the phrase most often uttered from the backseat was, "What?" Eventually, whoever was back there would tire from trying to be a part of the front-seat conversation and stare out the window or close their eyes, enjoying the driver-controlled music.

In London, we had purchased an updated car audio faceplate that had a USB connector. Brooke had her own playlist that she controlled when behind the wheel. Greg didn't have much of his own music so he piggybacked off my fourteen-hour-and-thirty-six-minute, two hundred and five-song "Mongol Rally" playlist when he was driving. It had everything from Jay-Z to Queen, Bruce Springsteen to Alesso. There were the no-matter-when-it's-on-everyone-will-sing-along songs like Oasis's "Wonderwall" and "Champagne Supernova," Red Hot Chili Peppers' "Under The Bridge" and Tom Petty's "Free Fallin'." Then there were the songs that induced silent reflections from all of us like Arcade Fire's "Rebellion (Lies)," or We Were Promised Jetpacks' "Keeping Warm," or Connor Youngblood's "Australia." Each song has a beat and melody that hijacked our soul and opened the once-sealed memories of loves we'd let go, of dreams not yet realized, of our place in the world and what it all means. The kind of road-tripping music that got us to ask ourselves: *Am I okay?*

***

We stopped for lunch at a rest area near Bratislava, Slovakia, having just hip-checked Austria on the drive by. Naturally, we were behind schedule but excited for a night in the center of Budapest no matter when we got there. Brooke had booked us at the Queens Court Hotel and Residence that even had a pool and a hot tub.

Before we sat down at the restaurant, Brooke said, "Goulash, guys. Goulash." She was right. When in the Holy Roman Empire... and we couldn't read the menus anyway. Brooke held up three fingers to the waitress and said, "Goulash?" The nod in return was all we needed to know that we were on the right culinary path.

After eating the savory bowl where even my spoon smiled, we stocked up on Snickers, snacks, and gas but noticed that while our brake lights worked, the rear lights did not illuminate when the lights were switched on. *Eesh*...Our daily race against sundown now had a new hitch. Did we keep driving on to Budapest knowing that we would have to drive a portion of it at night with no taillights? Or, did we stop for the night sixty miles out and tour the city the next day while we found a mechanic to fix our car?

We chose Budapest over safety.

I navigated the last sixty miles while Greg drove in the right lane with our hazards flashing. Brooke was turned around in the backseat, ready to announce cars zooming up on our rear. Anytime one did, Greg drifted over onto the shoulder in case we weren't seen. Looking back, the decision to ghost-drive into the city was an awful idea. We could have been steamrolled or pulled over by the first police officer who saw us, but we luckily avoided those or similar fates. Gradually, the illuminated cocoon of Budapest emerged on the horizon, filling our car with elation.

"Well, if we were going to stop before Budapest, we can't now that it's within view. That's a rule of the road, right?" Greg asked.

"Sounds about right," I concurred.

"Yup. Just don't kill us, Greg."

"Thanks, Brooke."

"Car coming fast!"

"Moving to shoulder!"

***

London is great, Amsterdam has a charm to it, Berlin balances the old and new, but Budapest buries you in its allure. When we finally came around the bend and saw the Danube River cradled between both sides of the city, our jaws dropped. Bridges, hills, monuments, palaces, churches, and a feeling of, "Oh, *now* I'm in the heart of Europe." And so, under nightfall, protected by our pulsating shield of hazard lights, we crossed the Danube via the Széchenyi Chain Bridge, the three of us simultaneously deciding we had to spend two nights here. We were robbed of our time in Berlin so we ached to get it back in a different European capital.

We paid extra to park in the garage of the hotel but it was a no-brainer. On the rally, "arrival" was always a three-step process: getting to the city we were supposed to be in, finding where we were going to sleep, and locating a place to safely stow Donata. The sense of adventure and glory came with getting to step one.

Once there, we had to pay our patience overtime rates to get through steps two and three.

Even with safe haven, we weren't quite ready for our post-driving exhale. We had to undo the straps that went around the cargo carrier and through the jerry can and spare tire so that we could get things out of our roof closet and then put the jerry can and tire in the car so nobody stole them. Each morning, we had to reverse the entire process. Like snowflakes, no strap assembly ever looked the same.

We kept the important items with us: money, documents, drone, and so on. Once in our hotel suite, Greg hopped on Facebook and found and wrote to Dave at Alpine Auto Shop—a local Daihatsu mechanic. Dave answered right away and said he'd be able to help us. Greg thought one of our front tires was a little too worn and it might be a good idea to replace it. Dave agreed to take care of that as well. We planned to meet him the next morning. This search and booking took all of five minutes.

Cheers, technology.

We headed to Liszt Ferenc Tér, a pedestrian street with restaurants stacked next to one another like bills in a wallet. No one sat inside. Each place had enough outdoor tables to accommodate a banquet and each maître d' or host subtly vied for our business, but all with a sense of decorum. No one chased us down the street with menus in hand. There seemed to be an unwritten rule that living or working in one of the sexiest cities in Europe demanded you carry yourself with a little more class than most.

We found a cozy place, ordered a local beer we'd never heard of, and ate enough food to feed a rugby team. As we leaned back in our chairs, we were now part of the life and flow of Budapest, no longer outsiders. That night in the belly of the old Austro-Hungarian Empire, my eyes wandered playfully, my feet tapped to the music, and my fingers pinched the beer bottle hanging by my side. In the serenity, I realized another reason I travel: *To be whoever I wanted to be in a place I'd never thought I'd be.*

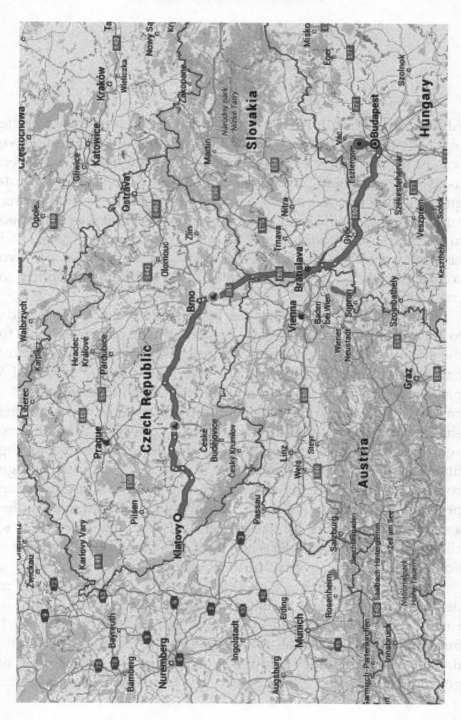

Day 5

Alpine Auto Shop turned out to be Dave's house in the middle of a residential neighborhood on the outskirts of Budapest. Dave was in his early thirties, spoke really good English, and assured us that the car would be ready later that day. Without any second-guessing, we handed over Donata along with all the pots, pans, tent, camping chairs, food, and everything else that was crammed in the marsupial pouch that was her back seat to a guy we had just met, whose full name we did not know. This trip across two continents would have been unthinkable without our ability to trust complete strangers.

Budapest used to be two cities separated by the Danube: Buda to the west and Pest to the east. We took the bus to the subway to the steep Buda side, meandered through the narrow streets, and had a great lunch overlooking the river. As if this fairy-tale of a place wasn't enough, I also fell under the spell of a woman at a bakery, the kind of immediate yearning where your breathing gets shallow and you start making relationship decisions like a fifteen-year-old at summer camp. Is there anything more enchanting than the prospect and perfection of fleeting love in a foreign country? When your life and dreams up until that moment can perish in the abyss of a dimple, or in the way a collarbone cradles a shoulder strap. When a pair of sleek calves perched on stilettos, click-clacking on a cobblestone street, can lure you into a trance you're not sure you ever want to awaken from.

It's not the ordinary high tide of sexual arousal that you're dealing with, it's a 3.5 billion-year-old tsunami of evolution rushing towards you, and your only defense is a measly beach bungalow of self-control. It's so tantalizing because there's no danger of losing your identity, of giving up your apartment, of getting rid of that cutting board, or "Until death do us part."

There's no risk of stagnation, ruts, or doubt. There's no sacrificing Saturdays for a deadbeat brother-in-law who needs help moving a kitchen table. It's a chance to have a lover who doesn't speak your language, to be that someone about whom she daydreams on a rainy day two years from now, wondering where you are in the world.

Luckily for my current life plan, we had to leave to pick up our car.

We took the reverse subway-bus-walk route back to Dave. Donata looked amazing. We tried to tip him but he wouldn't accept another euro. He wished us well, we hugged, and he gave us that increasingly familiar stare that said, "Not sure you're going to make it to Mongolia, but good luck."

With a shiny new tire and functioning taillights, we felt like we had just leased a brand-new concept car. Bristling with confidence, we went out to dinner and feasted on wine, steak, and seafood. We bounced around from one outdoor bar to another, bopping our heads to the dance music emanating from all directions.

"Do you think you guys could live here?" I asked, knowing full well that the question never presupposes bad days, struggles with employment, or making friends in a foreign country.

"I love this city. I don't want to leave tomorrow," Brooke said.

"Me neither," Greg chimed in while turning his head to follow an elegant blonde walking by. "Two days just isn't enough."

There is a feeling—half terrifying, half liberating—of being in a new place where no one knows who you are, where if you were to disappear, the world around you wouldn't skip a beat. I've felt that anonymous alacrity in in the streets of India, at baggage claim in Madrid, at a dodgy rest stop in Borneo. Along with that fragility, though, comes an elevated sense of self that tries to balance the weight of local obscurity. It's not a chest-pounding *yawp* brewing to be heard, but an outer-body calm that wants to fit in.

There in Budapest on our outdoor stools drinking beers and sharing stories, we *could* have been locals. We outsiders had blended in with what we didn't know and relished the sense of achievement that comes with being in a new place and feeling like we belonged.

That's why we didn't want to leave.

While there were opportunities to take the night into the wee hours, we all knew that we had a long ride through Hungary and Serbia to get to Sofia, Bulgaria, the next day—one of our longest legs of the entire trip. We would also have two major border crossings to contend with where we would undoubtedly *not* fit in. We had to push so hard because the night after Sofia we were scheduled to be in Istanbul for two nights at an Airbnb.

Stay charming, Budapest. Thanks for allowing us to be seen.

Day 6

Google Maps said the trip to Sofia would take eight hours. We knew better than to trust that duplicitous app, so we multiplied the time by 1.3, predicting it would take 10.5 hours. We sped towards the Serbian border on the M5 without much delay. We figured Hungary and Serbia were in some EU travel agreement, but our unfounded political assumptions were proven foolish when, within sight of the border, next to the town of Röszke (where the Syrian refugee crisis erupted in September 2015), traffic decelerated to a dead stop, like this was an abandoned highway scene in *The Walking Dead*. We learned that Google Maps didn't take into account the formalities of border crossings.

It was also hot as balls. "Balls" not being the most extreme level of heat on this trip, but when someone experiences an eight on a one to ten scale, without having yet to experience a nine or ten, he thinks that the eight might as well be a ten because there is no upper reference. Did I mention we didn't have AC?

In order to save gas and to keep Donata from overheating, we shut off the engine, put her in neutral, opened the doors, and, with our feet and arms, nudged her forward when we needed to. Peering eyes would look into our zoo cage on wheels and wonder what our story was. We were getting comfortable in our growing road-celebrity status. Some intrepid individuals hopped out of their cars and chatted with us. When we told them what we were doing, they always asked what we received when we finished the rally.

"Nothing."

The inhalation, parted mouths, and foggy eyes that searched for understanding communicated their silent response loud and clear: *You mean, you're doing this for – gulp – fun?*

The bathroom stalls were thoughtfully near the border. We were each able to pee and douse our shirts in water to keep cool, while the other two members of Marco Polover pushed the car. During our fragmented march to the border, I thought: *Man, I'm on the Hungarian-Serbian border. What the fuck am I doing here? Out of all the places on earth? How many people do I know that have stood exactly where I'm standing now? Two? None? Why was the border here and not one hundred meters ahead or behind? How many people died in order to have it be where it is? Who was it that gave the geopolitical globe a spin in one direction or another?*

"Shit! Some more lanes are opening up! Greg, turn the wheel."

We pushed hard but had to stop suddenly, forcing me to dive into Donata and yank the emergency brake before she bashed into the car in front of us. Getting into a fender bender under human propulsion on flat ground would undoubtedly be the dumbest accident in history. Eventually, we were close enough to the border guards that we all got in the car and started her up. Thirty seconds later I looked down and realized that I only had one flip-flop on and I couldn't find the other one. WTF? We had been wriggling forward for hours and the tarmac was hot as magma, there was no way I wouldn't notice a missing flip-flop. It must have come off when I dove in the car to pull the emergency brake.

I tiptoed barefoot back through the rows of cars (we're talking maybe eight or ten lanes), mumbling to myself like a madman, furious that I might lose the flip to my flop. Standing on the now melting balls of my feet, all I could see were cars, so I lowered myself to the ground in a resting pushup position in hopes of finding my AWOL, light blue, spongy beacon. Me crawling around on the highway put the one hundred people in my general vicinity into a state of heightened unease.

What's this bearded man doing lying on the highway with a foul look on his face?

My flip-flop was a whisker away from being run over by a van. I held up my hand like someone does in a movie when he's about to ask the driver to get out of a car so he can commandeer it. Back on the ground, I crawled under his chassis and grabbed my sandal. I waved it for all to see. There was no audible applause, but there were visible smiles. Just another one of those moments in travel, where in an instant, fifty complete strangers were looking at me. Never before did their lives shift because of some happening in my life, but today, they all had the same blip to react to.

There you go, Steve Jobs. I dinged the universe.

***

After an unplanned three-hour delay, we were in the Balkans. It was the first time of many when we had to buy country-specific car insurance at the border. Serbia was also the first place where we were a little...I wouldn't say *nervous*, but it was where we began triple-checking to see if our car was locked. I remembered the civil war there. I couldn't recall who was Muslim or Christian, if I was allowed to call a Serb a Bosnian, if the Albanians were the aggressors, where exactly Herzegovina was, and how did Croatia get on the fight card, anyway?

My knowledge of the region was of places like Sarajevo and Belgrade, and Russian tanks and Gavrilo Princip, Archduke Ferdinand, World War I, Slobodan Milosevic, genocide, Vlade Divac, and Drazen Petrovic. Of course, the depth and accuracy of this summary is embarrassing, but I'm being honest. Thankfully, as most preconceived, ill-backed notions turn out, there was nothing to be afraid of. Serbia is quite modern, and its highways are great, which was the measure by which we judged every country. And there were sunflowers everywhere. If sunflowers can grow here, what was there to worry about?

We still had to motor through the 334 miles of Serbia from Horgos to Dimitrovgrad, cross the Serbian-Bulgarian border, then get to Sofia, forty miles in from *that* border. We chose to avoid the Belgrade rush hour by taking the beltway around the city. This "shortcut" ended up being a one-lane road that coiled around the Serbian hills, setting us back two hours.

And so, for the fifth consecutive driving day, we motored on in complete darkness.

"What do you guys know about Bulgaria?" I asked.

From behind the wheel, Greg said, "Zilch."

Brooke chimed in. "I never thought it was a real country as a kid because it's where the movie *Chitty Chitty Bang Bang* was set, so I just assumed it was a fake place until I got older. I still think of the movie every time I hear the word: Bulgaria."

"Wasn't that Vulgaria, not Bulgaria?" Greg asked.

"Was it? I just thought Dick Van Dyke and the gang had shitty accents!"

We all enjoyed a hearty laugh, before I admitted, "I don't even know what 'chitty chitty bang bang' is."

Brooke and Greg couldn't believe it. "Come on, Bassam! So uncultured."

"Yeah, the only thing I have on Vulgaria with a 'B' is that it is the home country of Hristo Stoichkov, a soccer player I watched at the 1994 World Cup." This made my understanding of the former Yugoslavia seem scholarly in comparison.

Greg ended the conversation with, "Well, this should be fun, then." It was bizarre to purposefully enter a country we knew absolutely nothing about. *What are Bulgarians like?* Instead of delicately carving this cultural pumpkin, my lizard brain ended the exercise with one swing of its mallet. I was left with the shameful, *Darker skinned people previously living under Soviet rule. Watch out.*

The amygdala is surely the genesis of all racist thoughts.

At 11 o'clock we were at the back of a five-lane, 100-yard-long procession of cars that seemed to be moving across the border. Maybe we beat the system by driving at night, and since we were only sixty kilometers from Sofia, hopefully we'd still be able to make it to our hotel around midnight. Unfortunately, due to our underestimating the short distance needed for natural disaster-type delays in border crossing, there was no system-beating to be done other than the dismemberment of hope.

We plodded forward at the speed of trench warfare. It was the first border where we saw a budding economy alongside it: knickknacks, souvenirs, and money exchanges. This allowed passengers and drivers to get out, stretch, buy some cigarettes or soda, and do something other than stare into the distance.

There was nothing interesting to report about the two and a half hours it took to enter Bulgaria, until we had to buy a road permit. In the Czech Republic and every country thereafter, we had to pay somewhere between twenty to fifty dollars to drive for a certain amount of days (five, ten, thirty) in that particular place. Each country had a different fee and length of validity. We prepaid to use the roads in lieu of having tolls. Proof of payment was a sticker (called a vignette) that went on our windshield.

We knew we needed this vignette after crossing the border but it was unclear where we were supposed to get it. Greg pulled over next to the tens and tens of cars that were parked indiscriminately on a large stretch of pavement in front of a few poorly lit, makeshift stands, some of which were open (conducting business in I-don't-know-what), and some of which were shuttered by metal doors. Men opened trunks, moved goods from one car to another, or walked around aimlessly as if they had already reached their final destination and were now enjoying a leisurely stroll. None of it made any sense. One thing was certain, though—the women and children stayed locked in the cars.

With our car registration in hand and some euros in my pocket I got out wearing my flip-flops, shorts, and T-shirt to try to acclimatize. Sadly for me, Bulgaria was the birthplace of the Cyrillic alphabet so there were no Roman characters on the signage for me to interpret and it didn't look like anyone was eager to practice their English at 1:30 in the morning.

Everyone was smoking. I don't mean "everyone" to stress the notion that people in Eastern Europe like to smoke, I mean *everyone* in that I was the only adult not smoking. From overhead it must have looked like a brush fire had broken out.

After I had exhausted my stares and shoulder shrugs of confusion back to Greg and Brooke in Donata, one of the rolling metal shutters clattered up and the vignette office reopened, revealing a woman, smoking of course, inside a booth completely sealed in Plexiglas, save for the small hole to talk and pass money through. I happened to be standing very close to it, falling sixth in line. In an instant, the line ballooned to fifty but every man had the mind-set that he should probably be next. The swell pushed forward. Thankfully, I was big enough, assertive enough, and looked Bulgarian enough to get to the front window without being trampled like a dung beetle in a stampede. The woman in the booth waited for me to say what I wanted. Some sort of loud jumble of, "Vignette…need…only one day" came out of my mouth.

She rolled her eyes and asked me something I didn't know how to answer. I held out some money in the palm of my hand that she pecked from like a bird would crumbs on a floor, and then she gave me a vignette in return.

I wriggled out of there and found Donata, who was now legally cleared to run wild in Bulgaria.

Greg had been driving since 10:30 a.m. Most people would say that a fifteen-hour shift was excessive if not downright unsafe. He wanted to push through and make it on his own, though. I was his co-pilot but I had also known Greg for seventeen years, having witnessed his narcoleptic tendencies. The man could fall asleep on a couch, sitting up, holding a pint of beer without spilling it. So I supported his gusto but recognized his limitations. It wasn't just the fifteen hours or driving at night, it was about driving on an *unlit* road at night with headlights that had as much of an impact on darkness as a blister has on a wooden leg. It was exhausting. Paradoxically, following that anemic shaft of light through an ocean of darkness is hypnotic. Your body feels like it is dissolving into the night. The tarmac carrot that dangles on the end of your illuminated stick becomes the treasure you wade into the shadows to find, and the only thing delaying the black hole from completely enveloping you.

We blasted the music and I kept asking Greg if he was okay. He'd say yes but the mannequin stare on his face led me to believe otherwise. Suddenly, he released a detonation of sound that was part laugh, part yell, and part shriek, like a hyena had stepped into a bear trap. He wanted to get to Sofia but he had come unhinged. He could go no further.

I took the wheel, Brooke hopped into the navigator's seat, and Greg was in REM sleep before I got back on the road.

Thank God Greg passed over the reins when he did because a few minutes later he would have definitely thought he was hallucinating. We rolled into Sofia gradually. We never knew when a city started or not but overhead street lighting was always a good sign. Except here, these overhead lights revealed a ten-car-wide stretch of newly laid, shiny black pavement without one drop of white paint on it. It looked like we were driving on a pan of motor oil.

"Brooke, are we going to die?"

"I'm not sure."

Had there been a lake for us to drive into, it would have looked no different than the road we were on. This very Soviet-style main artery led us to some other streets and we were funneled onto a main thoroughfare. Our hotel was on the other side of this two-way boulevard, except there was no discernible way to cross the barrier separating the lanes of traffic: no turns, no exits, just us heading straight for a long time until a major intersection popped up. The streets of Sofia are great if you just want to drive, but not if you want to arrive anywhere in particular. It was like we were Pac-Man trying to get to a part of the screen that didn't have any pellets on it. And like our gobbling friend, we were solo in our pursuit of safety. It was so late at night that even crime itself was sleeping.

Unbeknownst to comatose Greg, Brooke and I centipeded around the city counting our lefts and rights, using various landmarks as reference points, until we accidentally reached the Best Western at a terrifyingly late 3:30 a.m. We dumped the relief from our bloodshot eyes and slumped shoulders onto the man at the check-in desk like he had rescued us from a hostage situation. *Thank you, sir! Thank you!* It was all we could do to not collapse on our knees and fall into his arms.

Momentary comfort gave way to a different form of distress when I looked at the clock on the wall. Counting out sixty minutes of sanity one finger at a time, I didn't even get to my second hand. Five hours. That's all the sleep we would get before we had to leave for Istanbul.

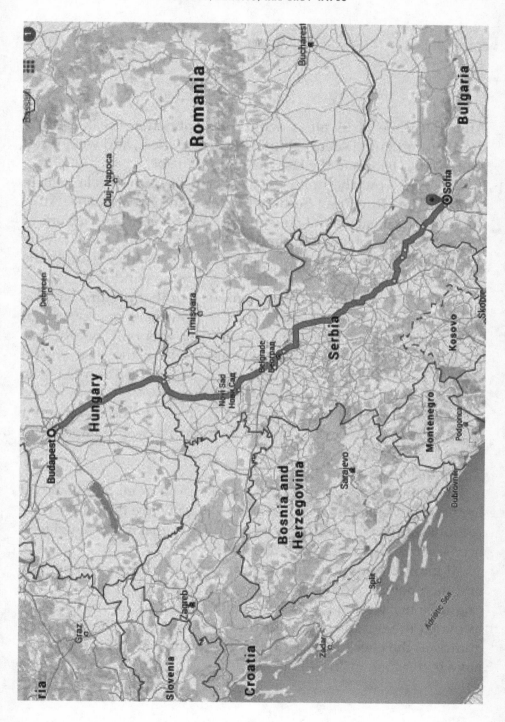

Day 7

After the three of us ate a delightful continental breakfast in a tired but contented silence, I took the driver's seat, and we headed southeast to Istanbul: the last bastion of Europe.

Up until now the only hot days had been the prelaunch in London, the Hungarian-Serbian border, and now this one. At 98 degrees F, the heat was all-consuming. Whatever tricks each one of us had to stay cool had long since been neutralized. When driving or sitting shotgun, we had to remember to constantly reapply the 30 SPF sunscreen to our arms dangling out the windows.

Turkey was the first country on our trip that required a visa. We'd need one to cross every border from here on out except in Kyrgyzstan and Mongolia, but Turkey was only one of two countries (Azerbaijan being the other) where the visa wasn't already adhered to our passports; it was a separate 8.5- by 11-inch sheet of paper we'd each printed beforehand.

Queuing at the border amid what looked like a vehicular diaspora, I asked, "Does everyone have their visa and paperwork ready?"

"Yup," Greg chimed in.

My question seemed to put Brooke in motion. She searched her bag for a moment and then asked, "Can I have the car folder?" A lot of things were in there, including our international drivers' licenses, but regrettably, not her visa.

"I know I printed it out," she said as she tore through her bag and then pawed around the back seat for any scraps of paper that might be her visa. Her internal temperature was assuredly rising to match the outdoor one. But the visa was gone. The Bulgarian guards at the checkpoint didn't have a printer but they said we'd have better luck in "no-man's-land."

Upon exiting Bulgaria around 3 p.m. we entered the no-man's-land between two countries. These areas can be hundreds of feet wide or tens of miles. We don't experience this sensation when flying but you know those duty-free spots in an airport after you go through passport control? That's you essentially between countries. You've exited and been stamped out of a country but you're not in a new one yet. I know it feels like you're in the same one because when you Instagram a photo of your plane tickets, you're still geographically *in* New York City, but you're not, politically speaking.

This "No Country for Sovereign Men" between Bulgaria and Turkey (Bulkey?) was about 500 yards wide and it housed a giant mall fitted with shops, eateries, a vignette office, and assumedly a printer. Once inside, we spotted a throng of people filling out forms, shoving their way up to a man at a desk. Our Spidey senses told us that this was the vignette we would have to acquire but we did not know where to begin the process.

Add this to the fact that our hunger level had reached DEFCON-Blinding and our bladders were about to burst. Unfortunately, to pee, we needed to pay a bathroom attendant a single Turkish lira, which we did not have. I was swamped with a sense of defeat, thinking that I was going to live out my golden years on a patch of land between Bulgaria and Turkey, because there was no way we were going to figure all this out.

Brooke was having zero luck convincing a travel agent to give her his email address so she could send him a strange attachment which he was supposed to then "open and print."

Sounds legit, crazy lady.

Nobody spoke English, and we barbarians had not learned a word of Turkish before today. Not hello, not thanks, not yes, and not no. Nothing. So we couldn't ask for help. Brooke and Greg decided to find a printer in another section of the mall and I was tasked with getting our vignette situated. For a moment, I watched the chaos to my left while standing motionless in the pariah boots the crowd had unknowingly shod me in. To my right, a large group of men stuffed packs and packs of cigarettes into their trousers, jackets, underwear, and socks in the hopes of smuggling them across the border. Folding, rolling, squishing, whatever… the only proof was the ever-growing pile of cellophane wrappings they kept shedding.

This was in broad daylight outside a department store. I'm guessing no-man's-land kind of rules itself. All the more reason our hopes of ever escaping this place were diminishing by the minute. Blank form in hand, my pride told me that I'd be able to "figure it out" when I concentrated on the Turkish words but my brain told my eyes, "No, I've never seen that alphabet in my life." This was not a translation problem; this was a frame of reference problem.

I entered the department store to get out of the fracas between the drug mules and the vignette mob. Maybe I'd have better luck connecting with the youth of Bulkey and their love of rock and roll, Levi's jeans, and Michael Jordan.

I was wrong. No one was remotely interested in me.

Out of options, I used the only weapon I had left. It's called the "imbecile in headlights" routine. It's when you give someone a blank stare, point at the form numerous times, point at your passport, and continue speaking in English while you wait until someone helps. I discarded my self-respect and crept up next to the guy at the computer everyone was dangling their paperwork in front of and began my routine. Before I could finish he said, "You're American?"

My whole body grinned. "Yes!"

"What on earth are you doing here?"

We laughed, I told him about the rally and the predicament regarding Brooke's visa.

"I'll help you out. I'm just about to finish my shift," he said.

His name was Emin. He was in his early twenties and had a warm face with an easy smile. Of course, I couldn't find Brooke and Greg at the moment I needed to and I had no way of contacting them (because our cell phones didn't work here), so I told this good Samaritan to wait with me in the middle of the mall until my friends found us. I wanted to wrap him in cowbells in case he tried to run off, but he was so kind that there was never any threat of him abandoning me. Brooke and Greg were spotted coming back from the bathroom (bastards!). Emin took us over to one of the windows (bank? insurance company? travel agency?) and even though he was speaking Turkish, the individuals he was talking to looked at him like he was bleeding from his eyeballs. There was no way they were printing this white girl's anything.

Emin had another idea, but before we took care of any state business, he needed a smoke and a cup of tea. *Ah…this seemed like Turkey.* His plan was to take Brooke across the fence to the side where the trucks get processed. He said he knew someone who worked in there who should have access to a printer. So to confirm the ironclad plan: Greg and I were going to leave Brooke (whom we could not contact) with a stranger to find a printer in some other grouping of buildings that was inaccessible to us. Seemed safe enough. Anyway, Greg and I were hungry and needed a Double Whopper with cheese. Any plan that allowed us to eat was shipshape in our book.

Wolfing down that burger reset my soul. The fates were shifting—we could feel it. Brooke came back with her visa a short while later and we endlessly thanked Emin for his time. He wouldn't accept money or allow us to buy him a tea. He said to go do something nice for someone else. I didn't know how to react to that and barely resisted shoving ten bucks in his pocket to rid myself of the guilt and the responsibility as Emin receded back among the swath of people, instantaneously morphing from a friend to a memory, exchanging his impact on me from the tangible to the metaphysical.

At the Turkish border, we ended up running into a few teams. One was Marcus, the guy driving the Ferrari. He was alive and well. The curve of his Herculean smile seemed to connect with the lines from the corners of his eyes in a complete circle. We shared some stories, laughed at the size of our car compared to his, and watched Brooke go off to get our car insurance for Turkey. I don't know how or why it happened this way, but since Brooke had been in charge of locating and sourcing the car back in London, she ended up being the person who put her name down as a contact. Hers became the name that had to go on the registration, and which had to go down as the name on the insurance. This isn't a big problem in places where women are allowed to do all the things men are, but we were now entering an area of the planet where sexism can reach startling heights and incomprehensible reach. I chuckled at the sight of this voluptuous girl with short blonde hair walking into the automobile insurance office on the Turkish border. Brooke's lack of male reverence that this part of the world demanded had to make every local man's head explode.

At last, we had our vignette and insurance and were on our way outside of the final checkpoint. The drive between the border and Istanbul was sublime. It was a combination of perfect highways, the excitement of entering another country, the manner the rolling hills revealed what the horizon was hiding, and the way the sun set in the rearview mirror. We even saw our first sign that denoted the distance to Tehran.

We definitely weren't in Kansas anymore.

It looked like we would make it to our Airbnb apartment in the neighborhood of Cihangir in the early evening (hours after expected, naturally), in time to enjoy the town a bit. A little hookah, a little *doner kebab*, and who knew? The traffic bloated as we got closer to the city. People told us that Istanbul was a vehicularly lawless place where motorists would often slice across five lanes of traffic, nary a blinker being activated, and do it in such a *laissez-faire* manner you'd think *you* were in the wrong. I didn't believe it until I saw it happen numerous times. Cars would cut in front of us at such an angle that I was looking through our windshield at their doors, not their bumpers. Because of this, buttholes puckered and hand grips tightened.

Istanbul is one of the most fascinating hubs in the world, not just because of its geographical position—it is the only city that sits on two continents, straddling the Bosporus Strait which connects the Black Sea to the Mediterranean—but because of the combination of Muslim and Byzantine architecture. Istanbul is like a Jenga puzzle. It is a metropolis limited by its footprint and landscape, so history and its invading aftermath could only build up, over, and onto what was previously there. Streets zigzagged and twisted almost 180 degrees on San Francisco-like hills, leading us under a narrow ancient aqueduct attached to a castle that men wielding swords on horseback had surely fought over for years. It was an irresistible city jam-packed with grace and antiquity, as well as Brooke, Greg, and I in what can only be described as a death match against every other car on the road.

We knew we'd never find our apartment on our own so we fired up Brooke's limited international data plan and synced up Google Maps to get us there. Brooke, I'll have you know, does a lot of things well but navigating is not her strong suit. It's her no suit, actually. There are rules of navigation that I assumed everyone knew. Unfortunately, I would get instructions like this from Brooke:

"Up ahead you're going to take a left."

Mind you, at the time, I was like a kayaker going down Class IV rapids, dodging cars, staying upright, and keeping us alive. "Ahead" didn't mean anything to me.

"Stay straight."

The road forked, so either direction could be straight.

"Take a right on Ku...zu...ku...lahhh...gi—"

Again, rapids, trying not to die, and street signs not written in phonetic Roman letters, but in Turkish...I was a bit on edge, to say the least. A few times I would catch Brooke looking around at the sights and then I would say, "Okay, Brooke, what's next?"

This would surprise her as if I'd woken her from a nap. "Oh, *umm*, left here."

"Great. Now I just missed that turn. Brooke, I'm going to need you to stay focused right now."

"I'm sorry! I'm trying to navigate and check out the city."

"No! There is no checking out the city right now. There is getting us to our apartment alive. That is all. I've never been to this city before. I can't read street signs. You have to give me specific directions far enough in advance. For example, 'Bassam, in three streets you'll make a left. In a quarter of a mile the road will split, you need to be on the right.'"

Silence.

Her Google Maps rerouted us. She remained cold but navigated well until we reached a red light and she said, "Go right."

I looked to my right and there were *two* rights: a 90-degree and a 70-degree right. I asked, "Which right?"

"What?"

"*Which* right?"

The light turned green. I chose the 70-degree one because it looked like the main road, but I chose incorrectly. I tried to keep my calm but it was challenging. Once more we re-spawned on a major thoroughfare to try that level again. The tension in the car was so dense I had to rub my eyes to see through it. Brooke gave me good directions until I saw another complicated intersection coming up.

I peeked down at Brooke's phone—because I trusted her less than Charles Ponzi right then—and to my horror, I saw the arrow telling us to go left on an overpass. "Brooke, am I supposed to turn here?"

"No...straight."

"Then why does the GPS tell me to go left?" I pointed at her phone in defiance because I couldn't get to the exit now.

The car filled with stillness like the woods before a hunter's gunshot...

"Brooke, I'm sorry, I'm losing my cool here but I just can't understand how powerless you seem even with a device telling you exactly where we need to go and when."

Greg stayed out of this conversation like a waiter filling the water glasses at a squabbling couple's table. Greg knew that putting an added burden on Brooke at this moment wasn't going to help her focus. At times, Greg and I could unintentionally stack the deck against Brooke, or maybe it just felt that way to her. We were both men, bigger and older, and he and I had known each other for decades longer than either he or I had known her. If there was a disagreement in the car between Brooke and either male, Greg and I oftentimes took the same side. Although her initial desire to embark on the rally had been to prove to herself that she could do it, she began to feel pressure to prove to Greg and me that she could. The worst thing Greg could do at this point was ask for her phone, so instead, he gave her psychological space.

These are the unexpected dramas that sprout in the microscopic fissures of long-distance driving in an enclosed space.

Emotionally sputtering, we eventually arrived at the neighborhood of Cihangir.

Only mountain goats and condors would find Cihangir's streets appealing. I've never seen steeper roads. So steep that when descending a vertical precipice, Greg wasn't sitting behind Brooke and me, he was sitting *above* us. I'd be in first gear, our front brakes feeling like wrists in a handstand, while my palm hovered over the e-brake, fully prepped to battle gravity with all the friction I could provide.

We safely reached our apartment and had the unbelievable luck of finding a parking spot right in front of our building at 10 p.m. on a Friday. We chuckled as we once again pulled into our destination in the pitch black. Brooke and I hugged, defusing any high-strung, end-of-day strain between us.

Greg and Brooke decided to meet some other ralliers who had put up a Facebook message that they would be hanging out in Taksim Square that night. I was beat. I honestly can't even remember if I had dinner that night or not. The knowledge that we didn't have to drive anywhere the next day was welcomed like liberators. I know we'd had an extra night in Budapest to stretch our legs but the last two days of border crossings, late night driving, and the chaos of Istanbul had eaten away at us.

So I masturbated for the first time on the trip, lifting the pressure release valve of frustration and angst. At peace, I vanished into sleep.

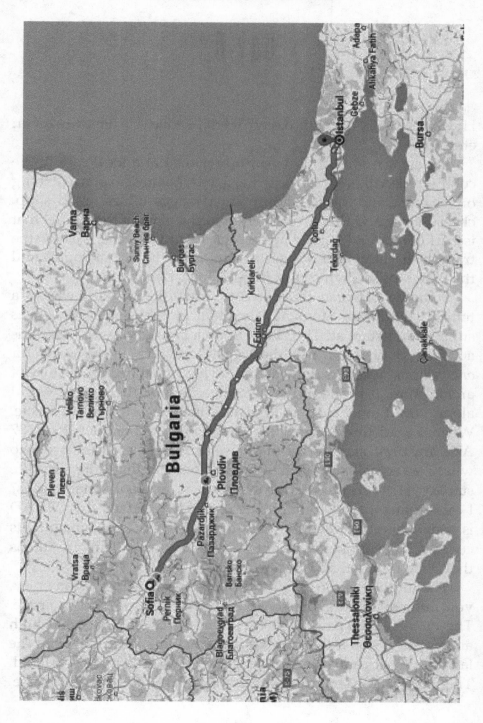

Day 8

How was it only the eighth day? It felt like we'd been away for an eternity.

We ate a tremendous Turkish breakfast at a local cafe in the cobblestoned hills of Cihangir. I ordered the most expensive thing on the menu and was not disappointed — eggs, olives, bread, soup, cheese. Greg and Brooke each embraced a glass of the jet fuel that is Turkish coffee. Hopped up on calories and caffeine, we took the tram from a stop near our apartment to see the Hagia Sophia and the Blue Mosque, which just happen to face each other.

Standing between these two treasures I felt like I was in a tourist singularity moment, uncertain of which horizon I was supposed to stare at. The Hagia Sophia is so impressive that it is actually confusing. It was the biggest cathedral in the world for *one thousand years*. Its dome is said to have changed the history of architecture. It is one of the seven wonders of the ancient world along with Stonehenge in England and the Coliseum in Rome. When I read things like, "It was originally constructed in 537 AD," my brain starts to ache because I am completely unsure as to what was actually happening on the planet at that time. Had life started yet? Were we still throwing spears at woolly mammoths? I can't remember, but after some research I realized that 537 AD is somewhere between the time of Christ and Charlemagne. Its construction commenced eight years after the Academy in Athens that Plato founded had closed. *Plato.*

The interior of the Hagia Sophia is spellbinding. Upon entry, you immediately have a sense that you're suspended in space. The curves, the spans, and the arches gracefully float so high above you it's as if the entire thing was built at a time when the laws of physics and structural engineering hadn't quite solidified. This improbable structure was grandfathered in by the universe, existing with the understanding that its shape and design would be an impossibility to replicate anywhere else.

I had to remind myself to breathe.

Most of the Christian elements sit under the Muslim ones but with the restoration, many of them now sit *with* each other. The mosaic of Virgin Mary and Jesus in the apse was created in 867 AD, a few decades after algebra was invented.

After that mind warp, we turned our focus to the visual ecstasy that is the Blue Mosque. It was built more than *one thousand years after* the Hagia Sophia, but that was still before the *Mayflower* landed in Plymouth, Massachusetts. Its beauty and breadth make it look like the Ottoman version of the Great Pyramid at Giza. I again shook my fist at the dark magic of architecture and construction, refusing to believe that something like this was physically possible. Six giant minarets surround it like sentries guarding a castle wall, walls that protect an interior so elegant and beautiful that even my camera said, "I wouldn't do it justice. Just put me away."

Outside, we walked through some gardens and eventually made it down to the water's edge of the Bosporus Straight, setting our sights on Asia for the first time during the trip. There are only two places on earth where a specific, narrow line of water separates two continents, allowing both lands to gaze at each other: the Bosporus Straight (Europe and Asia) and the Suez Canal (Africa and Asia). One could argue that the Straights of Gibraltar separating Europe and Africa is a narrow line of water, but that is 9 miles wide. The Bosporus is between 0.38 to 1.85 miles wide. The width of the Hudson River between Manhattan and New Jersey is about 1 mile.

To knowingly lay eyes on two continents in one fixed glance at sea level was a geographically grounding moment on the rally. For days on end, we were "somewhere in Europe" and soon enough we would be "somewhere in Asia," never truly sure of our exact location, only our relative position to the next waypoint because road signs told us so. But here in the face of a refreshing breeze, under three coats of a dark blue painted sky, we were specifically somewhere: right in the slender gap between two *continents*.

Later that night, we took a walk down Istiklal Avenue, the famous pedestrian street, enjoying our last moments in Istanbul: the music, the kebabs, the coffee, and the captivation. We wished we had more time here, but unfortunately our travel trajectory on the rally was so quick, our stops so brief, that we skimmed off the cultural cream of every place we touched, unable to be pulled into the gravitational center of a particular people or location. Even though we were deflecting stories and lessons untold, our interaction with various cities, villages, and nations was slowing us down on each "pass" so that the cumulative cultural and historical pull of the entire planet drew us into a new orbit of understanding and appreciation for it all.

Day 9

As we crossed into the vastness of Asia over the Bosporus Bridge we felt a kinship with explorers of old. From the Roman alphabet to the Cyrillic, from fair-skinned to olive hues, we'd just traversed the entire continent of Europe (2,300 miles), not as passengers in a plane or train, but in a car propelled by our own desires, at the mercy of highways, weather, other drivers, and engine mount bolts. We pushed eastward, each with one eye on the road and one eye on the calendar, because this next leg of the journey was all about Turkmenistan.

Turkmenistan is one of the top ten most difficult countries to enter according to nearly all lists that are made on the topic. You have to be invited by the government to even apply for a visa. Luckily, we had used a proxy provided by The Adventurists so we had the invitation but it was the date-specific, five-day Turkmen transit visa that we needed to secure. "Date-specific" is exactly what it sounds like. We could have gotten our Turkmen visa in London but that would have been on the back of a hope and a prayer trying to guess what exact five-day period we would be in Turkmenistan. The only other cities on our route that could offer us a Turkmen Embassy were Berlin, Istanbul, and Baku, Azerbaijan. Berlin was still too early and we couldn't get it in Istanbul because a) we were still a little too far from Turkmenistan to know exactly when we'd be there, and b) even if we did, we were in Istanbul over the weekend during a Muslim holiday called Eid. Due to Eid, every government building was closed on Monday and Tuesday. That left Baku. Baku was the most convenient city because it is the port city on the Caspian Sea and where we'd board a ship to Turkmenistan. However, rumor had it that the embassy in Baku was only open on Fridays and Mondays (why wouldn't it be?), hence our aim of getting there in four days—on Thursday night.

The real shit in our cereal, though, was this ferry from Baku. It was neither a ferry that had a confirmed departure time nor could it be referred to as a "passenger" ferry, but instead was an industrial ferry that left whenever its holds were full. There was no arrival time either — it could take anywhere from one to three days to cross the Caspian. No matter how we cut it, this was not a favorable situation with date-specific five-day visas ticking away in our passports.

This Turkmen visa situation was a nation-state example of trying to hit a moving target with a broken arrow. The disingenuous Google Maps said that the 1,360-mile drive from Istanbul to Baku should take thirty hours. Multiplying that by a factor of 1.5 to 1.7 gave us forty-five to fifty-three hours of driving time. To do that over four days would mean eleven to thirteen hours of driving each day. It was going to be a serious blitzkrieg across Turkey, Georgia, and Azerbaijan.

Turkey is huge. Its width is the distance from San Diego to Portland, Oregon. Our goal for the first day was the northern coastal city of Samsun (like driving from San Diego to San Francisco). We planned to stay at a campground on the Black Sea that Brooke had reserved online. The website indicated that we should arrive by 10 p.m. or we might be locked out. Having left Istanbul at 9 a.m., we surmised that we'd reach Samsun in plenty of time to take a swim, catch the sunset, and enjoy our first camping meal of the trip.

The northwestern part of Turkey is dry and mountainous, like the southwestern United States: reddish brown rocks; serrated, hilly terrain; and great open roads. Donata was somehow still going strong. Oftentimes we thought she was in fourth gear because she'd be screaming at 65 mph. I'd reach down to upshift but found the shifter already pinned in fifth, reminding me that this car was out here against her will. When approaching a hill, we would have to downshift into fourth gear far in advance so we could get enough speed and power to get over it, like a surfer paddling out to clear a wave before it breaks. If we mistimed it, we'd have to downshift to second or third, suffering the wounds inflicted by gravity until we crested.

***

Of course, by the time we arrived at the seaside town, it was the dead of night and just past 10 p.m. This wasn't a small waterfront municipality with one main street like in Central America or something. Samsun had half a million people, and boasted two universities, several hospitals, and giant, convention center-sized malls with every western brand imaginable spot-lit.

I know this because Brooke, Greg, and I spent three quarters of an hour trying to get to the campground. Nothing is as frustrating as driving for twelve and a half hours to get somewhere, only for that "somewhere" to gobble up forty-five more minutes. Compounding the problem was a paralysis of choice that entombed each of us as we navigated a city with a lot of streets but no discernable way to get to our destination. Every intersection demanded a decision. Decisions were made by opinions, some of which were conflicting among the three of us.

"I think we should turn here. It looks like it goes back towards the water."

"Didn't we see this road from over there? I think it dumps us back heading out of the city."

"I don't know."

"We should have turned on that street back there, I'm telling you."

We weren't mad at one another, but somehow we had to balance being an active part of the solution by chiming in, without causing derision or drama *by* chiming in.

There appeared to be tiered roads we had to descend to reach the water. We moved from one side of the city to the other like a metronome. We were always within a mile or two of where we needed to be but we...couldn't...get...there.

Finally, we made it down to the coastal road, hoping that a 10:45 p.m. arrival didn't really exclude us from getting into the campground. We pulled up to find the ten-foot-high, prison-like, sliding steel closed gate with no guard in sight. We could see parked caravans, parents sitting in lawn chairs, and children comfortably reading books in their pajamas on splayed picnic blankets. It was a scene so placid and pleasant that it magnified the difference between our collective realities on either side of the fence. We were *at* the right place; we weren't *in* the right place. This was the paradox of traveling. The distance between danger and safety, between foreign and familiar was paper-thin, but that gap was razor-sharp.

Brooke reached under the latch of the gate and found the lock unclasped. We were able to push it aside enough to let Donata through, careful to close it, just as we had found it. Trying to sneak our sticker-plastered car by all the caravans without drawing any attention was like trying to squeeze past two bare-knuckle boxers pounding each other inside an oil drum. Very quickly a man from the main building came over to see what our story was. Thankfully, he had our name on the manifest. We paid the nominal fee and were free to camp and cook in one of the open spots.

Home.

While Greg and I set up our canvas pavilion, Brooke was in charge of filling the stove's tank with gasoline from our jerry can. Within minutes she was swearing and claiming that our stove didn't work. Greg and I remained calm and continued with the tent, hoping that our poise and stick-to-it-ness would inspire Brooke.

In the meantime, another rally team showed up by pure coincidence. It was three Brits who looked like they'd just woken up on the floor of a Wild West saloon. Their car was a tiny, white, 1980s hatchback with a backseat so cramped, the guy who peeled out of it waddled like he had a slipped disc, but in fact it was the result of being sardined in a car for twelve-plus hours. Despite this underwhelming first impression, they each rolled out their self-assembling one-man tents. Poof! Done. Seconds after that, they had their stove on like it was a Kenmore, and before we knew it, they were in hoodies, sitting in camping chairs, spooning some sort of warm noodle dish into their gullets. Meanwhile, Greg and I were still setting up our command post, and our uncooperative stove was coated in a sheen of gasoline.

We finished setting up the tent and tried to help Brooke. With all the spilled gas, it looked like a raccoon had tried to get into the stove. I was a little concerned about having an open flame anywhere near it. Brooke said that the instructions stated to prime it around fifty times for the first ignition and then thirty times every ignition thereafter. She said she had primed it around one hundred fifty to two hundred times.

Dear me.

If this thing was in fact buggy or stuck, we were now arming an IED. I actually took a few steps back, found shelter behind some wooden pallets, and waited for the stove to explode into the ionosphere. After almost a year of prep and over a week on the road, this was a tool we needed to ensure our general survival, and we had no idea how to use it.

Greg thumbed around with our stove as I imagine a chimpanzee would a Rubik's cube. He determined that the valve had not been closed so nothing was being primed when pumped. Problem solved. Fire burning. Water boiling. Food coming soon. We sat on asphalt, slugged some vodka with no mixer, scarfed down peanut butter-and-jelly sandwiches, and looked at the shores of the Black Sea. We were proud of ourselves, as if we had done something truly noteworthy with our evening.

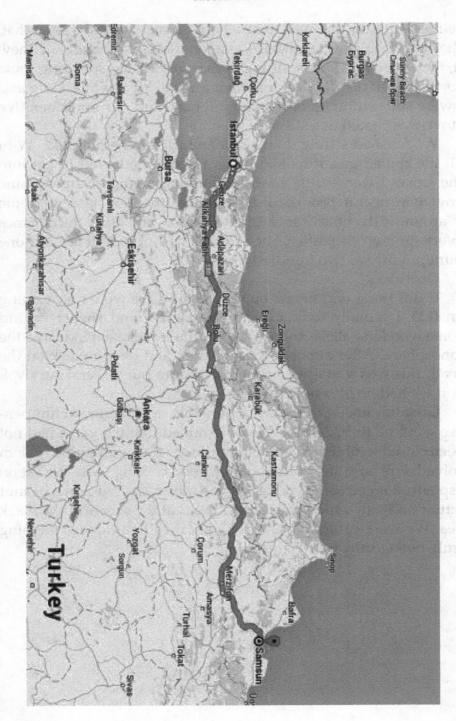

Day 10

Just like our camping experience in the Czech Republic, morning came with a blaze of heat and light. We were able to hop into the bay for a quick swim and enjoy the cascade of a warm shower in the onsite facilities before packing up Donata. It was Tuesday. Our goal was to cross into Georgia (the one that used to be "Back in the, back in the, back in the USSR!") by the end of the day. We had to get to Baku on Thursday to be at the Turkmen embassy early Friday morning.

But you already know this.

Brooke booked us at a camping spot on the Black Sea about an hour north of the border into Georgia. I know I give Brooke a hard time when it comes to navigating, but she was a gem when it came to finding places for us to stay. I'm sure if she were writing this book she'd have a chapter titled, "Bassam and Greg Are Two Controlling Sociopaths from Whom There Is No Escape."

We hit the road at 9 a.m. Google told us it would take ten hours to reach our location. We chose to not multiply that by 1.5 to 1.7 for fear of demoralizing ourselves. Greg directed Donata along the beautiful multilane road, kind of like the Pacific Coast Highway from Laguna Beach to Los Angeles, except the Black Sea was the size of California itself, so this ride took forever.

It was one of those beautifully boring days. Hour after hour, the summer scenery blended into an amalgam of stoplights, sand, water, and coastal cities. We rolled along to the hum of our tires, the raised octave of our roaring engine, and the unmistakable scent of sea salt in the air. Beachgoing traffic snarled our pace here and there, but our Zen-like road ethos reminded us that we were not stuck in traffic, we *were* traffic. Oftentimes, these exercises in patience brought rounds of "Would You Rather?" a game that asks players to pick between two hypotheticals, each more outrageous than the other. This process will undeniably teach you more about your friends than ten years of living together might.

"Bassam, what do you mean you'd rather have a triangular-shaped head than a spherical torso? It is completely illogical."

"You could wear a prosthetic head. I guess it depends on if the apex of the triangle is at the top of your head or if it's at your chin. If it were the former, you could get a spherical helmet head and push that on the tip of the triangle like you were juicing half a grapefruit. If it were the latter, that would be the tightest flattop ever, until you put your fake dome head on top of that, making you look like a single-scoop ice cream cone."

Or…"I think you are underestimating the horrors and insanity that would come with a lifetime of hiccupping, Brooke, not to mention the inability to have a conversation or hold a job that requires face-to-face interactions with human beings."

"And I think you're underestimating the public shaming that would come with colored wafts of ass following you for the rest of your life, Greg."

"For women, maybe. Everyone always assumes a guy farted, anyway. Might as well leave no doubt. Anyways, this can't be a smoke bomb amount of gas here. We're not landing helicopters next to my butthole. An average fart would dissipate into the ambient air in what, ten, twenty seconds?"

Real philosophical stuff.

In what was becoming par for the course, the sun began its descent more quickly than we were prepared for, although at this time of year and latitude she worked hard until somewhere between 8 and 9 o'clock. Because we were on the northerly curve in northeast Turkey, we witnessed daylight's exit over the water of the Black Sea. It was an impending collision of geometry until finally, and with prolonged precision, the aquatic blade of the horizon sliced through the glittering disc, sending a spray of glowing fragments across the endless sky. The sunset gripped us like we were theatergoers sitting unblinking and spellbound.

What a show. It was unquestionably one of the finest sunsets of the entire trip.

In the aftermath of that fiery adieu, while the sky still held a lingering radiance, my thoughts had the freedom to spread out in concentric waves from the singular phenomenon of self, to my friends and family, to my passions, to the reaches of the universe that encapsulate us all. The dots connecting the outermost fringes of my understanding and wonder (purpose, career, happiness...) became so tangled and secluded. I'd reach a unified conclusion about my life, simultaneously so heavy and so frail that this distant ripple of thought toppled under its own weight, leaving me unable to articulate what the hell I'd just realized.

This collapsed mental wormhole left me partially out of breath. I felt like a caterpillar accidentally awoken halfway to becoming a butterfly and then put back to sleep by the confines of the cocoon.

Maybe I wasn't ready to see things in a new light yet but something was billowing.

***

Idiotically, we thought Georgia would be a lawless land of barons and bandits, so we weren't going to risk entering with an empty gas tank. We stopped for fuel in the last town in Turkey — Hopa. It had the elegance of an abandoned concrete processing plant. With Donata's belly full and after spending our last Turkish dinar on a few bags of chips, it was Georgia or bust.

By 9 o'clock the roads were quiet...almost too quiet. We passed about a mile of tractor-trailers parked single file on the right-hand side of the highway. We assumed that trucks were only allowed to cross the border at certain times of the day. With two hundred meters to go to the checkpoint, we entered a tunnel, and still no traffic. Was border luck finally on our side?

Nope.

We emerged from the tunnel. Instead of passing through Turkey's exit gate, which was three cars ahead of us at our 1 o'clock, a smug police officer told us to make a U-turn, drive back on the two-lane highway that enters Turkey (the one that runs in the other direction and parallel to the tunnel we were just in), and queue up at the end of the line. Confused, we followed his instructions, now driving back into Turkey.

Moored in the left lane of this highway was a monumental column of cars facing the opposite direction. As we passed, each pair of headlights stared us in the face, almost ridiculing us for how fucked we were. There was a giant mosque right on the border as well as a jammed parking lot filled with sharply dressed Turks walking towards Georgia. What the hell was going on here? Dodging people, animals, food carts, automobiles, and buses, we drove in the one accessible lane trying to find the end of the snake of cars that was now reaching a depressing length. We passed under the "Welcome to Turkey" sign before we arrived at the back of the swine-class line, half a mile from the border, perplexed as to why this span of two hundred-plus cars trying to get out of the country wasn't on the highway that was dedicated to that purpose.

At this distance from the checkpoint, there were no streetlights, just a sea on one side, and a wall of rock on the other. We made a three-point turn, assumed the caboose, shut the car off, and waited to push Donata forward ten feet every minute or so along with the rest of the sorry lot who'd made the ridiculous decision of leaving Turkey in a vehicle. The treacherous thing was that about half of the cars that were driving into Turkey on this road weren't trying to join the back of our line; they were actually *driving* into Turkey. They zoomed by as if fleeing Georgia. Often they'd ride the bumper of someone who *was* looking for the end of the line we were on. We pushed Donata through the darkness, mere feet from this disaster-in-the-making.

Four hours of nothing gave us time to think and turned our conversations into a *Rear Window* on wheels. We'd comment on how many cigarettes one guy was smoking, or wonder how that entire family fit into one vehicle. We'd discuss the guys pushing carts, selling food and drinks to the people in line. The highlight of this border purgatory was when an intrepid driver making his way to the back saw a gap in cars and tried to cut in with a quick turn. A siren of honks and screams deterred the would-be shithead. Every now and then, though, a guy did make his queue insurgency a reality, at which point he was verbally berated by a horde of men who reached the car at a gallop. Sometimes the scumbag would stay in line, and sometimes he would be threatened enough that he would leave and go to the back. We just watched and talked among ourselves about what we would do if we were tough.

Why not have us line up on our own side of the highway in the tunnel to keep the cutting and the accidents from happening? Good question. Because then the cop directing traffic out of the tunnel wouldn't be able to take payments from cars looking to cut. That's right. Had we greased that policeman, we could have saved a good portion of our sanity. *Ah, corruption.* If only it didn't work so well.

***

Beyond the Georgian checkpoint was an economic circus filled with lights, cars, stores, opportunists, food stands, and money exchangers. Each one looked like a snake oil dispensary. We wanted to gather our thoughts and our nerves but the border-crossing process is like being on a conveyor belt with a cliff at the end of it, inevitably sending you freefalling into a whole new experience whether you're ready or not. We asked the friendly, English-speaking customs lady which way was north because there was no discernable way to drive through the fiasco just outside the gate, and even if there was, the signs were all in Georgian. The Cyrillic alphabet is a little different than the Roman alphabet, but the Georgian alphabet looked like a cross between Chinese and Arabic. She pointed into the distance and wished us well, and so, at around midnight, we entered Georgia. We parted the Red Sea with our Hot Wheels car, refusing offers of sausages and cigarettes as we proceeded down a dark road in a new country, with neither currency in our pockets nor an ability to read street signs.

Perfect.

Thankfully, a few miles in we came upon a gas station and a money exchange. This wasn't a government-sanctioned enterprise. This booth had the structural integrity and business legitimacy of a lemonade stand. Exchange rates were written haphazardly in ink. Ink isn't the inscribing medium of choice when dealing with fluctuating rates, but we did not care about economic accuracy right then. We knew that it was somewhere around 1.75 lari for one dollar so we took the 1.70/1 ratio as a fair deal.

Three teenagers sat on the curb, excited and unsure how to process three Americans who had found their ways here in the middle of the night, so we settled our silent kinship in smiles and head nods.

We picked up some water and beer, and giggled at the lunacy of filling up our gas tank in Turkey (five dollars per gallon) when we could have done it in Georgia for three dollars per gallon.

After a few minutes back on the road we realized why there were so many snazzy people heading out of Turkey into Georgia. About twelve miles from the border is a city called Batumi. It's a mini Las Vegas. In case you're not up to snuff on your history of the Caucasus, Georgia is a predominantly Christian country, whereas Turkey is a Muslim country. If debauchery is your thing, you're not going to find much of it within the borders of Islam.

We had to drive through Batumi to get to our campsite on the Black Sea, and each minute we got closer was another minute for us to think our eyes were playing tricks on us. Batumi at night looks like Crayola was in charge of the lighting, and a corrupt city official from the *Jetsons* oversaw urban planning that includes LEDs, neon, gravity-defying architecture, and casinos. We wished we could stop but it was the middle of the night and we wanted to sleep. Prague and Batumi are the two cities on the trip that we passed close to or had to pass through that I'd love to spend more time in. Batumi was that cool.

The winding, mountainous roads out of Batumi were respectable. Of course, when it was time to find our campsite, we played another round of "we just can't get there." Except this time, it was semi-dirt roads in the middle of a Georgian forest in a night so devoid of light it felt like we were immersed in tar.

No map would have helped because our directions from the man hosting us were "one mile after the end of the bridge there will be a turnoff on the left. It will be your third left. Follow this road for about a mile until you see an abandoned..." and so on. We ended up passing through a private gated area with mansions on either side. This was obviously not where we were supposed to be although we could hear the sea. No matter how much back-and-forth we tried, we couldn't find the campsite on Ureki Beach. There was a dark hotel back towards the main road but it looked like a horror movie waiting to happen. Greg and Brooke decided to see if anyone there knew where our campsite was or if they had any beds. I stayed with the car. The beam from their flashlights moved towards the hotel, then away from it, then bounced around in the trees above them as they tried to scale some kind of a wall, and then they were swallowed up in total darkness. None of these observations told me that they had ascertained any useful information.

Weeks earlier I would have been nervous in this situation, but being on the road fosters an atmosphere of indifference to discomfort. We weren't going to die. That, I did know. So much stress is reduced with that realization. Will we find our campsite? Maybe. Would we be driving towards Tbilisi (the capital of Georgia) tomorrow regardless of where we slept tonight? Yes.

I ate a partially melted Snickers, and quietly enjoyed the unplanned moment.

Eventually Brooke and Greg reappeared and confirmed that their recon mission had been fruitless. Just when we were about to give up and pitch our tent on the side of this dirt road, a man poked his head through a door embedded in a wall that protected his property. *Oh shit, now we were in trouble.*

He stared at us for a lengthy second before finally saying, "Brooke?"

Home.

We had driven by this spot five times. The man opened a gate that led into a sandy little enclave. We pulled in and turned off the ignition. The salty humid air off the water flooded our nostrils, expanding our chests with comfort. We were at the edge of the forest, about one hundred meters from the waves lapping against the shore in the dark distance.

There was space for us to cook and even indulge in a private hot shower. It made me think of the thin line between an ally and a threat when traveling, just like the night before, standing outside the gate of our Samsun beachfront campsite. Here in Georgia, this welcoming nook was only yards away from a forest wilderness. If we'd been forced to sleep on the dirt road, someone might have looked out the window and asked us to leave. *Strangers!* But a man Brooke had emailed opened a gate and we were welcomed. *Friends!*

Paper-thin. Razor-sharp.

Greg and I set up the tent as Brooke cooked pasta. At 2 a.m., with our bellies full and a beer to add to the peace, we fell asleep to the soothing sound of the water, to the feeling of warmth in our hearts, and to the thoughts of what the next days might bring. Not bad. Not bad at all.

Day 11

A beautiful morning was upon us and we arrogantly wondered if we could make it all the way into Azerbaijan by end of day. Our host advised against it, because the border crossing could take forever. We'd see what time it was when we reached Tbilisi and decide from there. It is amazing to look back and marvel at our complete disregard for border delays when planning our daily pace of travel.

Having left the campground at 10 a.m., we thought we'd be in Tbilisi at 2 p.m. After driving through what looked like Appalachia for two hours, we were famished from not having had any breakfast, and were tired of eating chips to stave our hunger pangs. Fortunately, we were on a road that had a tire store, a mechanic, and a bodega. We wanted a sit-down lunch but there was no "Georgian Fried Chicken" or "Pizza Barn" or even "Restaurant." Realizing that an obvious solution was not going to appear, we needed to physically pop our heads in a few places to see if they served food. We parked on a pile of rocks and rubble at the entrance to a construction site. Giant trucks rumbled in and out, kicking up dirt, cloaking our car from sight, leaving it vulnerable to being squashed. We locked our doors and hoped for the best.

The first store I entered looked like a shop you'd see in rural America in the 1960s at the onset of the *End of Days*. There was a kind, plump, older woman standing behind the smudged-glass counter who greeted me with a bright smile and wiped the dangling strands of hair from her sweat-covered brow. There were a few candy bars here and there, some sodas, and a dish detergent called "Barf" (I'm not making that up), but no real food. We all get that feeling of guilt, disappointed by a menu while the host is staring at us. We almost feel obliged to eat or to buy something. Embarrassed, I scuttled outside and said to Greg and Brooke, "No, no kebabs or anything, just snacks." We sauntered towards our car but the woman ran out, said something in Georgian with the word "kebab" in the middle, and motioned "yes" by waving us inside.

You don't have to tell me twice when it comes to eating kebabs!

Soon enough we met her preteen daughter and her husband, Michael. He had a Tom Selleck mustache, a tight friar haircut, and a big, half-dome belly. He was so honored and excited to have us there. It helped that he had lived in Spain and Portugal for years so I was able to communicate in broken Spanish. He told us to get comfortable while his wife and daughter cooked up a meal (in a hidden kitchen, presumably). He pulled up a chair and made us drink oppressively fruity white wine that he had bottled himself. He told us about how he was building a hotel behind this "restaurant" that travelers would flock to. His confidence was endearing. I tried to convince him that I was driving and that I should limit my alcohol intake. Michael dismissed that suggestion by giving me another glass of wine. *"Un poquito esta bien."* ("A little bit is fine.")

Si, un poquito esta bien. But because we were so hungry and the wine so sweet, it was like epinephrine to the heart. Eventually, bread, kebabs, and some vegetables came out to soak it all up. Our ten-minute stop had turned into an hour, but we were grateful.

We made it to the majestic city of Tbilisi at that time of day where shadows lose shape, becoming a mere forefront of darkness. We tried to memorize the architectural layer cake of Byzantine curves and Soviet formality before nightfall gobbled up its beauty. It was too late to make it to the border, so on an app called Maps.Me we found a group of hotels clustered together on the western side of the Mtkvari River. We used our best guesses for how to reach them since we didn't have a working GPS. (This is otherwise known as, "using a map.") We made some wrong turns here and there but it was no one's fault. There were secretive one-way roads and then all of a sudden, giant, ten-car-wide cobblestone lanes wound their way uphill like a grand staircase to a ballroom, eventually spitting us onto one of the ten bridges that spanned the Mtkvari.

"Oh, no-no-no, not again!"

We'd then have to scramble back west across the river, and start over.

After some back and forth, we found ourselves in the Freedom Square roundabout, pretty much dead center in the city. There were a few small hotels around but also a Courtyard Marriott that was singing to us like Odysseus's sirens. Brooke said, "Fuck it. I want to stay in a real hotel tonight. I have a ton of Marriott points and I'm willing to use them." Greg and I were not going to argue. Brooke's points got us a 50 percent discount, so Greg and I covered the rest and bought Brooke dinner. We, of course, paid extra for the parking garage. Knowing we could be in a shower in ten minutes, they could have demanded a kidney from us and we would have been cool with it.

Our room overlooked the splendor of Freedom Square. We were now eye-to-eye with a golden statue of St. George affixed on top of the Liberty Monument at the center of the plaza. He was on a saddled horse reared on its hind legs, and spearing a serpent. Dedicated to the Georgian independence, the statue was the ultimate show of power and victory. In that room we shared St. George's sculpted glory. Moments before, we had been a dirty, homeless trio looking for a place to sleep, and now we were staying in one of the nicest hotels in the city and enjoying the view of a lifetime.

Home.

Paper-thin. Razor-sharp.

We had a great meal and a few drinks at a restaurant around the corner. We thought we'd be in bed by 9 p.m. to rest up for the long ride to Baku the next day but that turned into 11:30 p.m. We had to enjoy a capital city a little bit. With the room lamps finally off, three lightning bugs of technology glowed for a few minutes longer. It was impossible to ignore some news, emails, Facebook, and Instagram when we lay in our beds, wrapped in the blanket of free Wi-Fi.

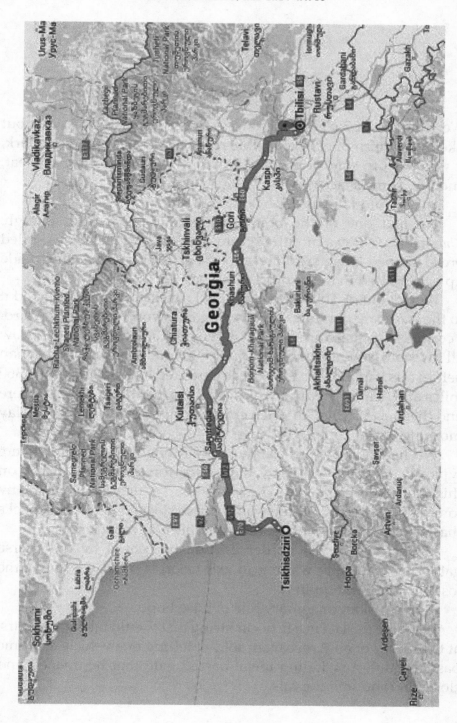

Day 12

We woke up at 7 o'clock hoping to be on the road by 8 a.m., but like our pattern of not being able reach a destination before dark, it was hard to start our day promptly. We still had to pack, eat, and buy some snacks.

This would take us three hours.

We had one of the best breakfasts in the world, though: *Khachapuri*. It was a mouth orgasm of freshly baked, cheese-filled bread shaped like a swollen canoe, with butter and a sunny-side up egg cradled in the middle.

We got out of Tbilisi with minimal confusion and hightailed it to the Azerbaijani border. Just typing that word still seems weird. I consider myself somewhat of a geographical whiz (I still know all my state capitals) but I couldn't point out Azerbaijan on a map before this trip. Brooke had already booked a hostel in Baku—360 miles and "eight" hours away—so all we had to do was get there and then head to the Turkmen embassy bright and early on Friday morning. What could go wrong?

We had heard stories about how Mongol Rally teams were typically used as ATMs by the police forces in two places on this trip: Azerbaijan and Kazakhstan. To defend against any tomfoolery, we had our big wads of cash stashed in our backpacks that were buried in the organized rubble of our back seat.

We arrived at the border cautiously excited by the sparse gathering of people waiting to exit Georgia. Had we found the lost border of tranquility?

Nope. Just an imaginary line of false hope.

We were the last in a fifty-car string that would take four hours, at the mercy of an Azerbaijani soldier letting one vehicle at a time pass through a swinging metal-barred gate that he opened and closed at random intervals.

There were a few rally teams in the queue. Some of them played cricket on the open pavement and some tossed a Frisbee. Most of the local families stared in wonder and judgment from inside their cars. Azerbaijan is a strict Muslim country, so seeing a bunch of secular white adults without any children or responsibilities, showing far too much skin, and clearly misunderstanding how to conduct themselves in public, probably didn't place us high up on the social respect scoreboard. Under the oppressive midday sun Brooke, Greg, and I stayed in our car.

When you're going into your fourth hour camped out on the strip of land between two countries, you start to wonder about all sorts of things:

Why do we need borders?

If a crime is committed in no-man's-land, whose jurisdiction is it?

How much would I pay for a burrito right now?

Eventually, our conversations floated into a stagnant sea. Conversationally adrift, we silently wandered through and experienced the abundant access to our own existence that only mindless waiting can accommodate.

It's crazy to think how the laws and governance of a country we were just in — all the bloodshed, revolutions, debates, trade, progression, voting, and everything else that became the bedrock of that civilization — can end on the same patch of road, among the same vegetation, under the same shade provided by the same rock outcropping where another country begins. *Poof!* Just like that! A new jurisdiction, new regulations, rituals, history…everything. The geography may not look different, but culturally we might as well have driven off a cliff.

When Brooke pulled Donata up to the inspection point, a whiff of militarism filled our noses, and a vest of uneasiness tightened around our ribs. We were unaware how border corruption worked but we were prepared for the guards to start asking us for money like we were passing through a tollbooth.

Our camouflaged, laconic inspector looked into our car. He didn't say much about the drone even when I opened it. He asked to see what was in the cargo carrier. This was such a nuisance for us because our cargo carrier was strapped to our roof much like if you placed a loose deck of cards on a cell phone and wrapped a rubber band around both objects, thus "securing" the cards to the phone. So anytime someone asked to look into our cargo carrier, it would be like taking the rubber band off and displaying a specific card in the deck, except our rubber band was a much more intricate series of loops, pulleys, and ties, wrapping into, through, and around a spare tire and a jerry can.

We got the "all clear," reattached the Rube Goldberg contraption to our roof in the customary knots-of-chaos method, and moved to the next stage.

Brooke had planned to handle the paperwork but for some reason the guards pointed at Greg because, obviously, the biggest man in the group owned the car, right? Brooke was relieved not to have to do it. Greg ran from window to window all over the outdoor complex getting the various vignettes, insurances, blood samples, firstborn child sign-offs, and whatever else was required. It truly was a feat to get all the right documents with the subsequent stamps when you're not speaking the language. Inevitably, Greg would miss a step, get yelled at, and have to go back to the previous window with a shrug and a smile to try to reconcile whatever it was he had done wrong.

Brooke and I spotted a poster at the customs window that had a phone number for the anti-corruption hotline of Azerbaijan. I don't know what would be worse: a government turning a blind eye to corruption or a government knowing that it was so rampant that it publicly created a division to help curb it. We were about to find out, as we had to cannonball-run the entire three hundred-sandy-mile length of a country patrolled by money-grubbing cops.

Finally, Greg had all the papers in order. We rolled towards the exit gate, where more guards asked to see some signature or stamp. The border process never seemed to end. A wad of forms, passports, receipts, and visas were fumbled through as we meandered the last few feet of one country, the feet in-between sovereign states, and first few feet of a new one.

In the end, it didn't matter how tight our paperwork was, how polite we were, how many times our car was searched, or how many border employees said that we were good to go. If the last military guard at the last gate didn't want us to enter his country, we weren't going to enter his country.

The man keeping us from roaming freely into Azerbaijan was a cadaverously thin teenager with a machine gun strapped over his shoulder. He asked for our passports. We gave them to him. He said something in Azerbaijani. We stared at him, puzzled and unsure if he had asked us for a bribe or something legit. He then pointed at our cargo carrier and said, "Top."

"Yeah, top...they opened it already."

He said, "Open," or made a gesture meaning as much.

We told him, "No, dude. They checked that already and it took us fifteen minutes to tighten it back up. We're not opening it for you." I'm not exactly sure where our gall came from. Maybe it was the miles on the road, maybe it was our urgency to get to Baku, maybe we were defending against corruption, or maybe we were fucking tired of opening and closing that damn thing, but for whatever reason, the guard gave us our papers back and opened the gate to the desert wilderness of Azerbaijan.

We were always enraptured when a country admitted us into her vitals, but this was different. We were floating in zero gravity. We felt like West German spies who had shaken off the Stasi in the streets of East Berlin.

There certainly wasn't much on display in the scenic department other than a visual lesson on aridity. The duvet of sand bounced the sun's rays into our eyes, leaving us with permanent squints. The driving rules were typical of this part of the world: if you could pass, you passed. Most people know how to drive extremely well. They're not as worried about rules as they are about getting somewhere without killing anyone else.

Since I was in the back seat, I tried to get a little shut-eye or shut-brain and take my mind off things and how hot it was.

***

I awoke to a panicked conversation.

"Shit…shit."

"No worries. Just pull over here. I'm sure he's not following us — okay, he is."

"Goddammit. Why did we get pulled over?"

"I don't know, Brooke."

All things considered, it's pretty impressive that this was our first potential ticket. Of course, whether we deserved it or not was another story. Like a black panther trying to stay hidden on a dusting of snow, our decal- and sticker-laden car was easy pickings.

There were two cops in the blue-and-white Ford Focus. One of them got out and took a self-satisfied walk up to our car. He was in his early thirties. He leaned into the driver's side window and began to speak absolutely no English at all. The dropped jaws and glassy eyes that he peered into gave him a good idea that his message was not being processed as intended.

He reached into the communication coffers and brought out hand signals, onomatopoeic noises, and facial expressions to get his point across. We still had no idea what he was trying to say, but Brooke stayed on the super-apologetic-and-ignorant-course, which was the best defense. After a two-minute game of charades, chuckles, and clarifications we deduced that we had passed a car on a solid white line as opposed to the dotted line. *Okay*, that was true, but *everyone* on the highway was passing like that. In fact, when we got pulled over it was because Brooke was following someone who was passing someone else over a solid white line.

She apologized.

The cop smiled.

We smiled.

And we all waited.

Again, he said that we crossed the white line. We pantomimed our understanding and that we were sorry. Could we go now?

No, we could not go. We had to pay a fine.

Let the corruption begin.

The cop asked Brooke to step out and took her to his car. Maybe this was how they read Miranda rights here. Looking back, this was complete insanity. How and why Greg and I allowed this is well…actually…what else were we supposed to do?

"What's happening, Greg? Can you see her?"

Peering into the rearview mirror, "Yeah. They just put her in the back seat. She's fine."

"Okay, what now?"

"Not sure."

After about fifteen minutes, the cop returned, put his arms on the driver's side window and leaned in as if to say, "So…" And we gave him our grins relaying the same message.

So…

He told us once more that Brooke crossed the white line and this couldn't go unpunished. He shook his head and practically trembled, chilled by the memory of the ghastly maneuver he had witnessed.

We get it buddy, and we know the game you're playing.

He returned to his car.

The cops were probably expecting Brooke to get scared and agree to any fine, but they didn't know Brooke. She doesn't give a shit about you and your intimidation tactics.

After ten more minutes Brooke got out of the cop car and walked up to our driver's side window.

"Okay, they want three hundred euros."

"Get the fuck out of here! *Three hundred* euros?"

"I know! And they started at four thousand U.S. *or* three hundred euros."

"Um, that makes no sense," I sleuthed.

"I know. Okay. Fuck these guys?"

"Fuck these guys," Greg and I confirmed.

She walked back and hopped in the cop car on her own like all of this was normal. Greg and I got comfy for what might be a long wait.

Shortly thereafter, Eric Estrada came back to our window. In the meantime, Greg and I had wrapped a pack of cigarettes with a twenty-dollar bill. This wasn't following the rule of the road of never directly offering a bribe. The guideline is to ask if there is a fine to pay. You let them lead and you try to keep up, but we felt that the rules of the road were for travelers who weren't as charming as we thought we were. This backfired when the cop stepped away and put his hands up like we'd brandished a gun in his face.

Whoops.

Luckily, he politely declined (see: our charming selves) and didn't arrest us for bribing a police officer in broad daylight. Instead he uttered, "No, no, no…two hundred."

Okay, so the price came down by quite a bit from three hundred euros, but we were still not interested in that offer. He went back to his car to do whatever he'd done when he went back to his car the other ten times.

Greg and I resumed baking in the midday sun. It was now pushing an unconscionable 100-plus degrees. At least Brooke had AC.

Part of us wanted to pay these guys so we could get on with our expedition, but when you're in this situation, the only thing you're thinking of is not losing. It's terrible and horribly shortsighted but it's something that gripped us fully because it was forcing us to deal with a visceral life truth: You don't want to be someone's bitch, even if you will never see this person again. Relationships have ended, companies have folded, people have died, wars were fought, and civilizations were destroyed all because a person did not want someone to get the better of them in an otherwise meaningless disagreement.

It was also about group ego. Greg and I didn't want to pay the penalty while Brooke was being the stalwart in the back of the cop car. And I was sure that Brooke didn't want to come off as a wimp to me and Greg by folding and having us pay a larger fine than necessary.

Stubbornness and pride...vines that choke the life out of every logic tree.

After ten more minutes, the cop came back to our car. He seemed to be confused we were not giving him what he wanted. He laughed. We laughed. He was nice enough. We never felt scared. He asked to try on Greg's sunglasses. They were a cheap two-dollar pair that Greg had gotten at a surfing event years ago. Greg flattered him with how good he looked and told him to keep the glasses, but our friend refused, like he could never accept such a wonderful gift. He returned the glasses and then slowly walked back to his car.

"Fucking hell, Bassam. How long is this going to last?"

"I don't know."

About five minutes later Brooke came back to our window and said, "Okay, guys. I got it down to eighty dollars total. What do you think?"

Brooke Blackman, everybody!

While Greg and I had fumbled with twenty-dollar bills, packs of cigarettes, and two-dollar sunglasses, Brooke got it done.

We pooled the eighty dollars, and were free to go.

We drove off, comparing stories of what we each dealt with and — *what the fuck?*

Before we knew it, about a half-mile later, a plump, clean-shaven, middle-aged police officer sitting in a lawn chair under the shade of a rock mesa just beyond a police station blew his whistle and waved his wand, pointing for us to pull over.

We were livid.

It was obvious that he and exercise were barely on speaking terms but he shuffled to our car with a general air of pleasantness. Before he could say anything, Brooke beat him to the punch. "I know. I know. We just got pulled over back there. Your guys got us. We paid our fine."

The cop chuckled and added, "Oh, so the Azerbaijani police got you?"

At least he spoke a little English. Brooke took her chance.

"So that's not why you're pulling us over?"

"No. Did you see the stop sign?"

On the side of the road, an uninspired stop sign hung on a railing that looked more like a rubbish pile than traffic coordination. Having never seen this setup before, we assumed they actually rolled this out *into* the road when they wanted someone to stop.

"We didn't know it was for us."

"It said 'Stop.'"

"We're trying to learn the rules of the road here and we just got pulled over half a mile back and paid a fine. We're just trying to get to Baku tonight."

He smiled and seemed sympathetic. He looked at Greg, who was sitting shotgun, and said, "Come with me."

"Me?"

Brooke and I said, "Him?"

"Yes."

Greg grabbed what is known in this part of the world as the "car passport" (registration, insurance, and so on) and followed our portly fellow into the station. Was this just one more jolt in the grand Azerbaijani shakedown that we were going to have to endure for the next 250 miles, or was this a misunderstanding? Brooke and I talked about food and freedom, unsure which was more important.

Ten minutes later Greg emerged from the police station. I stuck my hand out of the window and made a thumbs-up and thumbs-down symbol, fishing for a response. Greg gave us a thumbs-up.

Nice! Azer-not-so-bad.

He said, "Good news and bad news. The good news is that we are not getting a ticket but the bad news is that Brooke is not allowed to drive in Azerbaijan anymore. Here's how the conversation went:

Cop: Why she drive?

Greg: What?

Cop: Why she driving?

Greg: It's her car.

Cop: Okay, she no drive anymore. You drive.

Greg: I drive?

Cop: You drive.

Greg: Okay. I drive.

Azerbaijan is a secular state but it is 95 percent Muslim. This conservative Islamic country didn't want any bit of Brooke and her car-owning self.

And so, Brooke got yanked to the backseat early on in her shift, having only driven 120 miles. She was a little depressed, feeling like she wasn't able to pull her own weight. We quelled her concerns, reiterated how much of a badass she was, and told her that there were many more countries to come.

Having traveled a little over a mile, Greg was barely out of fourth gear when we came over the crest of a hill only to be met by *another* cop, standing in the middle of the road while his partner leaned on their car parked in the median of the two-lane highway. The cop pointed his wand at us and then waved it with the flourish of a magician, directing us to pull over.

This was absurd. We were hungry, we were tired, and we hadn't gotten anywhere in the last hour.

Since I was sitting shotgun and since this was a British car, when the cop came up to our window from the middle of the road, he saw me first. He was a stocky, irascible white man in his early forties, one of those guys who looked like he was born middle-aged. Had I not known he was Azerbaijani, I would have guessed eastern European, Russian maybe. He put both his hands on the door, leaned his small, pugnacious face into our car, and blurted, "Papers. Papers. Passport." I didn't so much hand him my passport as he took it out of my hands once I had removed it from my pocket. I don't know why I forfeited my passport instead of the car passport but it all happened so fast. It's easy to say what you would do or should do in moments like this but what you *do* do is anyone's guess.

Devoid of my passport, I yelled, "Why are we being pulled over? We just got pulled over twice and we paid you guys already."

He spoke less than no English and seemed about as dumb as a bucket of hair as he kept repeating, "Money."

"For what? What did we do? You tell us what we did and you'll get money."

Was word traveling among the Azerbaijani police ranks that Donata and her passengers were easy pickings? If we didn't stand up for ourselves, we'd be the country's prison bitches for the rest of the drive.

There was something wrong with this situation. Jason Bourne would have figured this out more quickly than we did, but the cop's uniform was a little tattered, his eyes were bloodshot, his partner was in plainclothes, and their squad car was a Lada with a crooked stripe painted on the side of it. (The Lada is a cheap Russian car that kind of looks like a BMW. Everyone has one and everyone overloads them. They are the iron mules of Central Asia and I want one so badly.)

These were bandits.

He was able to muster, "Speeding," and then kept blurting out the only other word he knew, "Money. Money."

We decided to play the slow game of "I...*uh*...I...don't... what?" I had eighty dollars on me while Greg and Brooke had around one hundred dollars each. Over our dead bodies was this knucklehead getting that.

He reached into the car and grabbed at our pockets, forcing me and Greg to say, "Do not touch me. We don't have any money." He sprang back and forth to each window, getting louder and louder, slamming his hands on our car, clenching his teeth, which gave a quiet, throaty intensity to his demands.

We did not know how far this maniac would go.

Needless to say, this was not good. How long should we stand up for what was right? It was a two-man debate between being bitched and being killed, with dignity as the moderator.

As things escalated, Brooke, never the one to be shy, said, "Fuck this guy. Greg, just turn the car on and hit the gas."

To which I replied, "Um, no, no, no! He's got my passport. We can't leave without my passport."

Silence filled the car amid the gibberish demands being spewed at us.

"Okay, Bassam, then on the count of three, you grab your passport, shove the guy, and Greg, you hit the gas."

Fucking GI Jane in the backseat.

"I don't know if I'm cool with that plan! What if I don't grab it? What if this guy has a knife or a gun? This could get bad quickly."

He's yelling at us. We're yelling at him. We're yelling at each other.

Anarchy.

Greg quieted the hysteria by slipping out a twenty-dollar bill from his pocket and offered it up. "Here, this is all we have." As the outlaw moved around the car in the desert sun to grab his spoils like a circus monkey, I too was able to sneak a twenty-dollar bill from my wallet and keep it loosely in my pocket.

Instead of taking a small win and going on his way, this buffoon was like a shark smelling blood. "More, more, more."

Fuck.

"We don't have anymore, dude."

"More. Money. Money. *Money*!"

Jesus Christ. I snagged the twenty dollars from my pocket and said, "Okay, here. That's it." He scurried around the car and grabbed it like Gollum snatching for the ring.

"More, more, more."

Somewhere, Pavlov was laughing.

He then said, "Five. Five," and followed that one-word message by attempting to poke his filthy paws into our pockets.

I hit his hand away and said, "Dude, you're not going to stick your hand in my pockets. I don't care who you are."

I have to admit, part of the strength it took not to fold like a bedsheet and give this psychopath all our money was that we didn't want to later meet someone who got away from this guy by giving him less than we did. The power of social hierarchy could get us killed in situations that should never warrant such an escalation.

Fortunately, Brooke's brain fired when we needed it most. "Greg, call the embassy."

Greg pretended to dial a number on his phone. The madman suddenly got skittish and said, "Okay, okay, okay," and handed me my passport. He ran back to his car with his minion who, not for nothing, didn't do a thing the whole time except stand on the other side of the empty highway, sucking on a lollipop.

Sigh.

We were thankful to have our lives and the majority of our money, but we were pissed. We had just reached the first "difficult" country and within one hundred miles we had been pulled over three times, fleeced twice, and were emotionally frazzled. A distance that should have taken us one and a half hours had taken us three. It was already 4 p.m. and we supposedly had five and a half hours to go to Baku (before any road multiples). This was the lowest point of the rally for us so far.

What the hell are we doing here?

We also hadn't eaten a proper lunch, but we didn't want to stop. Anyway, we couldn't. We still didn't have any Azerbaijani currency. On Greg's suggestion we agreed to drive the speed limit and not a mile over it. We didn't want to give these crooks one iota of a reason to pull us over, although I don't think it really mattered how fast we were going.

To add to our misfortune and frustration, the main highway had construction on it 50 percent of the way to Baku. And by "construction," I mean our entire side of the highway was closed because they were preparing to pave a layer of asphalt. I don't mind any country investing in their infrastructure, but they could have done it one piece at a time. Speed limits in the construction zones were about 25 mph, painful even for Donata's limited horses. We putzed on under the heavenly blue hues that sank deeper into the coal-like abyss of the night sky.

When it finally was time to get gas, we stopped at a well-lit, modern station. All the attendants were dressed exactly like Luigi from Super Mario Brothers: green overalls and the hat. They didn't speak English but they did accept credit cards.

Of course, when it was time to pay, our cards were about as useful as inflatable anchors.

"Try it again, please."

The manager even walked around the gas station, moving his portable payment device towards the sky, hoping for a signal. Instead, all we got was repeating ellipses followed by "Rejected."

Like they do in the movies, I had him try it again a third time. No luck.

We couldn't think straight because a sadistic cult of mosquitoes was mauling us. Where they had found standing water to breed was beyond me. To get out of there we offered the manager U.S. dollars at an unbelievably greater exchange rate than any bank, but he was by-the-book. No way. No how. We had to pay in *manat*.

Great.

The Luigis pointed down the road to a group of buildings and said "money exchange." We left one of our passports with them and drove until we found a generally populated road with some life and electricity but no discernable currency exchange. Greg parked and I hopped out.

I got looks from the locals but I didn't give a shit. I went into the first store I saw, held up the U.S. dollars, did a little "me-to-you" thing with my hand to the guy behind the counter, and he got it. He took his calculator out and exchanged my money at a fair rate.

I'm sure there were some places that served food here but we really needed to move on. It was well past dinnertime and we had already skipped lunch but unless it was a fast-food place, we couldn't take the risk of sitting for too long.

We paid for our gas, took some photos with the Luigis, and crept on until at one point around 11 p.m. I told Greg, "Dude, we have to drive faster." We were heeding the speed limit but everyone was passing us. We took a vote and decided it was time to accelerate.

With no streetlights, no markings and no signs, the driving became a feat of survival. When we looked straight ahead, the glare of the headlights coming our way rendered our depth perception useless. Imagine you and forty other people are taken to a giant basement in a house you've never been to. All the lights are off. You are handed a dying flashlight and a mirror to see behind you. Everyone else has a Maglite. They are told to shine it directly in your face. You are asked to navigate through the basement while not bumping into anyone. Everyone will be moving faster than you.

Good luck.

Half the time we felt like we were avoiding the incoming headlights through psychokinesis. The other half, Greg looked out of our windshield at a 2 o'clock angle so that he could keep us out of a sandy ditch. This went on for a mind-boggling distance.

The saving grace came when a massive semitruck overtook us and we could accelerate and ride in its wake for as long as possible. We ceded control of spotting any impediments on the broken highway and instead trusted that the truck driver would brake if he saw something that warranted it. Instead of looking at the road, we simply stared at its brake lights, waiting to react.

Sometimes the trucks would drive too fast, spitting out potholes quicker than our fast-twitch muscles could respond, forcing Greg to cut the tether and fend for ourselves. A minor divot to a truck was a major cavity to us. It was a neverending game of speed versus safety.

Baku became an enigma. We thought we were on the right road, we saw a random sign for it every now and then, but we couldn't ever get there. Were we close to the water? Were we not? Was that the bend we needed to take? We knew we were on the right track when street lamps began to illuminate the highway. It was the first time I'd ever heard my pupils sigh.

It was 1:30 a.m.

And so, once again, we rolled into our destination under the cloak of darkness.

Baku is the largest city on the Caspian Sea. People other than I have long documented its geographic importance throughout history. Nowadays, it's a visual manifestation of the lopsided wealth distribution that you see in a lot of oil-rich countries: grand palaces, fast cars, boutiques, and futuristic architecture, while everyone else in the country is living in the 1960s or 1860s. It's the modern-day moat and castle.

Our hostel was on a labyrinthian street in the beautiful old-walled city that dates back more than one thousand years. One hundred spy movies could have been shot here. We prayed that there would be accessible parking but had that wish firmly punctured by the "2-hour parking" signs posted everywhere.

When we reached our hostel at 2 a.m., we could not *find* our hostel. We were at the address listed but all we saw was a building under renovation and a super swanky restaurant with people above our pay grade enjoying dinner on the patio. We double-parked with our hazards on, blocking a Maserati. We asked around if anyone knew the location of the hostel but the maîtres d' put a stop to that and tried to wave us away like we were feral cats. Suddenly, from about five stories up in the building being renovated, a man yelled down to us. "Brooke?"

Home.

This was Mikail. He was the owner of the hostel. He came down and negotiated one of the prime spots usually reserved for German sports cars. We were sure Donata would be a smoldering piss bucket by morning but we were tired. So tired. We could find a new car tomorrow.

Our room was the *only* room in the hostel. It was a giant hippie den with four king-size mattresses and sliding shag curtains separating each bunk and bed.

Whatever. Fuck it. Two of the mattresses were already filled with guests so Brooke and I shared a bed while Greg took the spot above us. Mikail muttered some house rules that I barely absorbed and he handed us each a fancy key to our own personal locker.

We still hadn't eaten a proper meal since breakfast but we had no recourse other than passing out. I quelled the beast scratching his talons on the walls of my stomach by smothering him with a rag doused in Ambien.

Day 13

Four hours later...

Our alarms sparked the flames of consciousness. Where was I? What day was it? That fire was fanned by the winds of realization. *Oh, right. It's Friday. I'm filthy, sweaty, and starving to death in my least favorite country on the planet.*

We were hoping that the hostel would have food for us, but Mikail said that the full breakfast wouldn't be ready until 8:30 a.m. We couldn't risk being in the back of the line at the Turkmen embassy.

We packed up our stuff, but left a few things because by all accounts it would take us a full day to procure this visa and then at least another day to coordinate the ferry. At the time of our departure from the hostel, we had no less than three possible addresses for the embassy. That's right. Websites, directories, and blog posts did not agree, so famished and ambiguously directed, we drove into the madness of morning rush hour. Getting across the sprawling capital took a lot longer than anticipated because of the gridlock, the car horns, and the gigantic one-lane roads we didn't know how to exit. Like new trees reaching for the top of the jungle canopy, Baku seemed to be in a race to expand. It was a ten-pound city stuffed into a five-pound bag.

We arrived at the first address on our list but I had a bad feeling. "I think this is the actual house of the ambassador, not the embassy." We stopped, asked some people questions they didn't understand, and drove away.

The second address was from the reputable site, www. caravanistan.com. If you're going to any of the 'Stans, ever, let this website be your bible. It directed us to a back street. I was ready to move on to the third address but Brooke said, "Wait, let's check it out."

I said, "Brooke, it's a fucking embassy, it has to be a huge building with signs, flags, and all that. There's no way it's d—"

"Wait! Go back!" Brooke spotted something in the distance down one of the alleyways. We pulled up and sure enough, ralliers! Too many ralliers…Good call, Brooke. This was the Turkmen embassy. One green door attached to a two-story apartment in a nondescript alley, open two days a week. An economic war chest was clearly not something the Turkmen tourism board had access to.

Our brothers and sisters in adventure informed us we could park around the corner on a parallel street. There, we saw four rally cars lined up next to a construction site on a mound of rebar, glass, and various other tire-piercing debris. We tiptoed our wheels this way and that until we were sufficiently off the main path.

By the time we got back to the group with all our papers in hand, it was just after 9 a.m. Our aim of being early backfired and now we were last in a line of six teams, dreaming of the breakfast we had skipped.

After asking a few questions to establish what the process was, one of the ralliers said, "Dude, just talk to that guy in the striped shirt. He's taking care of everything."

Enter: Ishmael.

Ishmael was Azerbaijani but he also spoke Russian, Turkmen, and English. He was short in stature, good in looks, and had a little extra in the tummy. It seemed like he lived a pleasant life. I would have guessed that he was Indian or Pakistani based on his skin color and his just-long-enough-to-run-his-fingers-through-it jet-black hair.

Ishmael was a fixer.

Countless times we were at a literal or verbal impasse until someone with more local knowledge or a grip on multiple languages came to our rescue. A fixer can get you from point A to point B, geographically or logistically, when you can't do so on your own.

Within a minute, we understood the lay of the land. For twenty dollars per person Ishmael would be the liaison, guiding us through the whole process:

Translating document instructions

Depositing money into a local bank to pay for the visa

Taking new photos for our visa

We couldn't speak Turkmen, and we didn't know where the bank or photo store was.

Ishmael, meet twenty dollars. Twenty dollars, meet Ishmael.

Had we arrived ten minutes later, Ishmael and the current crop of ralliers would have already been headed to the bank and we would have had to wait until who knows when for him to return and make his next trip. With the prospect of more teams showing up as the day went on, and without knowing how long this embassy even stayed open, we wanted to be as close to the front of the line as possible to secure our visas. No time to eat. We asked Ishmael if he could "pin" the location of the bank on our Maps.Me app in case we get lost but he said, "Don't worry. Just stay behind me."

He obviously didn't want his jewel box of information to be shared with others for free, but staying behind someone in "Baku the Clogged" was like trying to continually hold the hand of one partner in a square dance. We traded an assortment of fist bumps, hugs, and handshakes with other teams/cars, like we were all about to jump into enemy territory from a plane.

"Good luck."

Good luck.

Greg drove so that I could navigate. Brooke was happy to be in the back.

Our daisy chain of clown cars entered the fray of Baku traffic, each vehicle more laughable than the next. Our sponsor decals, dragging mufflers, backfiring exhausts, and squeaky brakes drew glances, laughs, and doses of ire. We were like a gaggle of preschoolers crossing a street attached to a leash, each kid looking in a different direction, unsure of the destination.

Yeah, that was us.

Baku drivers would try to sneak in between us but we wouldn't let them, even when it was the my-lane/your-lane merging routine. We stayed undivided, like a funeral procession.

We navigated our way to the bank in twenty harrowing minutes, rolling into a stop next to a crop of parked cars on the right side of the highway, effectively turning ourselves into a double-parking squadron. In many places in central Europe and Asia, there is one sheet of tarmac and no delineation between where the road ends and parking begins. There are no real curbs or islands or anything like that, so when we double-parked we ended up blocking at least half a lane.

Ishmael assured us that it wasn't a problem. As he led Brooke and the other team representatives into the bank, Brooke stopped, seized me with the devil's grip, and implored, "Find some fucking kebab." She was right. Sadly, there was no kebab for sale this early in the morning, unlike in the good city of Istanbul.

The rest of the ralliers bonded on the side of the road. There were the Spaniards (Jorge and Osvaldo) in the black Peugeot 205 that I wanted so badly. There were the Irish (Mick and George) in the teal 1999 Ford Focus hatchback. There were the Americans (Team F.L.P) whom we had met on launch day (Parker, Emma, and Ryan) in their green matchbox car. There were the white-car Brits who camped with us in Samsun, and there were the red-car Brits (Rory and Stanley) in a 1985 Nissan Micra hatchback. All good people.

Even after a couple of hours, we were talking about how great it would be if we could all make the ferry together. Maybe this is what war is like when they say you are only concerned with the person next to you, the one who has been through what you've been through. As the saying goes, "God does not say that you won't suffer on this earth, just that you won't suffer alone."

Nothing bonds like strife.

Soon enough, the money was deposited and the Ishmael Train continued for fifteen minutes to a Kodak store. Since we thought we were only parking for a few minutes, everyone parallel parked illegally, again, but the store was closed. Ishmael knew of another photo store down the road, so we walked/jogged there at around 11 a.m. in the already searing heat. "Just down the road" was much farther than we had initially thought, so, woozy and ravenous, we filed down some treacherous steps and were greeted by a man who would happily oblige our polychromatic group. Brooke went first and when she was done, I returned the kebab request she had given me earlier. She went foraging in the streets for sustenance.

The rest of us stayed inside this small office thinking about the hilarity of where we were and what we were doing: in Azerbaijan, on the Caspian Sea, running around like lunatics so that we could get *into* a country that had seemingly done everything in its power to keep us all out.

Brooke was only able to locate some water. Fine. It was hot. We were all entering a state of hunger-induced delusion. We raced back to our cars, relieved that they had not been towed. Ishmael had been making good so far. He was constantly on the phone wheeling and dealing. Some other ralliers needed visas to Tajikistan or Uzbekistan. Ismael fixed everything, maybe too many things. I hated putting all our eggs in one basket but we had no choice.

With all the necessary visa documents, we returned to the embassy to practice our line-waiting skills. Of course, when we showed up, there were a bunch of new faces, people who wanted to get *their* visas, people who needed answers. Now we were the ones with the information and it was our turn to feel thankful for our place in the pecking order. We told them who to talk to and wished them luck. With an abyss in our guts, Brooke volunteered to stock up at a supermarket. Greg and I would wait at the embassy.

She returned with a couple of plastic bags of fruit, chips, peanut butter, and a small loaf of bread. We made single-ply peanut butter-and-jelly sandwiches. Those folded handfuls of wonder were a revolution in our mouths. We couldn't get too reckless with our consumption, though, because we needed to have enough food for the ship in case the crossing took two or three days.

Greg made friends with some local children who were admiring our vehicles. These kids were signing cars, taking photos in front of them, and I hope, not planning to rob everything we owned. That's not jingoism; that's a precaution.

Ishmael was constantly on the phone with the ferry office. In order for private cars to get on a commercial ferry, there needed to be enough of them (vehicles) so that the fees garnered offset the profit the ship could make with the goods they would otherwise be shipping. Basically, if there were four or more cars, we'd get on the next ferry. If we were by ourselves, we might wait a couple of days until more cars wanted to join us. Of course, there was no online booking. It was all shady deals: first-come, first-serve.

A little after noon, Ishmael hung up and said there was a ferry supposedly leaving at 2 p.m. (!) but the following one wouldn't leave until Monday. This was a revelation. In our wildest dreams we never imagined we could do the visa/ferry combo on the same day, but now that it was a possibility, I couldn't fathom staying in Baku another three nights.

It was 12:30 p.m. There were still three teams in our group that needed visas, and we were second-to-last. Ishmael said that we would be cutting it close. We desperately wanted to stay with the teams we had connected with, but we had the additional hurdle of not having checked out of our hostel yet.

We made a plan. Brooke would stay in line and manage the acquisition of the visas. Greg and I were going to race to the hostel, check out, and then meet back at the embassy. If we timed it right, it should take us about forty-five minutes round-trip. Considering that it took each team roughly half an hour to secure their visas, we should make it back before Brooke got out.

Fueled by half a peanut butter-and-jelly sandwich and one-third of a tangerine we sprinted to Donata. In the car, Greg and I were like a real rally team. "Greg, remember that road we came up to get here? Well, we can't take that same one back...second right and then your immediate left...fuck, traffic...take a right here." And so on.

When we were almost at the hostel, something popped in my head that threw me into an absolute blood-boiling frenzy. I started punching the dashboard.

"Fuck. Fuck. *Fuck*. Fuck. Fuck!"

"What the hell is going on, man? Talk to me."

A few deep breaths brought me off the ledge and negated any need for an exorcism.

"I didn't get Brooke's key to her locker. Did she pack her bag this morning?"

Crickets.

This was the million-dollar question. I had left my backpack and toilet bag at the hostel, Greg had packed all his stuff in the car, but what Brooke had done this morning was anyone's guess. If she packed her bag, it was in the back, covered in a tower of luggage.

It wasn't like our hostel was easy to get to. The old walled city only had two gated entrances. We chose the one on Neftchilar Avenue. *Whoops*. We were met by a single-file stretch of cars fifty yards long. I hopped out and told Greg to stay in line. If I returned before he reached the gates, we could slip out of line and steam back to the embassy.

I ran down the sidewalk, entered the old city, bounded up the six flights of stairs, and almost passed out from low blood sugar before storming into the hostel like it was a bank heist. Mikail wasn't there, but there was a boy on the computer behind the front desk.

"Where is Mikail?"

"Out to lunch."

"Can you call him?"

"I don't have his number."

Awesome.

I put my key in my locker and grabbed my bags. I yanked, pulled, and pried at Brooke's wooden locker and was on the verge of obliterating the thing, but I couldn't. I shouldn't. If we didn't catch this ferry, we'd still need a place to stay for a couple of nights. I was left to hope that she had already put her bag in the car. I hate hoping. Hoping was for people who aren't in control of their lives. Cortisol flooded my veins. Additionally, Brooke had yet to pay for the room. I remember her saying that it was forty-something dollars. I left forty-five dollars on the counter and told the dude sitting there surfing the internet to make sure Mikail got that money.

I sprinted down the stairs with my backpack and toilet bag, bolted around the corner, and saw Greg about to go through the gate. He couldn't back out at this point because there was a line of cars behind him. We explained to the guard that we were going to pull a U-turn and we weren't going to pay. He obliged...barely.

We raced back to the embassy, feeling like we knew how the roads and city worked. "Okay, Greg, here is that crazy plaza with that S-turn that has that dual-stop roundabout on the cobblestone streets. Stay left coming into the turn but then you have to get right to stay straight and go under the bridge and then...." Greg said, taking over, "take the second right and then my next left. Got it."

We zoomed through Baku, returning to our homing beacon—Ishmael at the embassy. Once we were across the Caspian, we would be left to our own devices, back on our own relative and general schedule, but until then, we were captives in Azerbaijan. Our only means of reaching Mongolia was contingent upon us getting stamps in our passports, boarding an industrial cargo ship, and sailing to and then driving through Turkmenistan over five specific days. We couldn't go through Iran because we didn't have a visa and we couldn't go through Russia because we didn't have a dual-entry visa, only a single entry one, and we had to save *that* for the Kazakh-Russian border.

We parked the car between the shrapnel pile and dust bowl, high-fived the local kids, and ran back to the embassy. Brooke had yet to go through. When she saw me she immediately had an apologetic look on her face. She said, "You're going to kill me."

I said, "I know. Your key...but please tell me your bag is in the car."

Her five-mile stare told the story.

She apologized and said that she chased us right after we left, only to see the back of Donata zipping away. I told her that it wasn't her fault at all and that I should have taken my time and made sure we had all our bases covered. This was true. I did blame myself. We'd all lost out minds.

So we'd have to go back to the hostel *again* before we could get on any ship. We debated whether to do that now or wait for Brooke to get out since there was a team behind us who still had to get their visas. What to do? What to do? We circled up with Ishmael, who seemed to be brokering international hostage exchange deals on his phone. Calling, texting, multiple languages, hand gestures, and the like...

The update was that we would have to hurry if we were all going to make the 2 p.m. ferry. It was now a little past one o'clock. That's when the team in front of us came out and it was Brooke's turn to go in. We told her to start our five-day visa for tomorrow. We were betting the house on us getting that 2 p.m. ferry. Greg and I didn't want to split the group up again so we decided to wait for her, then we'd all swing by the hostel on the way to the port.

So, after all that hectic insanity, we stood around and did absolutely nothing for half an hour. A nice gentle rain pitter-pattered on the surrounding roofs. Some other rally teams showed up and got the lay of the land. I didn't have the emotional energy to really engage with them and get to know them at all. I focused on locating my wits, dusting them off, and plugging any leaky holes.

We went over the plan a hundred times with Ishmael while Brooke was inside. When she came out, we would go to the hostel, get her bag, and head to the parking lot for the Seaport Hotel/

Marine Passenger Terminal, across from the JW Marriott Hotel. Ishmael and the other teams would wait for Rory and Stanley to finish and then all would head to the same parking lot to meet us. I even got Ishmael to mark the terminal on our map. He mentioned that the dock was a little farther down the road (a point he refused to mark) but this parking lot was the easiest place to meet. Brooke had his phone number in case of emergency but international service was spotty at best.

"Ishmael, don't leave without us. We'll be there. We'll be there."

Greg and I were acting like boxers before a prizefight, getting ready for Round 3 of the Baku Melee.

Finally, Brooke came out and gave the thumbs up. Our visas had been issued. We hugged each other and congratulated ourselves on fitting this piece into the puzzle. We said goodbye to Ishmael and the other teams who would be part of our convoy to get on the ship. They would all be going with Ishmael once Rory and Stanley—who went in after Brooke—had their visas in hand.

"We'll see you soon, guys. In the parking lot."

We were oh-so-close to boarding the ship and getting out of Baku in less than a day! But nothing was in our control. It was about getting Brooke's bag and reaching the meeting point as quickly as possible. The rest was wholeheartedly not about us—a theme repeated throughout the rally. We could only control what we could control and hope for the best.

We cut through Baku with the precision of a surgeon. We gave Brooke the rundown of how crazy a street Neftchilar Avenue was and that she had to get out of the car and run inside, while we illegally parked with our hazards on.

"So you have to hurry. Okay, Brooke? Hurry."

Brooke shot towards the Old City gate like she was legging out a 400-meter dash, but not twenty seconds after she darted did Greg and I see a cop in our rearview mirror moving his way up the line of parked cars.

Fuck. Fuck. Fuck. Not now, dude.

Thankfully, Brooke made it down in record time with Mikail, the saint that he was, carrying her bag and coming to wish us well. But we were like a race car at a quick pit stop: no gas, just tires. Time to go, bro. The cop was two cars away. Brooke shoved her bag in the back and we sped off before Mikail could even lower his goodbye wave.

However, we were now driving *away* from the port. We had to go straight for a hundred meters and then make a U-turn around Azneft Square. This was a dizzying multistage roundabout of confusion. Some cars went in front of us, some behind us. It was unnerving. There were police officers there to direct traffic. We were in the middle lane, and I wasn't sure if we were allowed to pull a U-turn but I told Greg, "There is nothing more important than getting around this fucking loop without getting pulled over. No pressure."

The cop spotted us at the front of the line waiting to enter. He knew we were easy money. I'm sure something was illegal about our car, our straps, our obstructed views, our steering wheel on the wrong side, or our general sense of foreignness.

He stared.

We stared.

I didn't know what was going to happen when the light turned green, but when it did, by God, "Greg, you get around this corner and head for the port!"

Green.

Zoom. Come on, baby. Come on, *baby*!

The turn was so tight that it felt like an elliptical slingshot around a planet. Thankfully, the cop shifted his attention to the thousands of cars crisscrossing in front of him, and he let us go on our way. I let out a cheer and a fist pump. Finally, we were in the clear.

Record scratch.

About a mile down the road, we approached the parking lot where we were supposed to meet Ishmael and the ralliers. Again, it's hard to describe the size of Neftchilar Avenue, but at this stage it had unfurled into an unpainted super highway, maybe seven cars wide. The parking lot we had to turn into didn't really have a designated entrance—it was a continuation of the tarmac into a giant open space in front of the Seaport Hotel. One could enter or leave the parking lot anywhere they wanted to along a 50-meter length of road.

"Brooke, text Ishmael and let him know we're here."

She did and he wrote back, "On our way."

Fuck. Yes.

We parked and aired out a bunch of our stuff on the pavement all around the car. Poor Brooke didn't even pee when she ran up to get her bag at the hostel because of the apparent severity in my voice when I said, "Hurry." She was now about to wet herself. She suggested finding a bathroom in the seaport although I didn't want her to go far. I was so concerned with getting on this ship that I didn't want to mess up one thing on our end. But the girl had to pee. I suppressed the Stalin in me and told her to go ahead. In the meantime, I walked over to a small newsstand and bought three giant bottles of water, a bag of raisins, and the black-tar heroin of snacks: Snickers.

So hungry. So tired. So thirsty. It was nearly 2 p.m.

Come on, Ishmael. *Come on.*

"He's gotta be showing up any minute, right?" I did my calculations of times, distances, and what streets he'd be traveling on. I walked to the edge of the parking area, looked at a different road, and confirmed that its one-way direction was away from us. Ishmael, if he *was* going to be driving by us, would have to come from the same way we came.

He should be here by now.

"Brooke, can you text him again?"

"He said he was coming. Maybe 'on our way' meant that they were finishing up and not in their cars yet."

"Better safe than sorry."

She texted him again but there was no reply.

One minute.

Two minutes.

Five minutes.

We had now been waiting at least fifteen minutes. There was no way he wouldn't be here by now if he came directly from the embassy. Maybe it was paranoia. Maybe we should have trusted the universe, but our collective resolve cracked. Brooke tried to call but had no luck getting through. Should we split up? Should we chill out?

"But we did everything right. How come..." This defeatist way of thinking was not helping me, but really, drowning in a sea of people and cars, we were an Ishmael away from being led to a ship that would take us into the open roads of Central Asia.

Where was he?

We had to do something. Greg suggested that he take a quick walk around the giant construction site to our east, to see if there was anything on the other side. Maybe we misheard Ishmael. Maybe they took a different road. I hated splitting up but we had to be proactive.

Greg left. He had no phone, no nothing; just a dirty man in flipflops searching for answers. He said he'd be back in five minutes max.

Of course, about two minutes after Greg broke off the mother ship's mooring, it happened. To this day it is one of the more dumbfounding moments of my entire life.

As Brooke and I leaned against the car I saw a flicker of color out of the corner of my eye. Down the *right* lane (the one closest to us) of Neftchilar Avenue came Ishmael with the five-car parade of ralliers behind him. He honked his horn and waved. I waved and then very quickly faced my palms upward in a *WTF?* gesture because instead of slowing down, inching his steering wheel one centimeter to the right, and coming to stop in the parking area, he pointed in front of him, informing us of the general direction we already knew we needed to go. But it was the specifics we were missing, the specifics he kept to himself to remain a relevant fixer.

This modern-day Judas continued at a steady speed around the corner where the construction site started, and just like that, our lifeboat out of this country, our opportunity, our key to the rest of the rally was gone. Brooke and I looked at each other screaming, "What the fuck was that?"

No time for contemplation.

We glanced at Donata, all five doors open with bags, socks, and sweaty T-shirts strewn everywhere, airing out in the midday sun. We threw everything in, however it would fit so that the latches on the doors would engage. Brooke dove in the back seat and I took control of the wheel.

We were, of course, missing a teammate. We spotted Greg running back towards us on Neftchilar Avenue. He'd seen Ishmael and the Stooges drive by him. By the time I reached him, I couldn't stop because it was a major road with no shoulder and he was on an elevated sidewalk. I screamed out the window, "Follow me. Follow me! Run!"

I drove until there was a small turnoff. Brooke and I scanned our surroundings as we waited for Greg to catch up. Nothing. No rally cars. They *had* to still be ahead of us.

Paper-thin. Razor-sharp.

I was swearing at a Greg who wasn't there. It wasn't his fault, but he needed to get his 6'3" laid-back frame moving.

He came barreling around the corner and dove into the front seat.

Wheels chirped. Engine whirred.

Greg asked several logical questions and I responded with, "I don't know. I don't *fucking* know."

And this is when the demon came over me. I was so angry I began laughing. It was that sadistic laugh where you exhale out of your nose and shake your head back and forth with a pursed grin on your face. That one that terrifies everyone around you because you seem to have gone full psychopath. Hungry, abandoned, scared, and now murderous, I was flying down the highway as fast as Donata would allow, slithering in and out of Baku traffic like a water snake. Memories of corrupt Azerbaijani police not deterring me one bit.

Why didn't Ishmael stop?

Brooke tried to call him but didn't get through.

It was now 2:45 p.m.

Could they be this far ahead? We should have caught up by now or at least seen them. Every second at a red light was a second we couldn't get back. On Maps.Me, Brooke noticed that there was a passenger ferry about two miles down the road. I could have sworn that Ishmael had said that the ferry we were taking wasn't that far from the parking lot.

This was too far. I knew it. We had to go back, but where? We were a lost ball in tall grass. We were at the mercy of a man who had to pick up his phone or text us back in the next couple of minutes or we were not getting on this ship.

Illegal U-turns were everywhere. I almost went the wrong way down a one-way on-ramp so I could get back to the other side of the street, but I had to remind myself that just because I had a death wish didn't mean my friends did. Were our lives really in danger? No, but it sure as hell felt that way. It wasn't about living or dying; it was about what was right and fair. Had we broken down for two days in Turkey and reached Baku two days later, that would have been fine. But there was an expectation that was eroding. There was a visa with an expiration date that could essentially end our Mongol Rally if we didn't get through Turkmenistan within five days. If we took the Monday ferry, we'd need to cross the Caspian in one day and drive the fifteen "Google hours" through Turkmenistan and into Uzbekistan the next day. Not likely. With no dual-entry Russian visa and no Iranian visa, this was the only way to get Donata and us eastward.

We were in a geographic dilemma. Ishmael was the solution.

"Brooke, I'll pay whatever fees Verizon charges you, just get Ishmael on the phone and tell him that he'd better hang on to the ship's anchor line if he values his life."

She dialed out. "Hel...Hello? Ishma—*Fuck*. It dropped."

She tried again.

"Ishmael. It's Brooke...can you hear me? Where did you go? Why didn't you stop? *Fuck!* The call dropped again."

Breathe in. Breathe out.

Legal U-turn! Alright, Ishmael, we're coming for you and we're coming in hot.

Fifteen minutes. We had to take a fifteen-minute detour because Ishmael didn't stop for *one* minute.

Breathe in. Breathe out.

"Hel-hello? Ishmael? Hi. It's Brooke. Okay, we're coming. Don't leave...I don't know fifteen minutes? You have to wait for us. Please wait for us. We'll be there. Okay. Okay. Bye."

"What did he say, Brooke?"

"'Hurry.'"

Chuckle. Shake head. Sit at red light. Stew. Hate Azerbaijan. Contemplate murder.

Ishmael told Brooke that he would send Rory out to the road to meet us where we were supposed to turn in.

I said, "Greg, take a look at the map and tell me if there is any other way for us to get back to that road other than going all the way around."

There wasn't.

Breathe in. Breathe out.

At the next red light, "Greg, what if I just turn here, isn't that our street parallel to us over there?"

"Yeah, but the road to get there is one-way in the wrong direction."

"But no one is on it."

Silence.

I went straight. Eventually, we turned back towards Neftchilar Avenue, passed the parking lot where we had been before, and passed the construction site Greg had tried to walk around. Oh, the double-looping we did in that city! We drove a bit farther and, lo-and-behold, there was Rory standing at an intersection. I could have cried when I saw him. He poked his head into our car and said, "There you guys are! All is well."

All *was* well, mate—except for Ishmael's life expectancy.

Rory hopped on the back of our car as we drove down *an unmarked road* (Ishmael!) and met the other the teams. We got out of our car like a three-man street gang, but our rage was dampened by how supportive and happy the other rally teams were to see us!

They'd been as stunned by Ishmael's actions as we were.

"We asked him, 'What about the other American team? You told them we would meet them there but you didn't stop. Ishmael, we can't leave without them.'"

His reply was, "Well, that's tough luck for them. They'll just have to catch the next ferry. Sorry. We have no time."

That answer launched me, Greg, and Brooke past the point of rage, orbiting all the way back to tranquility, and somehow to a place where we let everything go. I've never experienced that in my life. Maybe we realized that we had reached our goal *in spite* of being deserted, that we were survivors, and nothing was going to keep us from getting out of Azerbaijan. Maybe harboring that anger, let alone killing someone in broad daylight, wasn't going to help matters. Or maybe, it was a grand humbling by unimportance. Maybe Ishmael's actions taught us that our narrative was closer to being a lifeless planet floating aimlessly in a dark corner of the cosmos, than it was to being the center of anyone's universe. The collateral damage of his actions was so insignificant to him that he had to be reminded about us in the first place. It was like someone trying to ruin your marathon-winning celebration by pointing out the three ants you squished along the way.

I am not a big deal. I am not a big deal. I am not a big deal. Thank you, Ishmael.

But from that moment on, I didn't converse with him. He never apologized.

We filled out the paperwork and paid six hundred and eighty dollars to board the ship. One hundred dollars per meter of the car (ours was three meters) *plus* one hundred dollars per person *plus* eighty-dollar port fee in Turkmenbashi. Terrific. Whatever. Get me out of here.

We passed through a sliding fence where a guard checked our papers and told us to wait in a small gated area. Beyond this quarantine, we could see the ship at the end of a long pier. Soon, all the cars in our convoy joined us, including a Lithuanian rally team that appeared from I don't know where.

The name Baku means "wind-pounded city," but today it was as still as a painting. The sun coated us with invisible lava, and we still hadn't really eaten. We were mentally and physically exhausted and simultaneously elated by our good transit fortune. The Spanish team huddled with us in a triangle of shade under the corner of a tarp the Irish guys hung off their car. The Lithuanians and Team F.L.P congregated behind an eighteen-wheeler to stay out of the blistering sun. Some people slept on the ground between the cars, their bodies motionless, like crumpled flags.

We waited.

The Irish broke out some mini bottles of vodka to share, and within minutes, the parking lot filled with laughter and relaxation. But one hour became two, and two became three. Around 6 p.m., my hunger pangs went ballistic. I would have eaten a *polonium*-and-jelly sandwich right about then. We found out that there was a Papa John's Pizza in Baku. We took a poll and figured out that we'd pay upwards of three hundred dollars if four pizzas were delivered to the port right now. Brooke texted Ishmael—that serpent—to see if he would order for us, but he didn't respond. His work was finished.

Sporadically, some more people would walk towards the ship, allaying our fears that the Caspian crossing might be part of local mythology. The dock's guards came out and played American football with us. These grown men in military uniforms smiling, chasing one another, and tossing footballs for the first time in their lives was direct evidence that sports do have a way of cutting through boundaries, barriers, and bullshit.

The game ended. We waited, and we waited, and the sun set. It was now somewhere after 8:30 p.m., between the shallow light of dusk and night. When we were about to lose all hope, a man came out of the guard booth and told us that it was time. *Finally*.

Our energy surged, we revved our three-quarter-liter engines, and got in line, but the party was short-lived when the lead cars (we were fourth out of seven) turned off their engines and everyone got out.

The fuck?

We were told to grab our passports and Azerbaijan visa in order to process our departure. Azerbaijan visa? Why would we need that? We're leaving the country. The Azerbaijan visa was another one of the 8.5- x 11-inch printouts, like the Turkish visa. I honestly had no idea where I had put it, but I reached in my left pocket where my passport was and felt a folded piece of paper.

Phew.

Brooke had hers all set. Greg opened the back door and grabbed his backpack.

Zip. *Rummage…rummage…* Zip. *Rummage…rummage…* Zip. Zip.

"Greg…what's going on? That's one too many zips," I said.

Greg is one of the most orderly people I know so if it wasn't where he looked first, there was something to worry about. Now that it wasn't in the fifth or sixth place, I hung my head. So close, yet…just one stupid ramp onto a ship. We'd solve this. As much as I wanted to believe that, I didn't know if I had any fight left. I'd used it all up over the past thirty-six hours. Did Greg and Brooke have anything in their tanks? We kept our thoughts and fears to ourselves even when every other team went towards the booth with their papers in hand.

We got in the back of the line outside of the immigration booth. Parker and Ryan came out holding their passports and their visa, which, clear-as-day, had an exit stamp on it.

Cotton mouth.

There was one guard, gun slung over his shoulder, standing outside of the building ushering people into and out of the processing room. When he turned away I spoke under my breath to Greg, "Greg, go back to the car. They don't know how many we are. If this is the last checkpoint, who cares if they're actually stamping you out? You just have to get *into* Turkmenistan."

Brave words come easily in the dark.

He caught my drift and as soon as the guard looked away, Greg slipped into the shadows. When Mick and George came out they had sensed something was awry but didn't know what. I whispered to them to go to our car and check in with Greg.

Greg said to them, "Okay, there is one guard on the ramp. If he checks your Azerbaijan visa tap the brake three times." Greg watched them drive to the ship. They stopped by the guard who leaned into the car. Five seconds, ten seconds. "Maybe we're in the clear," said Greg.

Red. Red. Red.

That one last guard, probably an eighteen-year-old cadet, stood between us and the rest of the rally. Brooke and I didn't know any of this until Greg walked back up to us in line and very delicately shook his head, "No."

So this was it. This was our Maginot Line. One by one, the other teams vanished into the night, driving onto what was to be our floating chariot into Turkmenistan. We were the last team to enter the booth, to face our judge, jury, and executioner.

I was first.

"Passport. Visa."

I handed both of my documents to the middle-aged military man behind the window. He had an air of charisma and lightness about him. Maybe there was hope. He stamped my visa, asked me to stand back, cracked a joke to make me smile, took my photo, and handed my documents back to me. Brooke did exactly the same. Then it was Greg's turn.

"Passport. Visa."

Greg handed him his passport.

"Visa."

"I don't have it. It was stolen by the police when we got pulled over."

"Visa."

"I had it. I mean I got into the country but your police stole it and other documents from me."

"Visa..." This time the word was chaperoned by a shoulder shrug.

No heartfelt stories were going to get us through this, but Greg had an ace in his hole. He pulled out his giant Android phone and loaded up the PDF of the Azerbaijan visa stored in his emails. The guard looked at the phone closely and with the greatest of ease and matter-of-factness, made a stamping motion with his free hand on the phone and said, "Can't stamp phone," and handed it back to Greg.

This severed the power to our engines, leaving us listless in a tide of decisions. Who knew the Angel of Death wielded a stamp?

For five seconds, we could taste the silence in air thicker than velvet curtains. There were eyes that pleaded and eyes that prodded. I, for one, was out of ideas. I was already thinking about future ferries, one-day raids through Turkmenistan, multiple nights in Baku, six hundred and eighty dollars lost, or whether we leave Greg behind to have him meet us in Uzbekistan.

I wanted to melt away like a snowman in a sauna, but Greg had one bullet left to jam into his problem-solving musket. He said, "Do you have a printer?"

Sadly, that was swatted away with a resolute, "No."

We glanced at each other again. I was in the fetal position, but Greg pushed on. "Does anyone else have a printer on site?"

The guy thought and said, "Maybe Customs."

A spike of hope, like a preteen's erection.

Greg asked, "Where's Customs?"

I was picturing us having to run to another building in the complex but the guy motioned and said, "Next room."

Next room? Jesus, dude. This could have been so much less dramatic.

. 148 .

We agreed to have Brooke go out to the car and make sure the ship didn't leave. I told her, "Tell them that we are coming. Do what you have to. Sell your body. Provide favors. Whatever. You'll have plenty of time on the open road to get over it."

Greg and I ran to the next room waving his glowing phone, hoping to find "Customs." We did. At this particular time of day, "Customs" was a man with big headphones on, watching a movie on his computer, and enjoying his dinner.

Dinner...

Shit. Focus. Greg and I tried not to spook him but time was of the essence. Greg talked a mile a minute, mixing in platitudes, thanks, and requests in one run-on sentence. The man squinted in annoyance, paused his movie, and asked Greg to slow down because English was not his thing. Greg used body language and hand gestures to explain that the printer on the other side of this room was being requested to spit out one sheet of paper that so happened to be the document Greg was pointing at on his phone.

As if to extinguish all our dreams, the man interrupted Greg, "No. No connection."

But Greg, giving me a lesson in snuffing out ambiguity and dealing with miscommunication, asked, "It doesn't work?"

"No."

"Is it broken?"

"No."

"No?"

"No connection."

"No connection?"

"No cable."

"No cable? No cable! I have a cable!"

What the guy was trying to say was that he didn't have a way to connect the phone to the computer. Greg had his USB cable in his pocket. Our messiah got out of his seat, dinner in hand, and walked us over to the computer that was connected to the printer. I ran to the car to let Brooke know that we were going to make the ship. "Do not let it leave."

I came back inside to find Greg staring at the computer screen with the focus of a samurai. I had to combine the back-seat-driving encouragement of a man providing moral support with the Greg-make-this-fucking-work monster that was boiling inside of me.

As Windows 97-Azerbaijan was booting up, a man from the docks came in and told us that the ship had to leave. I fired back, "Just give us five minutes. We'll be there."

"It has to leave now."

"No, it doesn't have to leave now! We've been waiting for six hours so it can wait five more minutes."

He left. I felt better about myself, but who was I other than a white tourist shouting orders in a foreign language?

"Okay, Greg. Focus."

The inherent problem with Windows 97-Azerbaijan is that it is in Azerbaijan. We couldn't read shit. All we knew was where the start button was and what the Internet Explorer icon looked like. Not super helpful, but first thing's first. The computer "saw" Greg's phone but it was taking forever for the folders to populate. That was the other fundamental issue with Windows 97-Azerbaijan, it was seventeen years old, running on a computer that looked just as archaic. Was that a floppy disk port?

We made a joke to the guy in an attempt to whack through the awkwardness that accompanies three men staring at the spinning hourglass on a computer screen. He didn't laugh. Finally, three folders emerged.

Okay, okay. We were in business.

Greg had no idea what was in each of the folders. He double-clicked on one but we were immediately met with a big red stop sign. Each folder reacted the same way. "Customs" shrugged his shoulders and slurped some noodles. Greg and I looked at each other hoping that an intense stare would solve our problem. Greg then said to me, "It might be the cable. It's finicky."

To my delight, Greg reattached the cable and we were now able to see inside those folders.

Next hurdle. There were hundreds of folders and each one had filing-friendly nomenclature like "xkasdghfaksq2893dfhw." *Hundreds* of these.

As Greg searched for a solution, one of the dockworkers came in again and said, "Boat has to leave."

I batted back, "Boat isn't going anywhere! We're going to be right there. Just a few more minutes please." My eyes shredded this man to bits until he left the room. "Okay, Greg. Take your time. What folder is this thing in?"

He didn't know. Being in IT, Greg came up with the idea of typing "*.PDF" into the search bar which should give us every PDF on his phone. Genius idea except that we couldn't find where the illustrated magnifying glass was to reveal the way. We turned to our fearless leader and said, "*Umm.* Search...see...find." We mimed out what a magnifying glass would be and pointed to the computer. It's amazing when two *Homo sapiens*, the apex species when it comes to higher brain functions, can't communicate any better than a fucking gorilla and a squirrel.

Finally, he understood our monkey-see, monkey-do game, and with a mouthful of lo mein, maneuvered the mouse to give us a search field. Greg typed in his "*.PDF" and every PDF that was on his phone came up on the computer screen. The problem was, there were hundreds of *those*.

"What's the name of the file, buddy?"

He didn't know, but he checked the email attachment on his phone and saw that it was named "Greg Johnson visa" so we scoured the PDFs until we found our digital Hope Diamond.

Double click.

Wait for it...wait for it...*boom!* There it was.

We looked for the print button but the stupid thing was hidden, and ctrl + p didn't work. Eventually, the guard found the button. Electrons must move slower in Azerbaijan because it took a full five seconds for the printer to come to life. Then it slowly spat out Greg's visa.

Jubilation!

We were able to print a PDF from an Android phone on a computer running Windows 97-Azerbaijan. I think a Nobel Prize in Linguistics was in order.

We hugged the guard and then bounded back to Immigration with Greg holding up the sheet of paper. The immigration officer beamed. "Visa!" He stamped it, made a few jokes, and took Greg's photo. The weird thing was that now Greg had a visa with an exit stamp on it but not an entry stamp. I couldn't figure out how *that* was okay, but I wasn't about to bring up a technicality at this stage of the proceedings.

We raced to our car with shaky hands and shit-eating grins, but before I got into the passenger side door, I heard, "Hey! You! Stop!"

I turned around and saw our dining guard glaring at us. I pointed at myself and said, "Me?"

"You!"

"Me?"

"Both!"

You're never out of a country until you're out of a country.

I looked at Greg and then back to our guy. He waved us over. We were mystified. My brain thought of everything and nothing in that moment. What else could we possibly have to go through to get out of this place? We followed the man back to his office. He swung around his desk and as he sat down, he pointed at something. When I saw it, I wanted to cry and crawl to my mother.

In our haste, Greg had left all of Donata's documents on this guy's desk—our registration, our insurance, and our international driving licenses. Everything. Had we gotten on the ship without these, we would have never been able to enter Turkmenistan. Our rally would have been over. Greg had never been more apologetic and thankful. The man simply wanted to be rid of us like nagging mosquitoes.

Greg and I made the 50-yard walk back to the car in silence until I broke it with, "Consider this our talk, Greg."

"Roger that."

We got into our car, explained the snafu to Brooke, whose smile glowed like Excalibur knowing that it was one of us who finally had a major screwup but one that didn't end up affecting anything. We drove towards the ship on the pier of death. I seriously didn't know if our car was going to make it over this wooden travesty. We'd worked so hard to get out of the country and now we were one soggy plank away from plunging to a watery demise. To get on the ferry, we had to be guided by the dockworkers to maneuver onto, and then remain on top of, the caissons that connected the ship to the pier. We heard, "Wait, wait, wait!" which presumably was us almost tipping over into the Caspian Sea, since these caissons were spread the width of a normal car, not that of roller skates, like Donata's chassis. Thankfully, we made our way inside the hull, nestling next to giant railroad cars and behind the other Mongol Rally-mobiles.

Turn engine off. Remove key. Sigh.

One of the stevedores leaned into our car window and rubbed his thumb, forefinger, and middle finger together, which is the international symbol of money, and said, "For car."

I volleyed back, "No, no, no! We already paid for our car, sir." We handed him our receipt, bill of lading, visas, and everything else.

"No. Money to watch car."

"Watch car?"

"To keep it safe so nothing is stolen."

Fuck this.

"No, that's not happening," I said. "You know why? Because if anything is stolen from our car, you stole it. Okay! You stole it. We're not paying any more."

I had gone haywire, but I honestly didn't give a shit, and neither did Greg or Brooke. We were tired of cops, bureaucracy, inanity, fixers, visas, bribes, and hunger. We grabbed packs, all the snacks we could carry, and two 5-liter jugs of water (it might be three days at sea). Hopefully Donata wouldn't be scrap metal when we arrived in Turkmenbashi.

To get on the ship, we had to walk off the back of it and pass alongside it before boarding via the gangway. We got a, "Finally! Where were you?" from this crazy, forty-something Russian lady who was our handler on the ship. There were no rally teams in sight but she assured us that she would lead us to them. She instructed us to hand our passports to one of the guys I'd mouthed off to in the belly of the ship. Great. But rules are rules and ship manifests are ship manifests.

As we were about to be taken to our rooms, Brooke had a bright idea.

"Bassam, can I get my bag?"

"Right now?"

"Yes."

"Can it wait until we get to the room?"

"No, I need it now!"

I de-bagged and dropped everything on the floor so she could get her pack. Everyone was staring at her: me, Greg, crazy Russian woman, guy I pissed off, and another henchman. This sidekick with the wit of a balloon animal had an Angry Birds shirt on so Brooke took out her Portable PlayStation (PSP), pointed to it, and then to his shirt and said, "Angry Birds. I like Angry Birds too." It *was* kind of funny that in this most foreign of experiences in a place that was culturally and geographically as far away as we could get from home, there was a man wearing an Angry Birds shirt. I appreciated Brooke's effort, but the two guys looked at each other stupefied, then reached for the PSP while Brooke kept trying to explain the small-worldness of this instant.

Humor was nudged away by awkwardness. Brooke was left with, "Isn't that funny?" as she tried to grab her PSP back, much to the confusion of the two men.

"They think you're giving them the PSP as payment, Brooke," I said.

Whoops...

Brooke retrieved her PSP but now our shit was *definitely* getting stolen for making a mockery of these guys. First we yelled at them when they wanted a couple of bucks to protect our car from lord knows what crook on the ship, and now we'd ungiven gifts. We couldn't get out of there fast enough. Eventually, the tsarina took us down the ship and we heard familiar voices. Ralliers! We hugged. It felt so goddamn good to be with them again.

Home.

"Where were you? What happened?"

"Everything happened."

For the past year, we had heard how the rooms on this ferry were like medieval prisons leaking water and furnished with out-of-service toilets, but we got a pretty good deal. Our wing had one functioning shower (for now) and eight functioning toilets. We were on the *Queen Mary* of industrial ferries!

I offered the first shower to the girls but they wanted to wait, so I dashed ahead to beat all the guys. Yeah, the drain clogged, yeah, the water pressure was shit, but I had hot water and a relatively clean bathroom. I am constantly amazed by what hot water and soap can do to someone's psyche. Kafka's *Metamorphosis* should have been about how we felt pre- and post-showering.

Food was next. I walked up some stairs and eventually stumbled upon the kitchen and found the cook. He was a bit overweight and, based on how he searched for utensils like he was visiting a friend's house for the first time, I guessed he was not really a cook. I saw him making a plate of eggs so I pointed at them and then to myself. He nodded and then held up five fingers and then did the money rub with his fingers. *Five dollars for an omelet with ham, cheese, and bread on the side? Sure thing, buddy.*

Gradually, other members of the rally came into the kitchen, heard about my order, and requested the same. Someone handed me a beer as my omelet appeared. If Greg hadn't gotten his visa printed, we would have been driving around Baku trying to find a place to stay for the next three days, texting Ishmael about getting on the next ferry. Instead, we were steaming east out of the Baku claw and celebrating George's birthday over a golden omelet and a beer that tasted like liquid sunrise. There's no satisfaction liked the earned satisfaction when joy sits inches away from calamity. *Paper-thin. Razor-sharp.*

Now the only question was how long would this ferry trip take? But for tonight, that didn't matter. We got to sit back without having to make a decision for a little while. On a trip like this we were always fighting the "exhaustion of new." As humans, we save energy by connecting dots that are familiar, by not having to think about every stimulus or input. It's why habits can help us do things without having to consciously *choose* to do them. On the road, it was an onslaught of new, and new is tiring. Every day there were new roads, new signs, new languages, new colors, new tastes, new sounds, new people, new cultures, new decisions, new conversations, and new calculations. Travel springs forth the inevitable clamor of derailed intentions without checking to see if our seat belt was even fastened.

Emotionally five years older and ten years wiser than I had been two weeks ago in London, I crawled into my bunk and let the slow, almost imperceptible rocking of the boat lull me to sleep.

Photo Gallery

"Donata" is ready for the rally.

Launch Day!

Donata getting serviced in Herford, Germany.

Donata's 42 HP engine.

Brooke, Bassam, and Greg in Budapest.

Pushing Donata to the Hungarian-Serbian border.

The ceiling of the Hagia Sophia Basilica.

Bassam "heel-clicking" over the Hagia Sophia.

A street in the old city of Baku.

Waiting to board the ship in Baku.

Border guards in Baku playing football with us.

A shot from the drone in the middle of the Karakum Desert in Turkmenistan.

"The Door to Hell" near Darvaza, Turkmenistan.

How sleeping worked in the Turkmen desert.

Filling up on black-market gasoline in Khiva, Uzbekistan.

Inside the old city walls of Khiva, Uzbekistan.

Registan Square, Samarkand, Uzbekistan.

Brooke and Greg making the hike up from the Toktogul Reservoir, Kyrgyzstan.

Our campsite in the mountains of Kyrgyzstan.

"No photos!" Bassam after taking a bucket shower by a lake in Kazakhstan.

Camping at the Russia-Mongolia border.

Greg chatting with our soon-to-be convoy partners in Mongolia.

Ralliers killing some time with a local at the Russia-Mongolia border.

What one would bring to "the bathroom."

Entering Mongolia.

Bassam and a golden eagle.

A young Mongolian rancher.

At Manat's house in Ulgii, Mongolia.

Our Mongolian convoy after crossing through a muddy bog.

Dusty, windy Mongolian roads.

Nothing but aridness on the Mongolian roads.

Bassam, covered in Mongolian dirt from the drive.

"Micra Management" needing a tow across a river.

Taking a look at the engine of the "Skoda Boys."

One of the MINIs getting ready for the day.

The other MINI needed some work.

What an average morning looked like in Mongolia.

Final Mongolian campsite.

A snapshot of the Mongolian convoy (L to R: Welsh, Americans, English).

Marco Polover reluctantly drinking fermented milk
at the Mongol Rally finish line.

We did it!

Day 14

Although it's called the Caspian *Sea*, it's actually the largest landlocked lake on earth, with more than three times more water than Siberia's Lake Baikal, the next most voluminous lake in the world. By comparison, Lake Superior only has 22 percent of the surface area and 16 percent of the water that the Caspian Sea has. The Caspian is shockingly big (about the size of Montana). In fact, it accounts for 42 percent of all the lake water on earth. So this lake is called a sea, like André the Human is called André the Giant.

I ate another omelet for breakfast and before we knew it, we slowed down and came to a complete stop within a few hundred yards of Turkmenbashi, Turkmenistan. Rumor on the ship was that we would be docking soon. The one- to three-day ferry trip was turning out to be the less-than-a-day ferry! It wasn't a question of distance—Baku and Turkmenbashi are only one hundred and fifty miles apart—it was a question of when the port of Turkmenbashi would receive the ship.

With the way the government protected entry into this place, I was expecting to see *Elysium* out of my port window. Instead, I peered at a sandy, rocky, and unforgiving landscape; a godforsaken postscript of terrestrial evolution. If you open an atlas and turn the pages to Turkmenistan, the thing that you immediately notice is the absence of roads. You'd think that the cartographers miscommunicated about who was going to finish the map. There is one road that goes north-south through the entire country. One.

Turkmenistan has the human rights record of a Viking army. The 2016 World Press Freedom Index ranked Turkmenistan 178 out of 180—ahead of only Eritrea and North Korea. The 2017 Human Rights Watch says that Turkmenistan remains one of the world's most oppressive countries. We also heard from Ishmael that photography should be kept to a minimum in Turkmenistan.

We could be thrown in jail for taking a picture of a government building. Except for the desert conditions, this place was basically the opposite of Burning Man.

I'd go so far as to say that most of us lumped all the 'Stans (Turkmenistan, Uzbekistan, Kyrgyzstan, Tajikistan, Kazakhstan, Afghanistan, and Pakistan) into a category of "Places Where Bad Things Might Happen to Westerners." Once a 'Stan, always a 'Stan, right? This is due to the media's portrayal of the region combined with our lack of knowledge about this part of the world, but it didn't help that Azerbaijan was an emotional train wreck for us and it was only an 'An. We hadn't even gotten to the full 'Stan yet!

As the ship docked, all the passengers had to wait in the main galley. There were other families there with us. Azerbaijani? Turkmen? Whoever they were, we must have looked like aliens from the Crab Nebula to them with our white skin, hairy legs, sunglasses, backpacks, tank tops, and cleavage (not me, of course; I have some couth). I wondered what their story was. Where were they heading? Every day we pass people who we'll never see again but this moment was extra-special. Here were two groups of people whose paths miraculously and inexplicably crossed for half an hour. At any other point in time, we couldn't have been further apart, but right then we shared that space together.

This is what travel brings out on the bell curve of relatability. The average day has us in the middle of the curve. We see the same kinds of people. We have similar conversations. Even when we are on the subway, in traffic, or at the supermarket, we can look around at people we've never seen before and understand that they're not very different from us even if we don't know them. It takes an unusual occurrence for us to tell someone, "You won't believe what happened today," but even that story won't be too different from what we're used to hearing. Travel, however, activates a cerebral stretching at both ends, heightening our differences and our similarities at the same time.

In this moment, we were sitting in a room with people who had no idea about March Madness, the Mongol Rally, gap years,

Drake, 401(k)s, cabin pressure, or junior proms. But at the same time, if I smiled at someone, she would smile back. If I handed a child a piece of candy, he took it and coyly smirked in thanks. Kids snuggled next to their mothers and siblings teased each other. They had dreams and they had needs. They wanted peace, a roof over their heads, honest work, and a family who loved them. We were nothing alike and exactly the same. Our massive differences and our obvious similarities blended into the smoothie that only travel can concoct. When I consciously took a sip of it, time itself seemed to stop in the experiential brain freeze while I struggled to define what the moment meant to me.

As terra firma passed beneath us one tire rotation at a time, each experience was always connected to a place we had just left. Downtown London and this floating room on the Caspian Sea were joined by a pencil that never lifted.

Our differences are cultural but our similarities are human.

Before my mind melt dripped through my tear ducts, the captain's voiced garbled something on the loudspeaker and our fellow humans from a different part of the same world got up and departed the ship on foot.

Describing the sweltering temperature that hits you as you approach Arabia from the sea, T.E. Lawrence once wrote, "The heat...came out like a drawn sword and struck us speechless." This could now also be said about Turkmenistan. It was infernal.

We were led down to where our cars were, and whaddya know? Nothing had been stolen, at least that we could see. Donata purred as she always did: reliable and steadfast. We parked outside the Customs & Immigration building and gleefully entered the air-conditioned space. This began the least efficient paper-processing, bureaucratic nightmare anyone had ever conjured. Turkmen immigration was a grueling governmental scavenger hunt.

First, we all filled out our paperwork with the help of Siga, a Lithuanian rallier who was able to translate the Russian prompts on the form. We shared answers to things we didn't have, like a hotel and its address. Because we were on a transit visa (five days) we also had to mark out our proposed route through the country and pay the gasoline tax (it was peanuts) based on that specific path.

After the people who exited the ship on foot had gotten through customs, it was our turn to face the man behind the Plexiglas. He was a handsome fellow, this Turkmen. He had the features you might expect of a Mongolian—a more traditional Asian facial structure but darker skin. Maybe the journey across the Caspian crossed an evolutionary barrier as well. He had the mood of a wet weekend. One look at a ragtag group of white people entering his country didn't seem to put him over the moon. Marco Polover happened to be the first group in the line of ralliers and since Brooke was the car's owner, she approached him. Maybe not the best idea to send in our feisty jackrabbit to begin negotiations in a den of wolves...

The man fumbled through our mound of paperwork, passports, and visas a few times. He muttered something to his colleague in the next room and then turned to Brooke and in English demanded to know where our guide was. (On a regular thirty-day visa in Turkmenistan you have to secure a guide who stays with you from border to border, twenty-four hours a day. You have to pay him and for his food/lodging as well.) But we were on a transit visa, a fact Brooke could have gently let the border agent know. However, she took a less diplomatic approach. She leaned down to the window, mustering a scarce supply of respect, and said, "We don't need a guide if we're on a transit visa!"

Yeah, dickhead!

Behind Brooke, some of us chuckled, and some of us shrunk and looked away— reactions that were byproducts of disbelief.

Come on, Brooke.

Her remark stripped layers of serenity and patience from the man. He called his superior over, and gesticulated at us, his tone of voice implying that he wanted to throw us all into the sea. Whatever was said behind the glass between the two men proved that we had the necessary documentation to get into Turkmenistan. Since the officials wanted to move the line a bit, Greg and I paid the twelve-dollar entry fee, got our receipt, had our bags searched at customs, and then waited outside the immigration area while Brooke went through the various steps to get our car lawfully fit for Turkmen travel. Here's what she had to do:

1) Return to the first window, hand in receipt, and receive illegible form.
2) Take illegible form to a separate office, where someone then handed her an entirely different illegible form.
3) Take both forms to a new office and receive a stamp.
4) Take forms to a third, never-before-seen office and receive another stamp.
5) Exit the building with no set direction and walk around aimlessly until she found a green door, where a man presented her with another form.
6) Before going back into the customs area, go to the ticket office to exchange one form for another.
7) Return to second window (the one where she paid the twelve dollars earlier) and get yelled at for not having the receipt from the ticket office.
8) Go back to ticket office to mime the need for a receipt for something she was unsure of.
9) Return to second window, receive another receipt.
10) Go to a fifth location, where things seemed to come together a little bit with a man actually signing things, stamping, and all else.
11) Get handed a new form by said man.
12) Take that form to a sixth office to get stamped.
13) Somehow exchange six U.S. dollars for two Turkmen *manat* with locals who happened to be at the building and who didn't know anything about exchange rates.
14) Take money and form to a seventh office to get stamped and signed.
15) Bring everything back to the guy in the fifth office, where she now filled out the customs declaration.

I wish I were making this up.

Greg and I were resting on our bags, free to roam Turkmenistan, while Brooke raced in and out of the immigration area dozens of times with new forms or returning old ones, embodying the hapless rodent in an immigration official's version of whack-a-mole. It was a win for comedy that it was Brooke who had to be our team's representative, her frustration expanding like a balloon. All us ralliers who had not succumbed to the back-and-forth life cheered all rally car owners when they came in and out, walking next to them like they were marathon runners, handing them snacks or water.

When Brooke was released from the five-hour swirling nightmare of information processing, it was time to get our car searched, and no one searches cars like the Turkmen military. Everything had to be taken out of the vehicle, including the cargo carrier.

And then, we were asked, "What is that?"

"It's a drone."

I opened the case, flipped back the top, and revealed padded Styrofoam holstering a quad-copter, buttressed by a giant remote control, and three extra batteries with finger-length wires poking out of them like blocks of C4.

Tada!

The appealing, English-speaking military man with a bald head, one-thousand-watt smile, and a striking resemblance to a sun-drenched Andre Agassi, raised his eyebrows, giggled, and looked at me as if to inquire whether my intellectual deficiencies had been documented by a medical professional.

When he asked me what the range of the device was, I lied as I always did when answering that question. I said 100 meters, when in reality it was more like 300. After all, in their minds, 100 meters was a toy, 300 meters was espionage.

I had to show them the GoPro and prove that it was a separate camera. I had to show them footage that I had already recorded that was on my computer. The situation seemed grim for my drone but I think the fact that I was so nonchalant about it made it easier. I didn't fight to keep it but I used some Jedi mind tricks like telling them I was making a movie for our sponsors and for the poor kids we were raising money for, and that everyone at home was expecting a film but if they *had* to, they could keep the drone. I wasn't about to teach them how to use it, though.

Our bald friend seemed to take a liking to me. And by take a liking I, of course, mean that it was probably Brooke's perfect boobs that did the trick. Whatever it was, when all the cars were searched and we were waiting for the final decision, he waved from the drone towards the car, signaling us to take it and get out of here. We thanked him enthusiastically and were now free and clear to enter Turkmenistan.

Seven hours—*seven*—after we docked, we drove off into the desert just after sunset, not really sure where we were going but wanting to chip away at the 360 miles between us and the capital, Ashgabat, before we camped for the night. We gassed up for the comically cheap seventy cents per gallon, which cost us only five dollars and sixty-two cents total. We blasted our music and took comfort in the safety of our convoy being led by our united streams of headlights. The wide, unpainted road was immaculate, as if paved for our arrival. Turkmenistan's roads felt like the love child between Holland and the Indianapolis Motor Speedway...so far.

About ninety miles in, we found an old electrical station that was inhabited by a few soldiers. It was the only illuminated spot on the entire horizon. The flat ground away from the road was suitable for us. Thankfully, the Lithuanian team's ability to speak Russian helped sell our cause and we were welcomed to camp for the evening. We set up our tents in the blustery, cool night, made our dinner of ramen noodles with a side of potato chips, put out our camping chairs, and relished the power and joy of being huddled together.

Day One of our five-day visa was history. We hoped to make it through Ashgabat and up to Darvaza, by the next afternoon. We wanted to see The Door to Hell. Really.

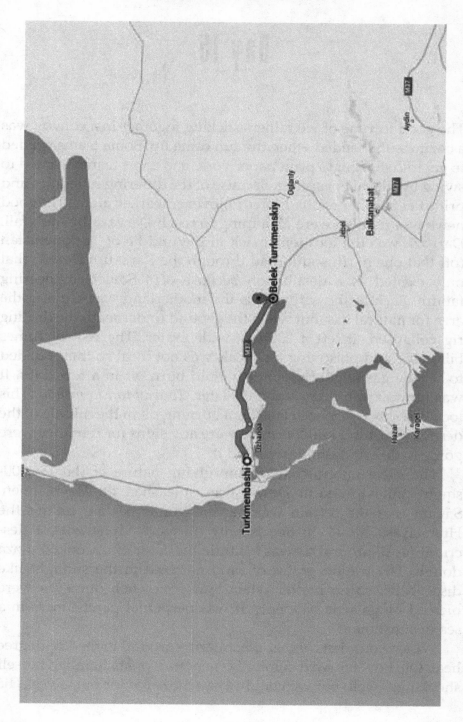

Day 15

The good fortune of we ralliers sticking together in a convoy was a coziness that ended when the sun came up. Some teams needed to get to Ashgabat to print paperwork, and some teams wanted to swing by a local hot spring. Because of the differing schedules and priorities of all the teams, Marco Polover embarked alone. The good news was that we were all aiming to reach Darvaza by nightfall. Darvaza was the location smack in the middle of Turkmenistan (off that one north-south road through the Karakum Desert) that only existed as a destination because of a Soviet engineering failure. Back in the early 1970s the motherland was tapping the area for natural gas, but when the ground underneath the drilling rig collapsed, it left a 230-foot-wide crater. The risk of fumes billowing and poisoning the locals was not ideal so they decided to set the gas alight, hoping it would burn off in a few days. It was now sixteen thousand days later. *To-may-to...to-mah-to*. This locally dubbed "Door to Hell" is a burning pit in the middle of the desert. We didn't know if there were any signs for it but we were going to do our damndest to find it.

The sheer enormity and unforgiving nature of the 135,000-square mile Karakum Desert was unleashed on Day Fifteen. Saying that the terrain was barren would be like calling the Himalayas "hilly." Justice is only meagerly done with a description. All around us was solitude the color of uncooked pizza dough. The trillion grains of sand glittered in the sunlight like disco balls, so no matter where our gazes fell, our eyes were pierced by galactic bayonets. It was perpetual parchedness in a sea of sunshine.

We saw our first camels, meandering around in the 120-degree heat. Oh, how far we'd come...Somehow, Donata handled herself shockingly well, but we couldn't say the same for ourselves. The breeze provided by the slipstream of our open windows felt like we were downwind of a fan in the boiler room of a frigate. The dry air was a straw sucking moisture away from us before we even had time to sweat. The struggle against the heat was an act of physical combat. Brooke could not withstand the assault. Under a makeshift hijab, she was constantly battling chapped lips, watery eyes, and blotchy skin. I kept reminding her to drink plenty of water because I was drinking twice the amount she was and my mouth had still turned into a desolate wasteland.

With Brooke wilting in the back seat, we followed the jet-black asphalt artery that twisted this way and that; its existence was not engineered, but conditional, determined by the desert's good graces. If the wind shifted, the sand could slither over the roadway, erasing our umbilical cord to civilization. Thankfully, the single-lane road soon turned into multi lanes.

Despite the unpleasant reception we received from the topography, one of the things I'll always remember about Turkmenistan is that random drivers on the highway greeted us with more friendship and cheer than in any other country. Either they respected that foreigners had figured out how to get into — and travel through — their country, or they knew about the rally passing by at this time of year. Whichever, we were rock stars.

We reached Ashgabat — capital of Turkmenistan, only five miles from the Iranian border, at the base of the Turkmen-Khorasan Mountain Range. It was home to more than one million people so it seemed to be a good place to get gas and load up on food and water because we weren't sure where the next outpost of civilization would be. Ashgabat is a strange city. The authoritarian grip of the previous leader, President for Life Saparmurat Niyazov (really, that's the title Parliament gave him), is everywhere in the form of golden statues, busts, plazas, roundabouts, and gargantuan hillside monuments standing sentinel. No matter which direction we looked, we were reminded whose country it was. As many old Soviet outposts can attest, the brutalist architecture of Ashgabat was as functional as possible. Large, white, geometric buildings —

all of them formidable, none of them memorable—sprinkle the length of the city. Conversely, there are great stretches of parks and green spaces, perhaps to afford people better views of the statues and monuments.

We stumbled upon a proper supermarket on the northern edge of town. As per usual in this part of the world, we stood out. Some locals took photos of and with us. Others gazed up at the white men in flip-flops towering over everyone else, while Brooke received stares like we were traveling with a jaguar.

We bought everything we could. Chips, canned goods, fruit, Aloe King drink, salami, all of it. We also got eleven gallons of water. That might seem like a lot of fluid but not when the heat was what it was, not when there were three of us, and not when a desert country larger than California had only one north-south road traveling through it.

We stuffed our car like a sleeping bag into its pouch. I actually saw glass bend. Looking at Donata from the back, our rear axle had the shape of a smiley face, not because of its mood but because of the elastic deformation of metal under gravitational duress. We filled up on gas for pennies. While we were under the sun's late afternoon death ray, deliberating over our Turkmen foldout map, a barely English-speaking local offered his help. We asked him about Darvaza and the best route to the Uzbekistan border from there. The map indicated that after Darvaza we had to go all the way to the northern tip of the country and then hug the Turkmen-Uzbek border in a southeasterly route to the border town of Dashoguz, but the local said that road was terrible, one of the worst he'd ever seen. He told us that there was a road that went east-west through a town forty miles directly west of Dashoguz, but it wasn't on our map. We didn't know if we understood him correctly but we made a mental note.

We drove north on the one road out of town, hoping to reach the "Door to Hell" and be reunited with our convoy. The great roads morphed into okay roads that mutated into shitty roads—potholes, caverns, tectonic fault lines, swells, and bumps. There was not much I could do in the backseat except cringe. Brooke was at the helm doing her best.

After an hour and a half, we passed a lone gas station, and there, miraculously, was our six-car contingent from the ferry! We embraced and hugged, happy that the Baku crew ("Ba-crew") had reunited. Had we been five minutes later, we would have missed them.

What followed on the road was pure freedom. Beneath a postcard-worthy sunset over the Karakum Desert, we snapped photos and videos, zigzagging and overtaking one another while trying not to kill ourselves in the process.

There were general rules to convoy driving.

Going first was always hairiest because you were the guinea pig. Your frame was the one exposed, your wheels and shocks were the ones that the rest of the convoy didn't respect. When you hit that pothole, we didn't, and we thanked you for it. The lead car, like in the peloton of a bike race, switched often so that the heavy lifting wasn't always on one team. Despite the danger, there was a certain pride in going first, knowing that everyone else was following the path you laid out.

I always loved going second or third because there were enough people in front of us to mine sweep and enough people behind us so that we were not alone in case we broke down.

However, if we weren't first and we didn't keep up, we ran the risk of falling too far behind the car(s) in front of us, essentially cutting us off, forcing us to decelerate to avoid the potholes as if we were leading the crew ourselves. Our dim headlights and tired eyes would then have to avoid the various terrors that might rip our tires apart or buckle an axle.

From the east, a few lonely stars dragged their black paint behind them, covering the blues, pinks, and oranges that the long-lingering sunset had brought. All of this, and yet still no fire crater...I don't know what we thought would happen when we reached Darvaza, but we expected some sort of sign, some sort of glow, some sort of tire marks, some sort of something. For those who have driven on I-95 between North Carolina and South Carolina, we were guessing it was Turkmenistan's version of South of The Border.

But there was nothing. We reached the railroad tracks, which according to our maps meant we had gone too far. You can imagine our dejection.

We asked a police officer stationed in a booth there. If anyone would know, it would be him. Turns out, he had *never* heard of it. Every single rally team we talked to who had done the trip had said that if we were going through Turkmenistan, we had to go see the fire crater at Darvaza. And this guy, who was from the country of the crater and probably the closest human to the thing, had never heard of it.

This would be like asking a Parisian taxi driver to take you to the Eiffel Tower and him saying, "The Eiffel what now?"

We decided to drive back south a bit to see if there was an inroad we had missed. In the eastern distance we saw vagrant car headlights ricocheting on the dunes. This must be a good sign. We soon found tire tracks veering off the road. A local drove by and confirmed for us, "Yes, big fire," so we were in business, except that "in business" was at the far end of a dark horizon buried in sand.

Some of the ralliers got out and assessed the path. The Spaniards in the Peugeot had the most muscle and had seven (not kidding) spare tires, so they made the first attempt into the dust. From the road, we saw the headlights carom back and forth, while redlining RPMs and bumper cracks saturated our ears. *Eesh....* I'm all for a side trip, but there's a difference between being adventurous and reckless. Our car was probably the least equipped of the group to make this off-road ramble, so like any smart team would, we let every other car go first to see if this jaunt was even possible.

The Irish, God bless their confidence, got stuck in the really loose stuff, turning their tires into sand flingers. After digging them out with shovels and pushing the car with all our might back onto some packed sand, the remaining vehicles found the line that provided the best opportunity.

At some point on a trip like this, you can't say no. You have to try, even if you think that there is no way you are getting out of the mess. With that, Greg drove into the powder. Donata huffed, puffed, swiveled, and screamed but she reached the hard sand intact. I was proud of her. Really. I'm not a car guy but it was one of the rare moments in my life when I truly anthropomorphized an automobile.

The next leg of the journey was ambitious. It was a slight uphill drive that ended with a steep climb that spit us out onto a leveled plateau. The Peugeot went first. We heard the growl of the engine and saw their headlights go skyward and then swing down like a guillotine when the car went back horizontal over the lip of the plateau. *Shit*. That looked violent.

The remaining teams eyed the path repeatedly and those not driving stood with flashlights highlighting the best line up the hill. Part of me wanted someone to fail so that we could say, "Maybe we shouldn't do this," but every car summited. And so it was Donata's turn again. Greg punched the gas and somehow maneuvered her up that hill and over the edge without tearing our sump guard or puncturing our gas tank.

He brought her to a stop behind the rest of the cars and we all celebrated our mini victory. Donata looked at us stoically, like an unheralded fullback. She acted like she'd been here before, that this was what she was made to do, that she was enjoying the Mongol Rally as much as we were. She believed in herself more than I did. I wanted to have sex with Donata.

Our celebration was short-lived. We were now further from help, had no real idea where the crater was, and the night was total black. However, we did see a group of headlights below us off to our left that turned out to be other ralliers. They told us we were indeed in the right area, but there was no way for any of our cars to get to the crater. For ten dollars each, though, some locals would shuttle us back and forth in their two Toyota 4Runners.

Right then, said locals appeared. The fifteen of us stuffed ourselves flank to shank inside the trucks and headed to the fiery pit of lore. Any notion that we could have made this trip in our own cars was erased as the 4Runners labored heavily for most of the twenty-minute ride.

Suddenly—*there it was!* Just as described. A burning hole in the ground about 50 yards deep and 100 yards across, spewed hell, fire, and brimstone in all directions. It might as well have been an open volcano. There were no railings, no signs, no nothing. If we had wanted to, we could have walked right over the edge without breaking stride.

When the wind shifted toward us, we had to hide our faces, turn, and run because it was too hot to endure. When the breeze was in our favor, we stared in complete bewilderment at what the earth hid in its bowels and what humans could do when they uncovered such power. It was one of the most shocking things I'd ever seen.

We rode the 4Runners back to our cars, made camp, and bundled up. The difference in day to night temperature was easily seventy degrees. In our hoodies and sweatpants, we wolfed down our ramen noodles and talked to each other about where we'd been, where we'd go, but most importantly, where we were in the moment.

The stars that littered the sky that night were something to behold. I couldn't help but wonder what thoughts I would have if I looked up at an illuminated sight like this without the luxury of scientific explanation. Or maybe *because* we have a scientific understanding of what "the heavens" are and our staggeringly small place in the maddening reach of the universe, our sense of wonderment and awe is even greater than those who had no idea what they were looking at millennia ago. Because the twenty-five hundred or so stars that enveloped my vision were enough to get me to hyperventilate at the incomprehensibility that what I was looking at was only 0.0000025 percent of all the roughly one hundred billion stars in the Milky Way galaxy. Fragile little me, spinning around on a rock in space, peering into a tiny spot of our galaxy, and yet that spot is the most limitless thing I could ever see with my own eyes. It was a mental M.C. Escher moment complete with Mobius strips, infinite planes, and stairs to nowhere. I felt like I was trying to hold gravity in my hands. I knew it was there, but I couldn't grasp it.

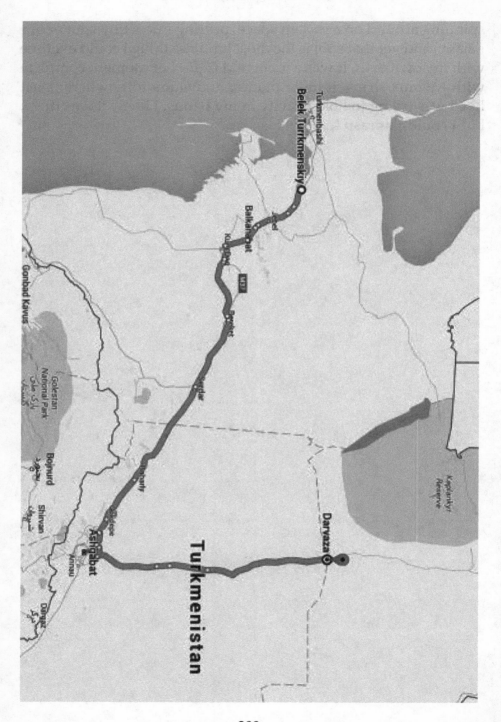

Day 16

When we opened the tent zipper in the morning, we realized how lunar the landscape was. Even on our elevated plane, we could barely see the road from whence we came. It was hills, dunes, and not even a tinge of a vegetative insurgency in sight. There were some teams who slept outside their tents because…well, because why the hell not? No mosquitoes, no crickets, no rain. Just sand.

I took a majestic shit that morning in what looked like a pre-dug grave. No matter, it provided the privacy one so desperately needed when squatting in the middle of a desert with a shovel, a roll of toilet paper, and a bag of baby wipes by your side. Having baby wipes on hand while going to the bathroom on the open road was like getting a star in Super Mario Brothers. You were now unstoppable in anything you wanted to do in life. That's how much of a game-changer they were.

After a couple of scoops to bury the deed, I felt like I was part Bedouin having a symbiotic relationship with the earth that not many other people shared. This was complete rubbish of course, because we were extremely privileged Westerners traveling for the literal shits and giggles of it, but it was still an electric feeling.

Then I scurried back to my tent in fear of scorpions and other icky things.

The sun dialed it up as if she had asked her husband to keep the sauce simmering on the stove overnight while she slept, only to wake to find the burner off, and now she had to get cooking. The heat was at playoff intensity although we were still in the preseason of our day.

The white-car Brits (the ones who camped with us in Samsun, Turkey) had some trouble with their engine and were now jury-rigging a contraption, but Donata was good to go. She was always good to go.

Eventually, our cars all scampered down the hill and made it back to the highway. If we reached the border before nightfall we would be into and out of Turkmenistan in three days. Plenty of time to spare, but as we knew, we were never out of a country until we were out of a country. We couldn't be complacent about distances and times.

After a few hours of wits-end driving, the roads improved tremendously and we came across some bits of civilization where we were also able to fill up on gas. Everyone's spirits were high until we proceeded north through a roundabout and encountered a road pummeled with shell craters. There were chasms ready to gobble our car like a Hungry Hungry Hippo would. We were snaking so cautiously that we had only gone about two hundred yards in five minutes.

This couldn't be right.

Wait a minute. Is this the road that the guy at the gas station outside of Ashgabat was referring to? Maybe we were supposed to go east at that last roundabout. We turned around and put our trust in that man, combined with the logic that if we drove east, we would eventually run into Uzbekistan anyway. But we also knew that based on our paperwork, we had to exit the country at Dashoguz.

The road ended up being that secret road we were supposed to take: paved, painted, and guarded with rails — three things that we rarely found together in the open land of Central Asia. And so, our stress of getting into and through this country suddenly — and without an ounce of pageantry — ended when we arrived at the border. The front gate to the complex was open, so we drove by the building and found the back gate open, too. Like a matador's *Ole!* It seemed a little ridiculous that we'd just be able to leave Turkmenistan, considering the rigmarole we went through to get into this place. Our free pass was revoked when some guards came out of the back of the building and pointed us towards the front.

The dog-and-pony show of filling out paperwork, going through metal detectors, and having our bags rummaged through made us feel more normal. Overall, exiting the country was a bit more streamlined than the tangle of forms and stamps that getting into it had been, but unfortunately, the Spanish ralliers messed up their Uzbek visa and technically weren't allowed to enter Uzbekistan for another six days. Their Turkmen visa would have run out by then, so they had to take a seven-hour cab ride back to Ashgabat to the Uzbek embassy, adjust their visas, and then take a cab all the way back to the border the next day.

Oof.

With our paperwork in order, it was time for the familiar game of having the car searched and its contents dumped. Greg and I, the nondrivers on this leg, had to wait in the building and couldn't help Brooke, even when the military guard was poking around at the drone asking her questions. I was yelling to her what to say but the guy didn't want to hear any of it and told me to go back inside. I felt badly about putting Brooke under the pressure of having to defend and explain the drone. I didn't care if it was confiscated—I just wanted to be the guy who fought for it. Thankfully, Brooke stayed on the right side of disrespect, working her magic as always, and we were free to go.

It was getting on in the afternoon, and borders close in this part of the world, so we were eager to dash through the final checkpoint. We passed through the last gate of document approvals, drove through some marshland (a marsh!), and then met *the* last guard, who was ten feet away from the gate that led into Uzbekistan. Hundreds or thousands of miles behind us, three feet in front of us, and we were still at the mercy of the Republic of Wherever. The closer we were to a border, the less important our opinion became, but that didn't stop us from venting to each other.

"What could we possibly be smuggling out of here? Sand?"

"Shouldn't they be happy we're leaving their country by now?"

"Motherfucking computers could help this situation tremendously."

Our assumed individual importance and thoughts on the proceedings didn't matter in the slightest. Crossing borders by car in Central Asia is a great lesson in humility and restraint. I'm a better man for it.

The guard stopped us, looked in the car, checked our passports again, and then asked us for…gum.

Sure, pal. Here's a piece of gum. Can we leave your country now?

So long, Turkmenistan. Your people were our biggest fans but your government scared the shit out of us.

On to Uzbekistan, the land that was positioned right in the picturesque oasis that once housed a section of the grain basket of the world: The Silk Road. On this day, the weight of the late afternoon sun was unbearable. A thermometer read 50 degrees C (122 degrees F). Average brain activity slowed in order to keep us cool. Brooke had it worst because once again the drivers had to stay with their cars while the rest of us were herded into a building with operable fans. We wished Brooke a pleasant heatstroke.

The forms and formalities took three hours even though our crew was the only people entering through the border. While we passengers waited for our drivers to get the cars searched, we concluded that the convoy was going to split up. Well, the convoy exiting Turkmenistan was two cars lighter than at the entry. The Lithuanians left earlier in the day because they were headed for a different border town, and the Spaniards were on their way back to Ashgabat to fix their Uzbek visas. Of the remaining five cars, the two British teams and the other Americans wanted to get as close to Samarkand as they could by nightfall to enjoy the city the next day. Greg, Brooke, and I didn't see the need for the rush, and neither did the Irish.

So again, just like that, friends we had traveled with intensely for a few days were going to disappear from the rest of our lives in the blink of an eye. We hugged, we wished each other luck, and then *poof!* we all went on our way, disappearing into the Uzbek countryside.

Not only did our companions change, but the landscape did as well. It was green! There was livestock and people playing outside. It was a tremendous difference from the intensity of Turkmenistan. The roads tried their best to be average, but we didn't care.

The most important thing for us to note was that Uzbekistan has had a gasoline shortage for years due to not playing nice with Turkmenistan, so gasoline has to be piped down from Russia. Evidently, the timely distribution of fuel was not on everyone's to-do list here, forcing us to find gas barons peddling low-octane fuel out of their homes. We were used to getting 93 or 95 octane for most of the trip but here it would be 83 or 85. (Not for nothing, "regular" in the United States is 87-octane. I'm not sure Donata could have made three back-and-forth trips across the continental United States — the distance of the Mongol Rally — on 87-octane.) The notion of there not being a gas station when we needed it was so foreign to me that I kind of thought that it was all bullshit and that when we wanted gas we would find it. That's how good my life had always been.

We didn't have a *Lonely Planet* guide, but thankfully Mick and George did. They convinced us to stay in the town of Khiva for the night, one of the main cities along the ancient Silk Road and our first encounter with the famed route. Like Baku, Khiva has an old-walled city that is separate from the rest of the town. Unlike Baku, the rest of Khiva was nowhere near as modern. Mick and George told us that there were a few highly rated guesthouses in the old city we could check out.

A little before sunset we reached the sand-colored fortifications whose shape reminded me of the rooks from a chessboard lined up in a row. The glow of the sun on the embankments protecting the old city put our insignificance in the grand scheme of human history into perspective. Rumor has it that Noah's son built a well here. *Noah's* son…The city originated in the 4th or 5th century

BCE. So the time between when Khiva originally existed and when Mayan civilization started to decline is the same amount of time between when the Mayan civilization started to decline and today. Khiva was the first location in Uzbekistan to be deemed a World Heritage Site, a fair designation indeed.

There are no cars allowed within the old city so we were forced to park outside the walls and travel on foot. Before we could even get out of our cars, a charismatic, multilingual, fourteen-year-old boy who could sell salt to the sea took us under his wing. His name was Shaxboz. His parents ran a bed and breakfast—Hotel Alibek—nearby. It was going to be cheap, they had Wi-Fi and hot showers, he'd help us exchange money on the black market, and we could park our cars in front of their place. Oh, and it was... right...there.

Sold. You win, kid.

The hot shower not only erased the dust and the stress of Turkmenistan, but provided the blank slate and euphoria that a full-body morning stretch does when you've just woken up. I moaned under the overhead spout and it was in that moment I became convinced that the delineation between the haves and have-nots of the world might be the availability and duration of hot showers.

When Shaxboz, our little maestro, brought back our Uzbek cash for us, it came in small garbage bags. The exchange rate in Uzbekistan wasn't so good. It was twenty-four hundred *som* to the dollar. The *som* come in one thousand-*som* bills. So if you changed one hundred dollars, you were left with 240 thousand-*som* notes. It's a lot. It's about one-inch thick. We exchanged two hundred dollars each and laughed at our six-inch-high stack of money.

The 600-square foot, open-air, covered upstairs balcony overlooking the old city would serve as our kitchen and bedroom for the night. We enjoyed a dinner fit for royalty, sitting on the floor around a large, rectangular coffee table. I can't tell you exactly what was prepared for us but it was a symphony of flavors. We washed it all down with a couple bottles of the local brew.

Afterwards, the five of us—me, Greg, Brooke, Mick, and George—spread out on the couches or on our sleeping bags, writing emails, checking in with various social media outlets, and catching up on some news, but we made sure to be quick and instead, revel in a truly happy travel moment. Our only job was to be exactly where we were, with the people we were with, in a country we couldn't believe we were in.

We told stories, jokes, and our hopes for the future. We talked about our childhoods, our jobs, and our loved ones. It was one of those rare conversations where every participant had left their circumspection at the door. We basked in the kind of moments that had inspired us to do the rally in the first place; the moments every traveler keeps in their treasure chest of memories; the moments that won't have any effect on the length of our lives, but will certainly alter the depth of it.

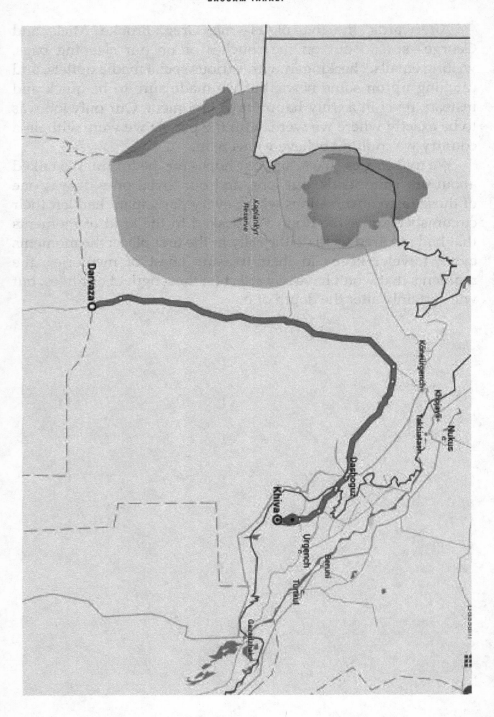

Day 17

What most of us call "hustling" is really stuff we choose to do because we don't have to scramble for a meal on a daily basis. Unfortunately, a good portion of the world does have to hustle for their next dollar, for their next bite to eat.

When it was time to go to sleep, the mother and daughter of the house were still cleaning, scrubbing, and tidying. They washed our clothes by hand. It was embarrassing how many times they had to replace the murky water due to our accumulated filth since Istanbul. And when we awoke at 7 o'clock in the morning, they were laboring over the stove, slicing tomatoes, cracking eggs, and concocting a breakfast more extravagant than we deserved, but much too good to be declined. There was no rest in their days.

Mick and George had to leave early since Mick had a visa issue that he needed to tackle at the Russian embassy in Astana, Kazakhstan. It was doubly sad to say goodbye to the Irish because we really liked them and we would be on our own for the foreseeable future.

It would have been criminal not to explore the old city before leaving. Khiva's interior was something out of the Old Testament. Apparently, it was the inspiration for the city in the animated film *Aladdin*. There was a giant cistern-like building that could have been mistaken for an ancient nuclear cooling tower if it weren't for the multicolored mosaic sheath in which it sat. This city was made for photographs: the sun cast just the right shadows, illuminating crevices in a yin-and-yang dance in the honeycomb of hidden alleyways, doors, and stories. Reluctantly, we stepped out of that time machine, beckoned by the call to once again, drive on, to see what lay ahead.

We needed gasoline, though. With no functioning stations, Shaxboz agreed to give me my first lesson in Gas Barons 101.

The reality of the situation settled like dust on a shelf. I was by myself in a car with a kid, going to buy gas from a place that wasn't sanctioned to sell it. I didn't have a phone, I didn't speak a lick of the local language, and I had no way to contact anyone if something bad happened. I was pretty sure that I was going to be fine but I didn't *know* that. Since I didn't know, I had to *choose* to trust the moment. And here was the heart of the rally: a fear of the unknown should not keep us from diving into it. Whether it was border crossing, ordering food in Hungarian, or hunting for fuel in Uzbekistan, I was constantly reminded that it's hard to shake hands if you're holding a shield.

Shaxboz was as cool as an autumn morning, and let's be honest, way more mature than I am. He told me how he went to school in Russia during the year but returned in the summer to help run his family's business. I was thirty-four years old, still unsure what I wanted to be when I grew up, and had so few responsibilities I could travel the world in a calamity of a car for six weeks.

We drove for ten minutes before reaching a house in the center of town. A few kids were kicking a plastic soccer ball in the small plot of land between the road and the house — a space so small that when Donata pulled up, there was not much room left for them to do anything at all. Sitting to the side was a group of older women chatting, their colorful flowing dresses provided the freedom to move and breathe under the solar noose. Shaxboz got out of the car and went inside while I stared and was stared at by everyone else.

Eventually, the house's matriarch came out and we agreed on a price per liter. By "agreed on a price" I mean that Shaxboz told me what I was going to pay. Whatever it was, it was cheap. The matriarch came back out with a beat-up metal funnel and the gasoline in an old 5-liter water jug. Donata had a 30-liter (7.93 gallons) tank but we weren't on empty so it only took about four trips to fill us up.

Back at the Hotel Alibek, we geared up, and thanked and hugged our goodbyes to our hosts. Before we knew it, we were again rumbling east on the planetary treadmill that spun west under our feet every minute of every day.

Our destination was Samarkand—the capital of Uzbekistan and the architectural crown jewel of Central Asia. It was also another stop along the famed Silk Road. Brooke had booked us into a hotel, which took part of the stress out of the day. Google Maps told us that it was "only" a nine-hour drive. Hitting the road at 10 a.m., we thought we'd play it safe and say we'd get to Samarkand by 10 p.m. Incorporating a three-hour margin for delay was us spitting at the realities we consistently chose to ignore.

The first part of the ride was uneventful other than the unspeakable heat corkscrewing into our skulls—the temperature rivaled that of the previous days. And then...our first Uzbek checkpoint. Being the driver, I had to enter a guard shanty, get my passport information recorded, and sign a book with dates and times. I chatted about the World Cup and had to turn down an offer of tea so that we could keep to our schedule. Yes, that's right—we were offered a sit-down drink of tea and a welcome conversation by the Uzbek police. Talk about hospitality. The other thing the Uzbek police force had was cohesion. Each checkpoint knew who we were and where we were going because they radioed each other. So we had to stick to the plot of where we said we were traveling, otherwise they'd accuse us of lying.

Things got interesting about fifteen miles northeast of Khiva when we had to cross the Amudaryo River over a bridge that was only made for trains. The bridge itself was about a half mile long and I had to be careful not to get our tiny tires caught between the rails. We made it across and it seemed like we would be able to link up with the main road, the A380, in eight miles, which would take us through Bukhara and into Samarkand. Easy-peasy... except, this eight-mile piece-of-shit road along the Pravoberezhny Magistralny Canal between the end of the bridge and the A380 was and will always be the worst tract of "paved" road on the entire Mongol Rally.

Inexplicable.

BASSAM TARAZI

We acrobatically descended and emerged from potholes at odd angles to save our undercarriage, or because there was simply no other way to go. Someone watching from above would have thought we were trying to draw a giant lightning bolt with our car.

It was always fun when a vehicle approached from the other direction. They'd be going straight and we'd think, okay, the road clears a bit up there, when suddenly their nose tilted down and their rear tipped up as they slammed on the brakes. Or maybe they had to dip their car off the mini cliff that was the entrance to the gash where Paul Bunyan had dragged his ax across the road. The other car would pop up on the other side and we'd see one side of it, then the other as the Z-turns came towards us.

The best part of the stretch was when we were able to avoid it. Every now and then sand gutters that Donata could fit into would appear on the side of the road. These provided a smooth but brief form of travel slightly faster than a jog. It took us more than an hour to cover the eight miles. Our reward was the A380 itself. It was one of the finer pieces of road in Uzbekistan: newly paved, freshly painted, three lanes in both directions, and hardly another car on the highway.

This long, mindless, hazard-free road invited one's brain to wonder and observe. Seeing hawks circling in the distance, a lean horse tied up to a shed, or shrubs clinging to any shard of rock they could get a grip on reminded me that every species on earth is engaged in an eternal resource war. While life may be very beautiful and aesthetic from a superficial human point of view, organisms are constantly evolving and creating different ways to dominate, kill, or hump one another. Life is ruthless. Venoms, toxins, shells, dances, packs, inflating, coiling, colors, camouflage, jungle canopies, salmon runs, coral reefs…one animal's "amazing" is another animal's "terrifying." We call this bit of evolutionary change "arms races" for goodness sake. Yes, it's beautiful that a cuttlefish can vary its colors to conform to its surroundings, but it's not beautiful if this stealthy squid is creeping around in the shadows waiting to devour you—then it's horrifying. Leopard seals are adorable animals with puppy-dog eyes and silly swirly motions that are *just so cute*, until they start ripping penguins' heads off.

It's no different for humans. Only a minute group of us don't feel that battle, day after day. We open the fridge and it's full. We turn the tap and water flows. We click on Netflix and watch (and chill). But we forget that if we're randomly placed at any point in the two hundred thousand-year human history, there would be a 95 percent chance it would be during a period of hunting and gathering. We'd be huddled in a cave, waiting to fend off a pack of wolves or an invading tribe while dealing with a case of whooping cough we couldn't shake and hoping the gangrene rotting the flesh off our uncle's calf wouldn't keep him from hacking a rival or two.

If, instead, we happened to be placed in the last ten thousand years (the 5 percent chance in the 200,000-year human history scenario), we wouldn't be rummaging around from cave to cave but there's still a 98 percent chance we'd be living at a time when the vast majority of humanity lived in extreme poverty. Chances are, we'd be battling typhoid, smallpox, the bubonic plague, Spanish flu, yellow fever, or smallpox epidemics while fighting for every bite of food and puddle of water.

A good portion of the human world continues to live a very real resource struggle. I know these things. Of course I *know* these things—my parents went above and beyond to raise me to be a responsible global citizen. I've traveled enough to *see* that the majority of the rest of the world lives in unimaginable poverty but I've never had to *feel* it. I've had a life devoid of great loss, pain, or suffering.

Central Asia is one of those places where there are not many white-collar jobs; it's collars with different hues of blue. Countless times we'd see people walking to…nowhere. Often they didn't have any water or provisions with them although the previous ten miles had been all grass and the next twenty were all sand.

But these people walked or stood there waiting for a ride or to catch their breath. I don't know which. We saw people tending a makeshift melon stand, napping under a disintegrating tarp, and trying to stay out of the direct broil of the sun. And that's what they did all day: sat and tried to sell melons to the intermittent cars that drove by.

Out here, for what people lacked in money, belongings, food, or leisure time, they made up for in faith. I don't mean in a fanatical sense, I mean in a letting go, of a trusting in something greater than themselves because it provided comfort against a backdrop of scarcity.

All animals struggle, but only humans have to *think* about that struggle.

***

Uzbek highway perfection couldn't last forever.

Suddenly, the road changed from spacious cushiony asphalt to a rickety, one-lane Brillo pad. At least the Uzbeks had the courtesy of employing some kids who sat in the back of a slow-moving pick-up truck with the gate down, throwing shovelfuls of bright-colored sand in the potholes to offer some contrast to the black pavement, thus keeping us from disemboweling our car.

We stopped for lunch at a little establishment on the side of the road as two other American rally teams traveling together were about to leave. I wished them well but when presented with the prospect of a five-minute conversation with teams we'd probably never see again, I let Brooke and Greg take care of the niceties. I wasn't an outright dick, but I wasn't accruing sainthood points either.

In general, I craved distance when closeness wasn't required because the "exhaustion of new" was always lurking in the reeds. Earlier that morning I had to trust Shaxboz because that's what the moment demanded of me, but now, like in the Czech forest after Darren and Myles were robbed, I was safe in disengagement.

I didn't want to find out if this group of Americans had car trouble or water shortages because then I'd have to care. The less I had to care, the more my wits could recharge to prepare for the peppering of originality that was always one tire rotation away.

It was alarming how quickly I could manufacture cultural contrast in order to limit my emotional exposure, but on this desert road my goals were to eat and move east. The rest was extracurricular. Such is the conundrum of life in a foreign land: How to immerse yourself without taking on water.

***

Now on our own, Greg, Brooke, and I savored being in the shade for a bit, but even so, the heat clung to us like a barnacle. While waiting for our unknown food items to be prepared, I embarked on a journey to The Outhouse of Doom.

A bathroom in this part of the world is usually a hole in the ground in some wooden hut in a back alley, a decent distance behind the main building, beyond a chained-up, barking dog, past a lone chair resting against a cement wall in a fallout shelter, and around a stack of tires or a dilapidated something or other. We avoided these structures at all costs (peeing on the roadside was perfectly acceptable in this part of the world, even for Brooke) but eventually solid waste had to go somewhere. Undoubtedly, this "bathroom" would have suffered unspeakable indignities before your visit. Once inside, you fought through the odor of a cholera hospital while simultaneously trying to remove one pants leg without falling over. Cradling your excess shorts in one arm, your clothing was now free from being irretrievably ruined by the friendly fire that comes with squatting and crapping into a pit. A wide stance is advisable for obvious reasons.

Like using the claw machine at an amusement arcade, finding the lateral (x-axis) crosshairs of your aim into the much-too-small hole in the ground is basic body symmetry, but judging when your sphincter is directly above the hole in an anterior/posterior sense (y-axis) is an impossibility. Gazing back under your what-have-yous with sweat falling off your nose while scuttling forwards or backwards on your toes and heels is like trying to find the target during a cloud-covered WWII bombing run. The best solution is to lower yourself as close to the ground as possible even as your knee ligaments howl in defiance.

The temperatures in these shit saunas would inevitably hit staggering heights. At this juncture, the menacing septic stench rising from the open tank below smelled so badly I could hear it. Mouth breathing and battling watery eyes, I comically admired the deteriorating state of the entire structure in which I was temporarily entombed, in order take my mind off attempting to actually defecate.

You'll have better luck finding the lost city of Atlantis in one of these bathrooms than a roll of owner-provided toilet paper, so once finished and with now trembling quads, you'll shuffle over to the toilet paper and baby wipes you brought and placed on a wooden ledge just out of reach of your squat position.

Upon reentry into breathable air, free and clear of the methane miasma of this desert dungeon, you'll give thanks to modern plumbing and make a mental note to send your local handyman a nice Christmas gift next year.

***

We pushed on after our late lunch, but Samarkand was still eons away — 211 miles to be precise. Traffic swelled, construction increased, but our speed did not. I was drained after eleven hours of driving on the sun's patio, so Brooke took over right around sunset. We thought that as we got closer to the capital the roads would improve, but that quality-versus-distance graph became an inverse relationship.

Driving at night on these unlit patches of asphalt was like the Coast Guard searching for survivors with a penlight in the middle of a midnight tempest. We'd strain our eyes to interpret general shapes in front of us when *Wham!* The whole chassis of the car would rattle...*Wham!* Again. Cars were close. Cars passed. Cars suddenly appeared right in front of us because their taillights didn't work or because our narcoleptic headlights could barely keep their eyes open, their seven electrons doing their best to brighten this charcoal world.

Peering through our dirty windshield, led by the smallest grotto of illumination on tires befitting a wheelbarrow, reminded me of the difference between water park fun and mettle-testing fun. The road into Samarkand didn't offer any jollification, only prayers to a God I didn't believe in and a strange sense of calm that this might actually be the last day of my life. I put my head back, shut my eyes, and ceded full control to Brooke and Greg.

If I die, I die. I'm not going to stress about it.

Brooke weaved and caromed her way into town—like a Plinko disk from *The Price Is Right* game—where the roads *finally* smoothed out a bit. We found the hotel around midnight. Instead of nine hours, it took fourteen hours, right in our 1.5 to 1.7-time multiplier that we kept ignoring. Adding insult to exhaustion, there was no street parking available and we were unsure if there was anyone awake to let us in. We weren't staying at the Marriott or Hilton here. A lot of these smaller hotels close their front desks after a certain hour.

We located our contact at the hotel and he told us we could park inside for the night. "Inside" wasn't visible to us until he opened giant wooden doors to reveal a courtyard in front of the hotel, large enough to fit four or five cars. But to get in there, we had to somehow ascend a steep ramp up to the unnecessarily high sidewalk. Steep ramps were trouble for Donata because she had the ground clearance of a lawnmower.

Brooke attempted to get up but stalled out each time. It is a true test of one's fortitude after navigating for fifteen hours of white-knuckled driving in the earth's broiler to be confronted with ten feet of ramp that might ruin everything. After she stalled again, Greg took over and tightrope-walked Donata up the ramp, making it over the top with only a minor scrape on our sump guard, barely avoiding beaching our ship. We were home for another night.

Paper-thin. Razor-sharp.

Every food option nearby was closed and we weren't about to go aimlessly walking around at midnight. The only thing that could conquer our hunger was fatigue so we headed up to our room. There we were in a hotel with beds and hot showers but we felt like we couldn't catch our breath. There was no chance to enjoy a local dinner or explore the nightlife, just time to get some crackers or a granola bar in our stomachs, go to bed, and repeat it the next day.

I hadn't masturbated since Istanbul twelve days ago, which was the first time all trip, mind you, so I didn't feel that a second hand copulation in seventeen days was out of line. I'm a man, not a monk. I chose to take the last shower in case I took too long, but I was finished in about eight seconds.

There might be no better rest than after a biological equalization.

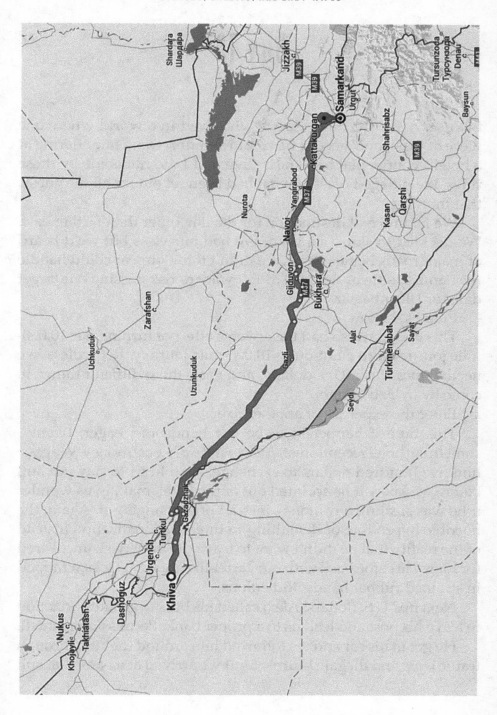

Day 18

I felt sorry for the other guests who lived in a world where one piece of toast, one piece of ham, and a muffin was a fair offering at a hotel's continental breakfast. Greg and I did not abide by those rules. We pillaged most of what had been set out for all the guests that morning.

We had no real destination for the day other than farther east. We decided to skip Tajikistan. We had our visas but we'd heard of major roads being closed, we didn't think our car could handle the Pamir Highway, and we didn't want to risk missing our target date for Ulaanbaatar.

Pussies. I know.

This decision also had the adverse effect of turning our 10,000-mile journey into a not-quite 10,000-mile journey. Regardless, we needed local cash, U.S. dollars, and gas — three difficult things to come by in Uzbekistan.

Enter the expertise of another fixer.

This time it happened to be our handsome, eager, twenty-something hotel receptionist, Alexi. First up? Local money. We gave him five hundred dollars to exchange. He told us to stay put and before we knew it he sprinted out of the hotel, making us wonder if he was stealing our money instead of exchanging it. Again, the horrible byproduct of defaulting to threat rationalization instead of the reality that he didn't want to leave the front desk uncovered for long. He came back with our cartel-like money stacks wrapped in strained rubber bands. Ridiculous.

Next up? U.S. dollars. Alexi called his boss to get authorization to leave his post and lead us to a proper bank. Permission granted.

He got in his car and we followed him around the city, through traffic jams and illegal U-turns, until we arrived at a bank that spit out fresh American greenbacks. It was a warm feeling to put my hands on those rectangular pieces of leverage once again.

Now for the gas. Alexi didn't seem optimistic about this because there was only one gas station in town. It was going to be crowded. We told him we had no choice.

How bad could it — *shit*.

I wasn't alive during the 1973 oil crisis but I've seen photos. This looked like a reenactment. There was a line of cars a quarter of a mile long waiting to fill up from one of the four pumps. What else did these people have to do that day? Did they take a day off from work to get gas? We couldn't wait in that line. Well, we *couldn't* wait in the "we're white, privileged, and can't be bothered to wait" sort of way.

This is when we realized that money might not buy happiness but it does buy "easier." We told Alexi that we would be willing to pay whatever he needed to get us to the front of the line without having him or ourselves stomped by a hostile mob. We could see the glares from those close to the front of the line fixate on us and our little expedition of fun on the other side of the road. They saw a man lean into our car, then run to the guys at the pump, then run back to us, then run back to the pump and wave us over. We blended in like a polar bear in a tomato factory.

We all kind of exhaled like this was as good a day as any to get shanked. Greg drove us down the road a little bit, and then U-turned and paraded by everyone else waiting in line. We got directed off to the side of the pumps for a couple of minutes. When a few cars left, the gas station attendant motioned us to back up into one of the vacated spots.

To our surprise, we didn't hear anyone honk or yell. After our experience at the Turkish-Georgian border, we were quite certain that we would be beaten with shoes and lambasted with verbal thunder, but no one said or did anything. WTF? I almost wanted them to, because it would make a better story. It's kind of like how we all secretly want that "Storm of the Century" to hit us (but we don't want to *really* suffer) so that we can tell everyone what we lived through.

The Samarkand public did not succumb to my shallow and twisted desires. Then again, with an 8-gallon gas tank, maybe we just didn't give people enough time to *get* mad at us. Or maybe, people aren't as mean as I think. That's probably it. I was assuming: Muslim country plus formerly Soviet plus waiting in line for gas plus Americans cutting line equals someone getting beheaded. But no, they acted in a far more civilized manner than would have been the case in any major American city.

Gas tank full, we wanted to tip Alexi but he wasn't having any of it. He said we were his guests and it was his job to take care of us no matter what. Damn it! What *is* it with these people, their outpouring of kindness and embodiment of honor? He and everyone waiting in line for gas made a mockery of everything people presume about "these" places.

Societies near the Fertile Crescent and Silk Road possess an intrinsic sense of Bedouin hospitality. These cultures were built on a foundation where *we* trumped *I* on every deal, where it was impossible to do things on your own because you'd be dead or ostracized if you tried. The American entrepreneurial zest has only created an illusion that the individual can be greater than the whole and that everything, even kindness, can be transactional. America is the teenager nation state to the elder desert wisdom. I'm not saying there's not value in each mind-set, but selflessness isn't exactly a high schooler's strong suit. America is a country built on "Fuck you."

Want to tax our tea, King George? *Fuck you.*

Want to have slaves, Confederacy? *Fuck you.*

Want to take over Europe, Hitler? *Fuck you.*

The words "American exceptionalism" are practically a synonym for "fuck you." God only blesses America. From sea to shining sea.

So it's no real secret that the elemental notion of going the extra mile for a complete stranger is a bit foreign to an American like me, who grew up without strife. Unlike my parents and grandparents, I don't have memories of war, of loss, of destruction. I'd never required the aid of a stranger in a time of desperate, life-altering need. On top of the good luck of living under the guidance of parents who gave me more than was ever required of them, in a land and at a time that had opportunity falling out of its stuffed pockets, I am an extremely autonomous person. Autonomy is the luxury of the fortunate. I've been mostly single, never married, and through switching various careers I've amassed an inordinate amount of self-reliance and self-discipline. These qualities undoubtedly shaped me as a person, and helped me do and attain the things I had. But I now believed that what had to be whittled away to get me to this point were various layers of empathy and selflessness.

Why are some of the nicest people you meet on earth also the people with the least? Because they can relate to someone who has nothing, and because they couldn't have made it this far by themselves. I, on the other hand, am extremely kind when I have nothing to lose, but when I might have to give something up (time, money, energy), my kindness becomes more calculated because I know I don't have an endless supply of it. I'm not asshole, but I'm not as naturally nice as I know I could be, as I was raised to be.

This notion was starting to burn a hole into the core of my being.

***

Before we left town, we needed to see at least one of the sights that Samarkand had to offer because all the books kept talking about them. We chose Registan Square. Good choice. It was made of three enormous *madrasas* (Islamic centers of learning) that enveloped the square on three sides, each one completely covered in Chiclet-sized mosaic tiles of myriad blues, whites, and greens. I couldn't help but shake my head at the sheer scope on one hand and the utter precision of it on the other. It was like a modern-day Angkor Wat. And by "modern day" I mean that the first *madrasa* was built in the fifteenth century and the other two in the seventeenth century.

While downloading the image of the square into our brains, we sat in the grass and enjoyed a tricolor ice cream with other tourists and revelers. Then it really was time to hit the road. We drove past some more squares and centers, and added Samarkand to our list of cities to return to. A half-assed morning look-see was insulting to the pearls that glimmered on every oystered corner.

**

The Uzbek summer made it feel like we were driving through a steel foundry, plus, of course, we had not eaten lunch, although it was after 3 o'clock. We always felt like we would eventually see something around midday but it never happened that way, and instead, we were stuck with making voracious decisions that never did anyone any good. When a group of hungry people tries to decide where to eat, everyone wants someone else to choose. "I don't care where we eat. Just pick something!" Of course, deep down, we really mean, "Pick whatever you want, just don't fuck it up."

After we passed the hundredth Lada carrying or hauling ten times its bodyweight, we saw a huddle of buildings with a pile of red patio chairs stashed in the back. If you've traveled before, you know that red plastic chairs usually mean food. We parked, ignored the stares, and walked around the building to see what was what.

"English?"

Nope.

I made hand gestures like I was scooping up food and putting it in my mouth, and I patted my stomach and moaned how good it was. This thought-to-be-universal description of hunger was not taken as such. I looked at a man and said, "Food?"

He shook his head, "No."

Damn it.

There was a small store there but we didn't want another Snickers or a bag of chips for lunch, we wanted *food*. As we were walking back to our car a guy chased us down and said, "Yes, food."

Thank God.

Never in my experience had an establishment changed its mind as to whether it served food, but I was glad this was the first time. The four of us sat in the shade provided by the tin roof. Four being, me, Greg, Brooke, and the blanket of heat that seemed to smother Central Asia. The gentleman who had called us back put down three sets of stacked forks and knives, each wrapped in a thin paper napkin—like red plastic chairs, a staple in far-off eateries—and awaited our order.

Only we didn't have any menus and he had none to give. This might be an issue, since our conversations with him had stunted at the miming phase. Greg realized he could use his offline Google translate app because this guy also knew Russian.

Greg typed things like:

Do you have a menu?

What would you order?

Surprise us.

We'll eat anything at all. Whatever you suggest.

There was now a group of kids reading Greg's phone but none of it seemed to translate the way we had wanted it to. Their reactions had an air of:

Surprise you? I don't know any tricks.

What would I order? Who cares what I want? What do you want?

Lo and behold our knight in shining apron came back with photos of various food items. He pointed to a soup.

"Yes. That. Bring us three of those...and three large waters."

***

. 225 .

That soup, though…

It was called *laghman*. It was one of those hearty-looking stews that couldn't *not* be filling. It had some noodles, meat, vegetables, and potatoes. I know that the superlatives in life always hijack placement in time, but this was a lifetime top-five meal. Sure, there was the hunger and low expectation factor, but the overwhelming truth was that it was one of the best things I've ever eaten, period. These spaghetti-like noodles were only like spaghetti in the same way that Neptune is "like" Earth because it is a planet. But you wouldn't want to live on Neptune, just like you wouldn't want to eat spaghetti ever again after you had these sublime, fatty noodles that were in our soup.

It wasn't a case of the same singular great food taste either. Anything I stabbed my fork or spoon into was a madhouse of flavors. That giant potato wasn't a potato at all, it was a dumpling filled with…holy shit! That must be dry-aged unicorn marinated in mermaid tears. And the broth was a new element on the periodic table, a truly noble gas in its liquid state. It's like my mouth had only eaten in 2-D until this meal.

Unprecedented.

We looked at each other in confusion and elation. I wanted to impregnate this soup.

The *laghman* definitely entered the FOSO GIMMA realm: *Food So Good It Makes Me Angry.* I got mad because I've been eating soup my whole life but it never tasted like this before, and I was mad that other people have been eating this for years without my knowledge.

FOSO GIMMA — use it.

The soup cost us four dollars each but I would have given my spleen for it. After being sated to a higher state of being, we floated out of there like kids departing their family for summer camp. We gave hugs, we said thank you, we took photos in front of our car, and then we moved east again.

Checkpoint after checkpoint slowed us down, but the cops never *shook* us down. On a map, Eastern Uzbekistan looks like octopus tentacles poking illogical reaches into Tajikistan and Kyrgyzstan. It was in these far-flung stretches where we pushed on looking for a place to camp just as the sun disappeared behind the mountains and a few cosmic lighthouses twinkled in the eastern sky. We had passed a couple of turnoffs but it was still too light out, there was no tree cover, and too close to the road. As with the selection of places to eat, no one wanted to make a camping decision. A how-about-here? suggestion would be lobbed hesitantly by one of us as we were passing a random off-ramp at a high speed. Worthy or not, it was inaccessible now. Brooke and I sloughed accountability to Greg since he was driving, but he was in an "I'm driving, so you guys decide" mode, scattering indecision through our car like shrapnel. This hamster wheel of decision-making happened when it was time to find a place to camp no matter who was driving.

Our dream of stopping before complete darkness became a fool's paradise when we began going up, down, over, and around a giant treeless mountain range between the cities of Angren and Chadak. The road had one lane of travel in each direction, forcing us into a game of pass or be passed. It's amazing the risk we would accept overtaking even one vehicle. I bet, had we decided to not pass anyone on the whole evening's endeavor, we would have been delayed ten minutes, max. But there is something psychological that happens when we are moving slower than we think we could, where it feels like our life is slipping away from us. A traffic jam is one thing, but no one wants to be told that the person directly ahead of them controls their destiny.

Once we passed the person in front of us, we didn't just physically overtake them, we passed them on the social hierarchy too. It was *us* telling *them* that we live a better life, that our partner is sexier than theirs, that our jobs are more important. Before, the car in front of us had been an impediment to where we wanted to be, but now in our rearview, it was swept into the metaphorical trash bin of insignificance, no longer disrupting the possibilities of the rest of our lives. It's like breaking the shackles of automotive slavery.

How else could I explain that we had traveled thousands of miles, had been delayed hours and hours every day, but I was fully on board with Greg choosing to risk our lives far too many times to gain one link in a chain hundreds and hundreds of cars long on our race to…nowhere? Stress, fear, flashing lights, accelerations, skidding—it was all suddenly worth it.

Adding to the excitement was that when driving in a British car on the right side of the road, passing becomes a two-person game because the driver couldn't see the middle of the road or the cars coming the other direction. This is where the navigator came in, which was my duty on this leg.

Greg would want to know if it was clear, so he'd poke his left side past the median so I could see the status of oncoming traffic. I then had a split second to decide if it indeed was clear. We had a rule in the car that we couldn't say "go" or "no" anymore because it sounded too similar and we didn't want to die in a fiery head-on collision because of an "Oh, I thought you meant *go!*" so we changed that to "green" and "red." But we'd forget, and on any given day we'd have an exchange like this:

"Go."

"No?"

"Go! Green! Move! *Now!*"

We added hand signals too. Showing all five fingers on a hand meant, "No." A finger pointing forward meant, "Go." However, the spotter always wanted it to be the driver's choice at night because with no streetlights, depth perception is like guessing which star in the sky is farther away than another. The driver would ease Donata into the other lane, the navigator would say, "I don't know. Your call," and then the driver would make a life-or-death decision.

The elevation description on a graph per mile driven in this leap-frog over the Uzbek mountains would look like a heart rate monitor. It was up, down, up, down—forty times in twenty miles. Some ups and downs were smaller than others, but the elevation changes were unrelenting. We reached the pass at a height of 7,500 feet and proceeded to descend to 1,652 feet in twenty-five miles. That's a 4.4 percent average grade for twenty-five miles. It's a long way down.

Of course, the downhill trip did not prevent us from zipping around cars we deemed to be impeding our progress. This was a truly reckless plunge. It was pitch black at the bottom of the hill and we had no sense of the topography. We were in for a night of commando camping—basically, find a spot of land where our car was hidden enough and the ground was flat enough.

Easier said than done.

We tacked down a few empty side roads abutting farms, contemplating parking Donata near or in the bushes. We'd stop and put on our camping headlamps to get a sense of what the terrain was like, all while trying to stay inconspicuous in the wide-open farmland. If a car drove by, we'd turn off our lights and hide behind Donata. I was getting so desperate that I was ready to pitch the tent right next to the outdoor bathroom in the backyard of a giant house where the residents were either sleeping or out of town. Greg and Brooke nixed this and made fun of me for the rest of the trip for wanting to pitch our tent in a cow paddy field.

We did find a small enclave at the corner of a farm that gave us enough room to lay flat and kept Donata kinda-sorta covered. Of course, when morning came and the sun was blasting, we would be visible to any farmer plowing his fields or any car driving by, but at least we'd get some shut-eye before a confrontation. Rest before stress. That's all that mattered. And around midnight, that's what we did.

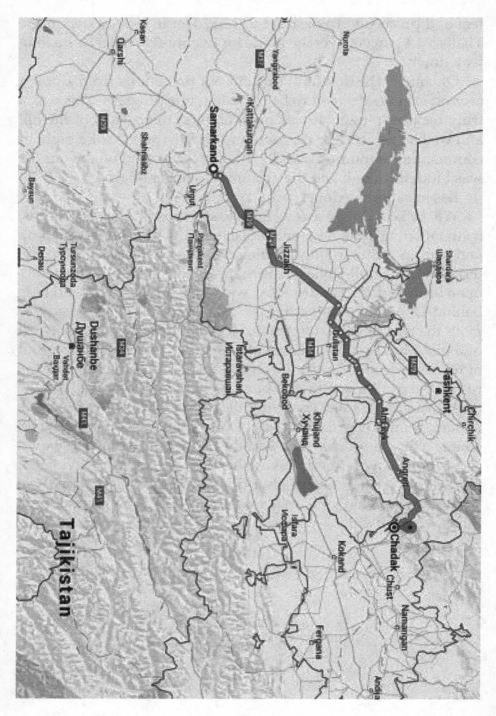

Day 19

As usual, the sun's photon party was raging out east far earlier than desired. There was no sense in fighting it so we packed up and hit the road by 7 o'clock, happy we had made it through the night without a farmer poking holes in our tent with a pitchfork. The construction barriers and svelte lane widths in the surprisingly modern city of Namangan made it feel more like were in a chute than on a road. I joyously navigated Donata through a fleet of white taxicabs packed as tight as toothpicks in a shot glass.

It was unclear what road we were supposed to take but the good news was that on a map this far eastern region of Uzbekistan looks like a mangled penis engaging in cartographic intercourse with Kyrgyzstan's borders. The good news being, Kyrgyzstan now surrounded us on three sides. Eventually we'd run into it if we drove in any direction but west.

We figured we'd see signs for the border town of Uchkurgan but found none. Maybe we would be absorbed into Kyrgyzstan. We asked some farmers, "Kyrgyzstan?" They didn't seem to agree but they pointed in a general quadrant of a direction.

Affirmative, gents...

Soon, we descended a small hill where painted tarmac gave way to what looked like a dried seabed. It must have been a border because it was absolute bedlam. Cars faced in all directions, dust swirled in the air, vendors pedaled trinkets, and pedestrians slithered among it all like water around rocks. Wading through the masses, we were most certainly that morning's entertainment.

Eventually, the crowds thinned out but there was no border.

Hmm.

Before we completely left the throngs and continued onto the fairly quiet country road splayed out in front of us, a man waved his finger at us as if to say, "No, no, no."

What did that mean?

We flashed the "No thank you, sir" smile and glanced away, but then he dropped the bags he was carrying and made a giant "X" with his arms over his head.

That couldn't be good.

In a fit of indecision, we let inertia take over, aimlessly driving straight past the man. He stared at the back of our car, dumbfounded we were not heeding his instruction.

Crazy old man! What did he know?

We felt that any border we would have to cross was to our left somewhere, but there were no roads going in that direction. We also knew that if we drove straight, we would eventually run out of Uzbek road and hit Kyrgyzstan, but just because we reached a geographic border didn't mean we'd reach a political one.

After driving for five minutes, we realized that the guy wasn't telling us that we were unwelcome—he was telling us that there was no border in the direction we were going. Well, where the hell *was* the border then? We weren't looking for bone fragments in an archeological dig; we were trying to locate a country the size of Nebraska that everyone agreed existed. It couldn't be that hard to find.

Before we turned around, Brooke had to pee, but in her haste to exit the car, she accidentally spilled her water bottle on the dashboard and I snapped. She hadn't appreciated my reaction, so there was a fog of tension in the car to add to the stress of finding a country.

We returned to the mayhem of people, cars, and animals because someone had to know where Kyrgyzstan was. We fit in like a sea urchin at a balloon festival. Eventually, we approached a young cop directing traffic, although judging from the gridlock we drove through he wasn't doing a good job orchestrating. He was so close to our car that we could have picked his pocket. Instead, we looked at him, shrugged our puzzled shoulders, and asked, "Kyrgyzstan?"

And he said, "Kyrgyz?"

"Yes, Kyrgyz."

He gazed at us quizzically as if wondering how many wrong turns we must have made in life to be on the Uzbekistan-Kyrgyzstan border still looking for the Uzbekistan-Kyrgyzstan border. He pointed off to our left (which wasn't where we'd planned to go). *Sweet.* We had our cardinal direction. We tried to say, "And then what?" but he continued pointing in the distance beyond a swarm of people. We hoped that the next turn would become apparent.

It wasn't.

Soon enough we came to a fork in the road and then another, all the while trying to point our car in a north or easterly direction. Suddenly, at what felt like another dead end, we spotted a building in the distance. Maybe they could help us. We approached and saw a soldier.

This was the border—a nondescript road, in the middle of the field, without a single sign or another car.

Okay…

We again pointed and asked, "Kyrgyzstan?" in the manner you would if you were asking for concert parking.

The soldier's look said, "Yes, you idiots. The giant country you are looking for is right behind me. Now get out of the car and go process yourselves and your passports."

***

Eventually, we were released from Uzbekistan unscathed and told to continue down a hundred-yard Podunk road to Kyrgyzstan's underwhelming immigration hut. There can't be an easier border to cross illegally than the Uzbekistan-Kyrgyzstan border near Uchkurgan. Americans didn't need a visa to enter Kyrgyzstan so it was pretty laid back to begin with, but the border guards we met could have been stationed there on a costume party prank. They were just two skinny dudes in their late twenties hanging out in a shack. Beyond this shack was a group of people on foot waiting to come into Uzbekistan. The only thing keeping them from entering no-man's-land was a one-bar, WWII-style vertical swinging gate that opened when someone pressed down on the far side of it.

We had to wait, though, because the generator that ran the building's electricity was down, which meant that their computers were down, which meant that they couldn't process us. We asked our guards about changing money and if there was a bank nearby. They said the closest bank was in Bishkek, the capital of Kyrgyzstan, more than a day's drive away.

Super.

I was able to exchange about sixty dollars' worth of Uzbeki *som* for Kyrgyz *som* with the border guards, but that's all they had. Greg talked to the people on the other side of the gate, but they didn't have anything to exchange with this scary white yeti towering over them.

I needed to pee. One of the guards pointed me to a crumbling shed in the bush on one side of the road. Before I reached the hut, the other guard yelled out from behind me in broken English, "Wait. Don't go there. This morning there was a cobra there." He made a snake face and hissing sound. Very well. I peed in the grass.

Back at the car, Greg, Brooke, and I chatted with the guards about life, America, Michael Jordan, LeBron James, and all that. Their English wasn't perfect but Kyrgyzstan was a country we couldn't spell correctly until that day, so we weren't going to split hairs. We were individuals sharing a laugh. I wonder if they still think about us at all. I wonder if they know that I think of that moment often, and that now I've written about it in a book. Maybe that moment was another one in a monotonous million for them. Even so, for those few minutes, we were the only people in one another's lives. Some far from home, others right at home—but all humans.

Soon enough, the generator was back up and running, the guards registered our passports in their system, and we were free to enter Kyrgyzstan. *Kyrgyzstan*! It is a country that boasts the presence of wild snow leopards and the three millennia-old city of Osh that had been a pit stop on the Silk Road for centuries. Kyrgyzstan was definitely a place that I had never dreamed of visiting before the rally. I don't know what I expected to see but what we did have were quite pristine roads and remarkable views. Up and around we swooped and turned amid rocky terrain on a road by the glowing, translucent turquoise of the Naryn River. It looked like the Caribbean was coursing through the Grand Canyon or a slice of St. Tropez was weaving through New Zealand. It was an absolutely stunning convergence of mountains and water.

The beauty led us to the Toktogul Reservoir. This thing could have existed as a location shoot in *Avatar* because it was cascade green, approximately 10 miles across and 6 miles wide, with jagged mountain peaks studding the circumference while rolling Irish-looking hills hugged close to the water.

"Did we just stumble on one of Earth's secrets...or are we dreaming?"

"How would we know the difference?"

A row of cars was parked at the rim of the lake, their owners enjoying a swim. Brooke made a passionate request that we stop and swim instead of getting to an arbitrary point on a map before sunset. Greg was neutral. I was the one fighting it. I was worried about the car because we would have to traverse a rocky, sandy road to get to the beach. We watched other vehicles inch downward and I was honestly unsure if we'd be able to get back up. I wanted to keep moving. I always wanted to keep moving. I had an almost maniacal grip on our timetable. We had to be in Ulaanbaatar by August 23 so we could all be back at work on August 25. I was so against the idea of only making it as far as we could on the rally. In my eyes, we *had* to reach Ulaanbaatar. We *had* to finish the task at hand. Anything less would be a failure. The closer we were to Mongolia, the more Mongolia weighed on my shoulders.

But the water was too perfect, the day was too hot, and even on a trip like the Mongol Rally that was created to encourage you to live a little, I was convinced that I needed to live a little more.

Greg walked in front of the car, tossing any sharp rocks out of the way. We made the half-mile crawl down to the beach and reached a bunch of people enjoying a summer's day. I was almost surprised that people in a place like Kyrgyzstan knew how to relax, smile, and play. This was, of course, me mentally regurgitating all the 'Stan brainwashing that I had been bathed in by the media. It was shocking that even someone like me—half Palestinian, half Dutch, who had traveled to sixty countries by that time—was succumbing to a previously painted picture of the mysterious and dangerous *they*. Even peaceful and amicable Kyrgyzstan, which has done nothing to the United States, which didn't require Americans to have a visa to enter its borders, which was guilty only of being in a part of a world that was unfamiliar to us.

Shame on me…

Brooke whipped up some prepackaged noodle concoction on the stove, we all went swimming, and I took the drone for a flight. A small group of local guys loved it. They loved it so much that we were able to download the video onto my computer and then transfer it to one of their cell phones through his USB cable. They'd be able to share views of the lake that no one had seen before. Technology.

We also had to pose for multiple group photos on everyone's phone. Radiating from all their faces and exuded in their shirtless stances was pride. They were proud to be Kyrgyz and they were proud to be hanging out with Americans who were visiting *their* country. It's easy to forget the profusion of possibility that is (right or wrong) still embodied in the idea of the United States throughout many parts of the world. These guys wanted to show their friends and family the photo they took with people who came from a land where you can do anything and become anyone.

Once I saw that look of dignity and honor in their photographed faces, I, too, stood with a little more fortitude for every subsequent picture we took, proud to be with these guys in their achingly beautiful land, proud of who I was, and thankful for the gifts of opportunity in my life that brought me to this moment.

Was I *worthy* of the gift? That's still debatable, but the dip in the lake and the human connection really had been the refresher I needed. It removed the push of *getting somewhere* and replaced it with the joy of *being* right here, like that dinner on the deck in Khiva, Uzbekistan. An interesting life isn't only about the accomplishments, but the people we interact with. Somehow in my pursuit of "finishing" I had forgotten all this.

I took Donata back up the treacherous road while Greg and Brooke walked behind me. Their weight would have been too much otherwise. As it was, Donata spun her tires, kicked up some dirt, and had a hard time getting out. When she made it to the flat road I could almost hear her sigh.

Like every other day, late afternoon arrived too soon and the thought of having to find a camping spot increased in urgency. Distances were not traveled at the speed we had anticipated, but my goodness, things were pretty. We snaked through canyon after canyon with snowcapped peaks popping up around us. The grass went a little farther, the animals roamed a little longer, and people bundled up a little tighter. This was the wilderness. We also saw our first *gers* or yurts, those cylindrical/conical white huts. Forget about Kansas, Dorothy—we weren't even in Uzbekistan anymore. We kept driving, higher and higher, so high that we had to close the windows and yank the cold weather gear out of the depths of our bags, although we had been sweating and swimming in a lake a few hours before.

The high point of the mountain pass was 11,500 feet. That's five hundred feet higher than the top of Mammoth Mountain in California. With the sun's last flicker doing its best to light our world from behind the western peaks, we found a side road on our descent back down the mountain that led to a 20-foot-wide flowing brook, providing a spot to park our car out of view of the main road. We were in heaven. Nestled in between the Kyrgyz mountains, we felt like we were as far away from what we knew as we'd ever been.

"Greg, did you GPS us?"

"Let me do that now."

We had a Spot GPS device that could broadcast our signal to ten preset email addresses. We pressed it once a day so that our families knew where we were. Oh, the look on people's faces when they saw those coordinates!

Where the hell are they?

We're *in it*, that's where we are.

The wind kicked up and the temperature dropped. Greg and I secured the tent before we lost the light altogether. Brooke boiled water from the river and began to prepare dinner. A few farmers saw us but had no problem with our presence. The sky was unafraid that night, peacocking in a full show of its capabilities in the crisp, 40-plus-degree air. Locking eyes on Orion took the otherworldly experience of the moment and brought it back to the familiar once again. *Oh, right. Those guys at the lake look up at night and see Orion when they wonder about their lives, their dreams, and their place among the stars too.*

Huddled into our sleeping bags, we talked about how the finish line was close enough to deserve a mention now. We were still about two weeks out (hopefully) but we only had three borders left! Were we going to make it? Could we make it?

I churned through countless hypotheticals until, with sleep finally lurking near the edges of my mind, I settled into its nothingness.

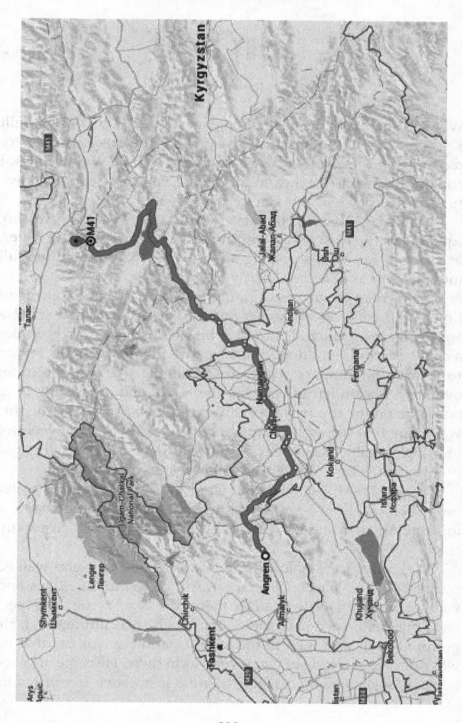

Day 20

When I unzipped the tent door and stepped into the moonlit Kyrgyz valley at 3 a.m., it was as if I had entered a sublunary realm. Even though there was absolutely no one within miles, I couldn't just shit diarrhea in an open field. There are primitive rules of decency hardwired into our DNA.

I walked upstream a bit (not sure why I didn't go downstream), squatted on a small ledge with my ass hanging over the water, and leaned forward, shivering and praying that I would not fall into the river as I peed out of my butt.

Later, when dawn was beginning to break, I woke up a second time. With cold sweats and a hunched back like I had spent a week digging a ditch, I moved a bit downstream to shit under a small overpass so I'd at least stay partially out of sight. Trying to balance on slippery rocks while clinging like a beetle to an overhead I-beam left me cursing the world and everything in it. Someone on the trip was bound to get sick and I was hoping this was a bug that would leave my body as quickly as it took control of it. I felt terrible. Really terrible. I tried to sit in silence in the cold morning air, letting the chills wash over me.

Brooke was still sleeping but Greg was up and had put water on to boil. While we were positioned in our camping chairs, a local elderly man and his wife pulled up next to us in their pickup truck.

The man got out holding a thermos of some sort and walked over to us. The skin on his face was a collection of ridges and valleys, proof of a life lived in the fields. We stood up out of respect and anticipation of an altercation for which I was unprepared. He gestured to us and then to the thermos and we realized that he was offering us a swig of whatever was in there. He came in peace but barely showed it, cracking a smile just above freezing. His offering of welcome was a sense of duty (not contingent on his mood, like mine might be at home). With my stomach balancing on a unicycle, I was wary of putting anything in there that would cause a digestive fuss, but cultural mores cannot be negotiated. Greg handed him our two mugs and the man filled them with whatever was in his thermos. He then poured himself a cup. We saluted and drank it, slug for gasping slug.

It was a warm, bitterly pungent taste that caused the muscles in my lower jaw to pulsate, which was, of course, vomiting's shot across the bow. I begged and pleaded with my body to keep down the devil juice. It was like a group of people having to keep back zombies from barging through a rickety barn door. Thankfully, the hinges held.

When we didn't die upon ingestion, Greg pointed to our now boiling water and then to the package of instant coffee in his hand. The man nodded. Greg poured the *boiling* water in the man's mug and mixed the coffee in. He gulped the scalding coffee down in three giant swigs without so much as a grimace. He nodded in thanks. We took a photo with him and his wife and then they went on their way. Not a word was ever spoken by the four of us during this whole encounter.

Bedouin hospitality, Kyrgyz style.

Culture is what makes *Homo sapiens* the higher ape. It's our proclivity for art, ritual, and communication that unite us as a species, but it's the variety within these expressions that make us different. Where there are two flags, there are two truths, two ways of life. But there is always common ground. We don't have to give up what binds us to our tribe in order to experience what unites another. If we don't venture out, we risk never walking a mile in someone else's clogs, sandals, or moccasins; we risk never tasting chicken, fish, or *laghman* soup for the soul; we risk never sharing a warm cup of coffee, tea, or God knows what we just drank.

***

There wasn't much excitement on the road to Kazakhstan, but we hit a snag upon leaving Kyrgyzstan when the last guard asked to see a document we didn't have. It sounded like he was seeking some kind of customs form. Through Google Translate, we were able to communicate in Russian and English, typing back and forth and trying to fill in the blanks where the translation didn't completely match.

Each time he typed something, we had to wait for the software to compile and translate. During that period of processing, we were on pins and needles, looking at the screen and hoping for the all clear. Here's how the typed conversation went.

Greg: We don't know what form you mean.

Him: Customs form.

Greg: We never received a customs form upon entry into Kyrgyzstan.

Him: You must have.

We looked at each other, confused. We looked back at him but he was unmoved by our confusion.

Greg: We're being honest. We never received anything. These are our documents.

He went through our documents a little annoyed but then typed:

Him: Where are you traveling from? To?

Greg: We're driving from London to Ulaanbaatar.

The crazy look on his face led us all to chuckle and alleviate the mood a little bit. He peeked into our car again, and did a few cursory glances.

Him: Gift?

Greg hopped into the car and pulled out a San Diego themed deck of playing cards. The guy opened them up but didn't tip his hand as to what he thought of the gift. He then said something in Russian and pointed at our car.

Fuck.

We didn't move. He pointed at us and then pointed at the car again. We had no idea what he meant but his voice was rising. Did we fall into the bribe trap or something? Did he want us to get more stuff out of the car? He repeated his statement in Russian again but we were palms up.

He grabbed Greg's phone, typed something, and then handed it back to Greg. We huddled around the phone and then the app popped up its one-word translation: *Godspeed.*

We erupted in laughter and gratitude. It's amazing how eight letters in a particular order can change everything. We shook the man's hand and he pointed us towards the Kazakh entry building.

As had become standard, Greg and I went through on foot and had to wait in sovereign Kazakh territory for Brooke to come through with the car.

"Can you believe we're in Kazakhstan, Greg?"

"No. Can you believe we can still see, Kyrgyzstan?"

"Nope."

I took out my phone and kept zooming into and out of the map of the world, giggling at the marvel of where we were. We found a bathroom in the strip mall just beyond the gates, and fully embracing our pioneering selves, we stocked up on aloe water and Snickers bars. Everyone in the area knew we weren't from around there but in the carefree manner Greg and I stood, sat, and chatted, they knew that we were fish from a different pond, but we were not fish completely out of water, flopping around hysterically. There's a difference.

After about an hour's wait, Donata came into view, her beehive engine buzzing audibly, and Brooke behind her windshield, arm draped over the door confidently, giving us the thumbs up, her gills clearly handling the new water with ease.

Atta girl, Brooke!

Only two borders left on the trip.

We left the gate at 7 o'clock. Since Kazakhstan is the largest landlocked country on earth (approximately twice the size of Alaska), we were going to have to cross it in chunks. Our goal that night was the town of Almaty, about 130 miles in from the border. Brooke had booked a hotel, probably the last one for a while. We wanted a good night's rest and some actual food before the boondocks of Kazakhstan, Russia, and Mongolia engulfed us.

Almaty is the biggest city in Kazakhstan, home to 1.5 million people, about the size of greater Milwaukee. As we entered, traffic fused together. Without the need to mind the road as intently, drivers honked and waved in support when they got a good look at our car. One guy even leaned out of his window and asked us what the hell we were doing in Almaty. We told him we were on our way to Mongolia and he said, "Mongolia? But there are no roads in Mongolia." A few weeks ago, someone might have looked at us crooked if we told him we were going to Kazakhstan. Now we were in Kazakhstan and they were looking at us crooked for going to Mongolia.

We found a parking spot right in front of the hotel and treated ourselves to a fancy dinner at the house restaurant. Because we never knew if we were going to reach our destination each day, arriving where we were supposed to arrive always created elation far greater than the event may have merited.

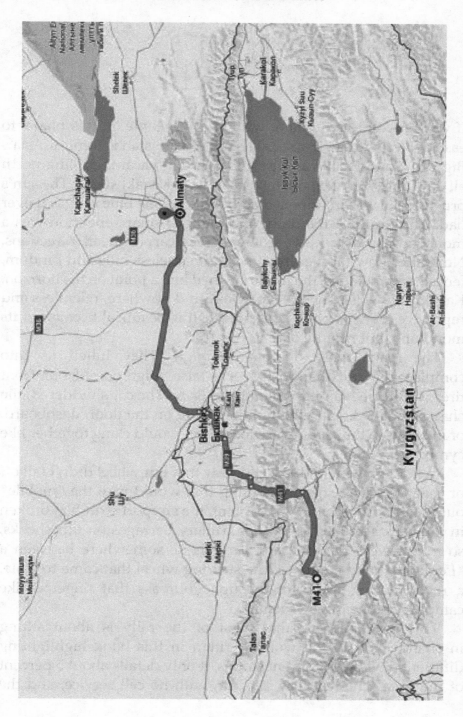

Day 21

If you're wondering where we could fit people on this planet to ease overcrowding, it's Kazakhstan. Kazakhstan is Central Asia's Big Sky Country. It's almost unbelievably vacant. Driving north all day long, we asked ourselves, "Why is Kazakhstan?" The sun's brushstroke was unimpeded across the largest blue canvas it ever had. The result of the daily onslaught of solar repetition was a monochromatic, treeless, golden grass carpet in all directions. No matter how far we drove passed nameless hills and random, fenceless cemeteries, the road vanished into a point on the horizon. Kazakhstan was at once everywhere and nowhere, relentless and repetitive, but somehow enchanting. It is beautiful because of its monotony, not in spite of it.

The roads were demonic, though. They lulled us into complacency and then just over a false ridge one of our front tires would free-fall into a sinkhole. *Bang.* The car shuddered, the chassis moaned, and whether they were on the floor, dashboard, or in between the seats, every loose coin would clang together like cymbals.

In that moment of doom, I'd pray that our wheel didn't fall off or that we didn't snap something that would take the "mobile" out of our automobile. At this point, the support strut had broken in the back seat from previous artillery barrages on our shocks, so if you were the sad sack back there, somewhere between a "Look out!" and a whip of the steering wheel that came too late, a reverberation was sent through your ass that lingered like campfire smoke in a sweatshirt.

This reminded me that most of the rally is about sitting in silence. For all the words written in this book highlighting different days and different stories, it only details about 5 percent of the time. The rest was in a car, with no cell service, and the only thing to comfort (or scare) us was conversation, music, or the thoughts in our heads. There's something about the emptiness of an open road that allows the brain to unwind that tangled ball of mental yarn, where rogue thoughts and free radicals can bounce around without being smothered by a blanket of brunches, work, Facebook, Instagram, email, or routine. It was a void of thinking established not by organized meditation but by forced depletion. The speed with which the world comes at us at home was replaced with the longevity of a random thought suspended in the hypnotic trance of all-day driving. The Mongol Rally let the primordial soup of our brains create new life, giving us a mound of mental clay with no instructions.

I asked myself countless questions like:

If my parents had never met or if another sperm beat out the sperm that was called "Bassam," would the brain thinking these thoughts today exist in another body some other day, some other time?

Wouldn't it be easier to die young in life so I don't have to go through any grand sacrifice or loss?

I'm thirty-four. I've had three intense, short-term loves during my twenties. Is there a fourth out there somewhere? Do I want there to be? Is love a choice? Have I outmaneuvered the idea of love now?

Do I need to reproduce to live a fulfilled life?

Do I really want to coach entrepreneurs anymore?

Why do recreational joggers run in place waiting to cross the street? There is no professional athlete on earth that runs in place on the sidelines or in between plays. It's only white people trying to get back in shape who do this.

Is there any way to eat a Nature Valley Crunchy bar without half of it ending up in your lap at the end?

How did Troy not get arrested for attempted murder when he drove Brand and his bike off a cliff in The Goonies?

We root for Maverick in Top Gun *but he really is a dick. Iceman is a much nicer and considerate person on all levels.*

Thoughts that I had buried for years rose to the top like air bubbles from the bottom of a thawing block of ice. As if shaken loose when our car hit a pothole, those once dormant or untapped inclinations wriggled and bounced in my head for days or weeks, eventually reaching my consciousness, evoking emotions I wasn't ready to have at that particular moment, on that particular day. Sometimes my eyes would well up with pure joy, and sometimes I'd think the weight of the world was burying me.

I'd suddenly find myself in a mental maze where I could see past and future versions of myself from a point of view I'd never experienced. The Real Slim Shady was trying to stand up. I got a glimpse of him looking out the window on the Autobahn. I saw him while sitting in bumper-to-bumper traffic in Bulgaria. He taught me something new looking out into the expanse of the Black Sea. He oversaw my growth on the A380 in Uzbekistan.

Strip away all our comforts and distractions and there is self-awareness. It's what yoga preaches you can get in a thirty-minute session. Unfortunately, unless you practice diligently, you keep scraping back the same superficial buildup each week. Maybe out on the open road I moved closer to enlightenment in my cerebral thaw. Before I left on the rally, my life was focused on how I was perceived by my readers, clients, and the invisible *they*. Without these endless validations, I was changing slowly—so slowly, I couldn't label it. I started to speculate that at home we get to find out who we want to be, but out on the road we find out who we really are.

All I know is that somewhere in the middle of Kazak...

Bang!

Unfortunately, the spinning hum that for the time being separated my mental reality from the physical one—like scientists isolating plasma from blood—fused together when a pothole readjusted my spine. I would have to travel to that higher mental plane some other time.

As the sun got closer to swan-diving out of view, we knew we had to find a place to camp. We had pushed the envelope a little bit at first, but we were rally veterans now, knowing that having a campsite *and* being set up by sundown were preferable to driving a few more miles. We found a small dirt trail next to the main road with a strip of trees in the distance that could provide some cover, ultimately securing a small enclave next to a soybean farm. Greg and Brooke drove back to buy some beers in a small town that we had passed five minutes before, so I sat there, flew the drone, and indulged in the insanity of being by myself, on the road less traveled, somewhere in a southern corner of Kazakhstan. Beyond the eastern edge of the largest dish of edamame in the world was the reddish glow of a mountain range still receiving the sun's full gaze, while the moon poked its head up from behind the peaks. It was like a set change in a magnificent play and I was the only person in the audience.

Bravo, Earth. Encore.

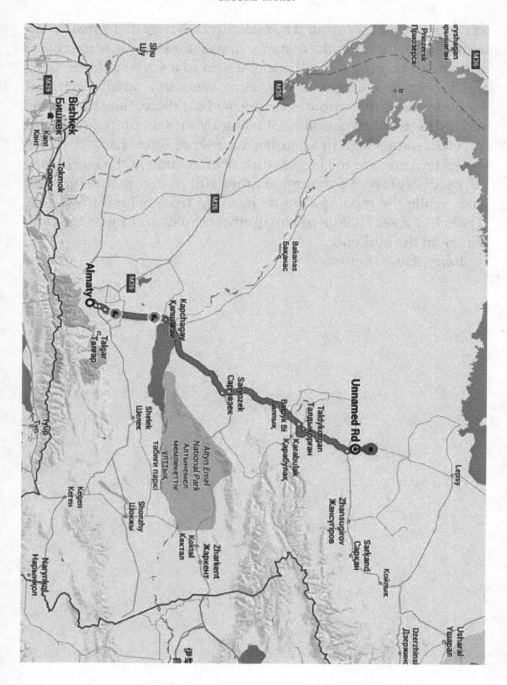

Day 22

Like an impatient parent, the sun woke us up when it wanted us up, not when we wanted to *get* up. Five a.m. We unzipped the tent and saw the mountains in the distance and the soybean tapestry in the foreground. It was beautiful, but as always, we couldn't stay long. We had more of Kazakhstan to drive through. After a quick oatmeal, coffee, and tea breakfast, we packed the car with an efficiency that only weeks of camping can teach.

No day on the rally provided less stimulation than Day 22. We saw various animals on the side of the road—cows, goats, whatever—mindlessly eating grass, ignoring the twenty-first century as it rumbled past them at 42 horsepower. We watched the sun draw an arc in the sky as we continued north for hours. When looking at the map, it seemed strange that we couldn't veer east into Mongolia from Almaty, Kazakhstan, but that would mean driving through China, and it was nearly impossible to get a visa there. This is why we were on this grand north-northeasterly arc heading towards Russia.

Snacks were hard to come by in places like this so every now and then I would pull out the magic *stroopwafels* that I had taken with us from my cousin's house in Holland on Day 2. During the unrelenting heat of the deserts of the 'Stans, the caramel had melted, fusing the three remaining cookies together. I took a small bite out of the tri-waffle and then slowly moved my hand up in between Greg and Brooke in the front. They reacted like dogs spotting a tennis ball you were about to toss.

I had to set the ground rules. "This is a tri-waffle. You will take a smaller than average bite so it can last!" The sugar rush from that cookie was the closest thing to an orgasm we would experience for days.

Proper meals were as scarce as snack food. Inevitably we'd find a restaurant attached to the only gas station within one hundred miles, but the restaurant was like a garrison behind enemy lines that hadn't been supplied in weeks. The ten-item menu, all in Russian, forced us to select items based on our favorite numbers, but everything we pointed at was returned with a shake of the head by the only woman working at the place. We then went down the list item by item until she nodded. We chose three different items in stock and waited at our table while everyone else in the joint stared at us. When the three plates came out, each dish contained a dumpling with a small side of rice.

What I loved about Central Asia was that there weren't too many "No Trespassing" signs. We kind of just went where we wanted as long as our vehicle could handle it. Greg had pinpointed on our map a lake not too far ahead that would make a good camping spot. And so when the lake was over the hill on our left, we found a tiny dirt track and crested the hill as the sun was setting.

We were so off the beaten path that there wasn't really a path anymore. We drove gradually down into a valley and set up the tent next to a small forest that abutted a river. Greg and Brooke went to rinse off in the lake and I stayed behind to transfer photos from my cameras to my laptop. The rise of the Super Moon looked like the Death Star ascending from the mist, almost too big to be real.

I didn't have too much time to bask in it because when you are next to a lake and a river at sunset in the northern Kazakh summer, it means that the mosquito swarms are athirst. As Greg and Brooke were returning from the lake, I was applying bug spray to fend off a black ops platoon of mosquito aggression. They were calculated, precise, and the size of small dragonflies. I put DEET on every exposed part of my body so that I could enjoy dinner, but the little vampires persisted...persisted to the point that one Olympic diver of a mosquito found the small space between my dense thicket of a beard and my closed mouth. Almost immediately, my lip went numb and swelled like a blowfish.

We were so wrapped up in trying to keep these goblins off us that Brooke and Greg couldn't see my face. I didn't want to be dramatic and cause a scene but I also didn't want to die in the Kazakh steppe, because as my lip expanded, I had thoughts of West Nile virus, beriberi, and Jabba the Hutt. I swooped over to the car and devoured a Motrin to help deflate my lip tumor. I was on the verge of asking Brooke to stab me with the EpiPen to cancel the death serum injected in me (that's how an EpiPen works, right?), but slowly the swelling maxed out and I simply looked like I'd been punched in the face by a grizzly bear. Crisis averted.

We finished dinner and relinquished the outdoors to these flying hyenas. In the confines of our tent we did a headlamp mosquito check of every corner and agreed that we had established quarantine, although I was half expecting them to saw and laser through the tent walls like a Sentinel from *The Matrix*.

I'm certain "mosquitoes" means "motherfuckers" in some language, somewhere.

Before nodding off, we talked about the upcoming border and what might happen. Americans with a drone entering Russia... should be interesting.

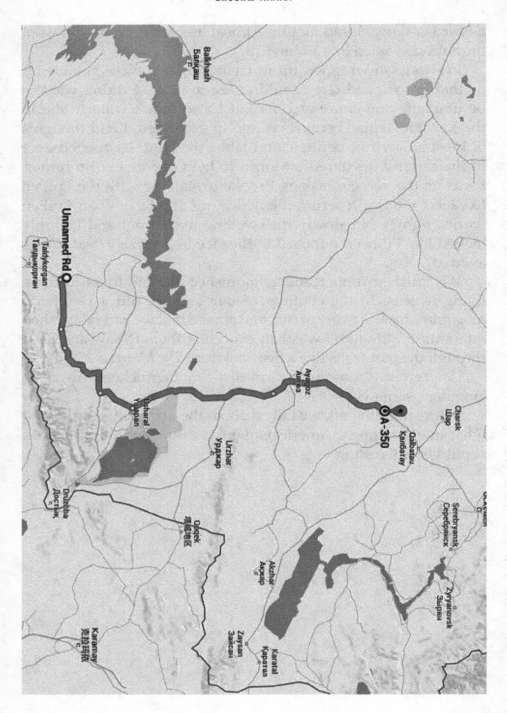

Day 23

Having spent more than three weeks not getting much sleep, we were all rundown, but the prospect of reaching Russia just north of the town of Shemonaika boosted our energy. However, our eagerness to reach the border was mitigated by Kazakhstan's shitty roads. As if on cue…

Wham!

Brooke hit a pothole dead-on. It was one of those impacts where I cringed, clenched my teeth, and held my breath all at once, half expecting the car to explode or career off the road with rims sparking.

Anytime we hit a pothole the driver felt a little guilty. Sure, some just couldn't be avoided — they either appeared too late or there were too many of them — but still…guilty. So after Brooke hit that one, Greg, being the navigator and his always team-playing self, said, "Damn, that one came out of nowhere. I didn't have enough time to holler it out."

No harm, no foul. No problem.

The duties in the back seat were complex because while I trusted the two people in front, what if the driver or navigator didn't see something I did? It didn't pay to bite my tongue but I also didn't want the driver to feel like she or he had two members of the peanut gallery in their ear the whole time. But Brooke had a tendency to brake or maneuver later than Greg and I would while we were driving, so we had the unenviable decision of "We see this thing but I don't know if Brooke has seen it, hasn't seen it yet, or will never see it." It's a tough line to walk. On one side is an accident, on the other an argument.

I tried to keep my comments from the back seat to an absolute minimum, but a few miles down the road…

Wham!

Bone-jarring. Deafening.

Greg consoled Brooke with, "Ooh, that one hurt a little bit, but we're all good. You might need to slow down around those blind turns so I can help spot you a little better."

The car got quiet again and we kept moving towards the border. I never truly felt comfortable when anyone else was driving. I don't think my teammates always felt safe when I was driving either. I made more aggressive decisions in traffic than they did. I once passed a truck while a car was coming the other way, temporarily making our wide two-lane road into a tight three-lane road. It was stupid but it was my only way around the truck. This was the nature of driver/passenger relationship. The driver always felt in control and the passenger feared someone was taking liberties with their life.

About twenty miles from the border...

Ka-boom!

I'm honestly not sure why the chassis did not collapse like a grass hut in a hurricane. The vibration of metal hitting metal hung with us like a tuning fork, and this time Greg didn't hold back. "Okay, Brooke, you need to fucking slow down! I'm sorry, but right now your driving is putting the car in danger and it's making me feel unsafe."

Ka-boom. Emotionally.

Brooke fired back, ceding no ground. "Unsafe? *Unsafe!* You and Bassam drive way faster and more recklessly than I do. You guys almost killed us in Uzbekistan passing cars in that traffic jam."

Neither Greg's nor Brooke's comments were unwarranted. It had been over three weeks of being together 24/7, of me and Greg ever so slightly ganging up on Brooke, of two guys versus one girl, of a seven-year age difference, and of us being so close to our ultimate goal that a pothole hit at a speed a couple of mph too fast could set us back days, if not derail us completely.

The air teemed with words unsaid. I could tell Brooke was fuming and I could tell Greg was trying to figure out a way to appease the situation. Thankfully, we reached the border within thirty minutes, pulling up at the end of a one-lane line. I decided to remove myself from the car so that they could have a one-on-one conversation without relying on me as a buffer. I navigated piles of human shit that led to a spot behind a building where I could pee one last time in Kazakhstan. I avoided the car for almost fifteen minutes and when I returned Greg and Brooke were still ironing things out. Brooke was in tears.

I took another lap around the stagnant column of cars and trucks, trying not to catalyze the drama in Donata, but eventually I needed some shade because the brutal sun had no regard for the drama between my rally mates. I got back in the car as discreetly as possible, and what I witnessed was to this day a master class in crisis management and stress diffusion by Greg, who's had his rough edges exfoliated by the San Diego surf over the past ten years.

Here's what I heard:

"Brooke, you understand that what I said was said because I want the best for us. I apologize for how I said it or if I insulted you in any way. It was a heat-of-the-moment comment and, at the time, I felt unsafe."

"You guys make me feel unsafe all the time with decisions you make and things like Bassam going three-wide to pass on a two-lane road."

See. Told you so...

"And you're right, you are. We've all made questionable decisions over thousands of miles but I personally have been put in charge of car health on this trip and we've come *so* far. The two most important things are our safety and making sure the car — *You call her 'Donata' goddammit!* — can get to Ulaanbaatar. I don't get a lot of feedback from you when I'm your navigator. I say things, I point things out but you never give me a nod, an acknowledgment that you saw what I saw or that you agree. So I never know if you're annoyed with me, didn't hear me, or disagree with me. If you disagree with something I point out when we're driving, say it. But say *something*. Your silence keeps me confused."

That now calm conversation paused when it was our turn to park our car in a small lot before processing out of Kazakhstan. Brooke still seemed more pissed-off than a badger being poked with a stick, so when we were about five people away from the booth, which was de facto eight feet from the Kazakh border, I leaned in close to Brooke and said, "Brooke, listen, we just got word from the people of Kazakhstan that they have one last question for you…are you ever going to smile again in their country?" I gave her a serious look and playfully held an imaginary microphone to her face.

Her eyes turned to me, mixed with murder and surrender. Eventually, she released the slightest twitch at the corner of her mouth but still held tight to her granite glare. I took the imaginary mic back and said, "It looks like Kazakhstan will be robbed of their smile." I kept things light without belittling her because I didn't want to let one tiff in the car spoil our entry into Russia.

Before we knew it, we were ushered into no-man's-land. I couldn't help but wonder how many Americans had crossed the Kazakh-Russian border by car at this spot. It's a bit of a long ride between checkpoints and we had time to wonder about a lot of things. Who mowed the lawn in this area? Who owned the trees and the flowers? Once again, being in diplomatic and sovereign limbo led to discussion of the strangest things. We were here, on earth, but we weren't *in* any country. Is that Russian grass? Are those Kazakh birds?

The mood in our car was fractured but not broken. We had to be united. After all, we were entering a country in conflict with the West. Vladimir Putin had recently invaded the Ukraine, the same country where a Malaysian Airlines plane had been shot down a couple weeks before.

No turning back!

After about ten miles, we reached a rolling hill and saw the checkpoint. Although it was eighty degrees in the shade, a chill crept through me when I saw the first set of Russian soldiers. It was the exactitude of their gait and the rigidity of their shoulders, as if Russian ballerinas had hoarded all the country's grace. It just all looked very...*umm*...Russian.

The short and stocky guard with piercing blue eyes asked for our passports without even the suggestion of a smirk or curiosity. Looking at all three passport covers he said, "Amerikanskis?"

We nodded. *Da, comrade. Da.*

He asked us to wait while he ran our passports into a one-story building, the only structure visible. He returned shortly thereafter and told us to get out of the car so he could inspect it. Stern but not psychotic, it wasn't the most invasive search we'd had. Turkmenistan was much worse.

Contradicting all our previous notions (I'm sensing a theme, here), the guy ended up being pretty cool, moving around the car, opening Brooke's medication pouch, and having her explain what they were. That was always an interesting conversation.

"Um, this is for...um..." pointing to her stomach and then putting her hand to her butt and firing it away as she made a poop sound with her tongue and mouth.

"This keeps me from getting..." then she would open and close her hand over her head, miming a pulsating headache.

"This is..." and then she turned to me and Greg asking, "Any ideas how to charade menstrual cramps?"

I know I am painting Brooke as an escapee from the loony bin toting bottles of lithium and horse tranquilizers (she wasn't) but it was funny to see this Russian soldier thumbing through a clear Ziploc bag asking what each bottle contained. Brooke, to her credit, used the simplest physical expressions possible to explain each pill, making sure to distinguish each interpretation from the previous one.

And of course, the soldier eventually got to the giant, shiny, silver, hard, rectangular cuboid and pointed to it. I, without hesitation said, "It's a drone."

He stood in thought, his elbow resting on one hand and the other hand resting on his chin, directing me with his index finger situated under his lower lip.

"Open it."

I took the case out of the car, put it on the ground and popped open the top. The guard turned to me, eyebrows raised. I returned his gaze with a grin. He said, "Wait," and walked into the building. There was only one car behind us and another car coming down the hill in the distance, its dust tail flowing.

Greg, Brooke, and I took bets as to whether this was the end of the road for the drone. The over/under was set at "probably." I wasn't concerned about the loss, as it was a good six hundred-dollar investment of fun footage no matter what happened. After a couple of minutes, the soldier came back and with a sweeping hand gesture instructed us to put everything back in the car. Then he pointed to the drone and said, "Not this."

Brooke parked Donata off to the side as a higher-ranking Russian colonel or military attaché came out in full camouflage. He was in his early forties and stood at 6-foot 1-inch. His English was great and he had a whiff of charm about him, hopefully someone who attained his position via politicking, not cracking skulls.

"Hello."

"Hi."

"So whose drone is this?"

"That would be mine," I said.

"Why do you have this?"

"I'm making a film. We are part of the Mongol Rally, a charity event driving from London to Mongolia, and our sponsors donated money and in return we were making a movie of our experience."

"Are you a spy?"

"Am I a spy? No, I am not."

"How do I know that?"

"I assure you. Well, I guess I can *only* assure you."

Pause.

"What is the range of drone?"

"One hundred meters." *Wink. Wink.*

"How long can it fly?"

"Per battery, eight minutes."

"Do you have paperwork for drone?"

"Yes."

I retrieved the instruction manual from the car and gave it to him. He thanked me and asked us to go through the immigration process in a room on the far end of the small building while he took the drone inside for a detailed inspection.

The immigration room looked like an abandoned cabin in the Canadian Rockies. There was nothing but weathered wood in there. A few other families waited, carrying some hand luggage and a baseline level of apathy. I didn't get the impression that the Russian people are a particularly comedic bunch. The two immigration officials were definitely not enrolled in any improv classes.

We filled out our paperwork as best as we could, ignoring some of the spaces that didn't translate correctly. As always, Brooke went first because she was the car's owner. From the immigration officer's reaction, you would have thought that she scribbled on her customs form in crayon. He poked at every line and since our fearless Brooke didn't exactly win any awards for silent composure, everyone could hear her verbal frustration.

Our foray into the motherland was turning out swimmingly.

Greg was called up by the other official while the first one continued to rip into Brooke like a raccoon into a bag of garbage. Almost immediately I could tell there was a problem with Greg's form as I watched him lean in, trying to communicate with the agent. I was the only one left behind with a bunch of Russians who were watching the scene in disgust. I gave everyone a half smile as if to say, "Psssh. Americans. Am I right?"

Greg was scolded for not following the unknown rule that every passenger in the same car had to be processed by the same border agent. Greg returned to the herd and waited his turn to be flayed by Brooke's guy, Igor. Eventually, she made it through.

When Greg and I proceeded, Igor was noticeably friendlier. In fact, I even got a giggle out of him. Either he got his day's quota of lambasting out of his way on Brooke, or this was an example of Russia's male-dominated society, and how dare Brooke own a car?

We now had our passports, stamps, and visas in hand, ready to enter the country for two weeks. We had our car that could drive us around said country for that time, but we did not have my drone. We were told to wait underneath a small overhang off to the side of the car staging area, out of the blistering sun.

After fifteen minutes the guards asked Brooke to follow them inside to answer some questions. Smart, these Russians. Ask the girl who doesn't know anything about the drone to see if she will counter anything I've already said, thus proving my clandestine operations in their country. While Brooke was enduring God-knows-what, Igor came out to practice his English with me and Greg and ask us why on Earth we were bringing a drone into Russia. He was tall, maybe 6-foot 2-inches, and had a deep, baritone voice to go along with his long, narrow, crew-cut head.

"Why not a camera, like normal people?"

"Because I am not normal people, sir."

We had the Obama versus Putin conversation that I'd *imagined* could happen between Russian border guards and spoiled Americans, but one that I never thought would actually happen. I was playing diplomatic Twister to make sure I didn't say the wrong thing and send us to a Siberian prison, but Igor was really cool. Before he went back inside, he asked us if we had Skype so he could practice his English. I gave him my actual Skype name. Clearly, I wasn't a spy.

After about twenty minutes, Brooke came out by herself.

"I don't know, Bassam...I don't know."

"What happened?"

"Promise you won't be mad at me?"

"How could I be mad at you? You did nothing wrong."

"I don't think there is any way you're getting your drone in. I'm sorry."

"It's all good. Don't even stress. What did they say?"

"They said you lied. You said the battery lasts eight minutes but they looked it up online and it says it lasts twenty-five."

"They are looking at the second version of the device and I have the first one. We'll be fine."

We waited a bit more until the colonel came back out and asked, "Is there a camera attached to the drone?"

"It's separate. It's a GoPro that attaches to the drone."

"When it records video, does it stream it directly to a computer or do you have to download it after it lands?"

Aka, if we shoot it down, would you still get that footage?

"You have to download it after it lands."

"Okay, thank you."

He went back inside.

More waiting. More wondering.

Finally, the colonel came out smiling and from a distance too far away to engage in normal conversation said, "Everything is okay. It's okay. We're sorry." He got a little closer and continued, "You are good to go now. We did some research online about the drone and we did some research online about you (pointed at me) and we are very sorry. Please enjoy your time in Russia."

My minor (*very* minor) online celebrity at the time convinced the Russians that I was some kind of influential American personality. The last thing they needed was me blogging about a border incident where my toy was taken from me. We shook hands and we were on our way.

I was in the backseat when we pulled out of the parking lot, but my dick was surely swinging up by the front seat.

"Guys, you show me the respect I deserve in this country because I'm big in Russia."

"Bassam, shut up. Which way do we go?"

We had reached our first fork in the road in the biggest country of the world and we didn't know which way to turn. We correctly guessed left and were now northeast on the path that took us towards Barnaul, the city 250 miles away where we would grab the road to the Mongolian border.

It was getting late and we scoured Maps. Me for what might work as a camping spot on this long, straight, two-lane road. Up ahead we saw that there was a lake about a half a mile from the highway. This lake idea had worked for us in Kazakhstan, so we pulled off and drove on a path through a corridor of long, gilt grass that reached above our car. There were tire tracks so we felt we were at least doing something other people had done. The further in we went, though, the boggier it became.

At one point we got to a 15-yard-wide puddle whose stick-tested depth of 2 feet kept us from crossing it. This was the end of our off-roading experience. However, this wasn't the easiest place to turn around due to the high dirt walls and mud bogs everywhere. Our three-point turn morphed into an asterisk turn with a whole bunch of "Stop, stop, *stop!*" and "Whoa, whoa, *whoa!*" Tension continued to permeate our car because Brooke was still driving and she had it in her head, dead to rights, that Greg and I thought she was a terrible driver. So, anytime she struggled or stalled, we could see her patience narrowing to a very sharp point. Greg and I tried to verbally massage the shit out of this, though. We would not allow our team to suffer a nervous breakdown in head-high, Russian grass, while the mosquitoes sharpened their triton straws.

We bounced back to the civilized part of the path and saw a small clearing. It had less grass because most of it had been rolled up into a giant, twelve-foot-high hay sphere. We debated putting the car and tent on the western side of it to protect us from the sun in the morning but that's when, once again, Greg and Brooke trumped my laissez-faire approach to camping locations and decided we'd head back to the main road to find something else, even as sunset fast approached.

Western Siberia is flat, and it's all farmland. Farmland as far as the eye can see. Imagine trying to find a private camping spot off the highway in the middle of Kansas, with the equivalent of a circus tent in your trunk. After a few miles we saw a small dirt trail to our right. These trails were traversed by giant trucks carrying wheat and barley somewhere, but since it was getting late we didn't think they would be schlepping stuff in the dark, which reduced our risk of being spotted on land we weren't authorized to be on. This particular trail was also next to the tiniest of forests, if you could call it that; maybe an acre at most. There were rumors of bears in this part of Russia, so that didn't make us feel great, but could there be bears in a one-acre forest? There's nothing like the baseless reassurance of "I don't think so..."

We found ground that was flattish, where, after matting down some knee-high grass, we could precariously set up our tent between the edges of two small drainage ditches. We were in view of the road and some drivers would honk (in support? anger?) but we stayed steadfast, put the tent up, and cooked our dinner. Eyeing the setting sun in this pale, seamless sky was an exhibition of what nature can produce if left alone. Watching it disappear behind the horizon was like witnessing a lens being dipped on the end of a string into a bath of orange light, its diameter seemingly expanding with each passing minute, until the whole thing was swallowed by the Siberian Beyond, leaving the sky smoldering in its embers for another hour. It was the finest sunset of the entire rally.

Emotions from earlier in the day were still not fully settled and I decided to fix that. "Listen," I said, "we had a tough day today. Other than the Azerbaijan exit debacle, maybe our toughest day — certainly our toughest when it comes to team unity. But I'll be damned if we are going to carry over a frustration from one day into the next. So while we sit in our camping chairs, on uneven ground in the Russian heartland, with possible bears and certain mosquitoes in that mini forest stalking us, let's get off our chest what we need to say. Each of us will have a chance, without being judged or interrupted. Fair?"

Obviously, I was the mediator of sorts and although Brooke claimed that she wasn't afraid to tell us what was on her mind when things went bad, she rarely spoke up, so I needed her to talk. Finally, she did. It was heated at first and I had to stop Greg and Brooke from interrupting each other so that they both could finish, but after twenty minutes, we realized that we all loved each other, that all we wanted was the best for one another, and that it was the *way* we said or didn't say things that caused struggles. Everyone apologized, and we hugged and agreed to put to bed any frustrations because we needed to be a united force through the wilderness over the next week to ten days.

When we laid our heads down that night, Brooke faced me and said, "Thank you so much for that team-building Kumbaya shit you just pulled. It meant a lot. I fucking love you."

"I love you too."

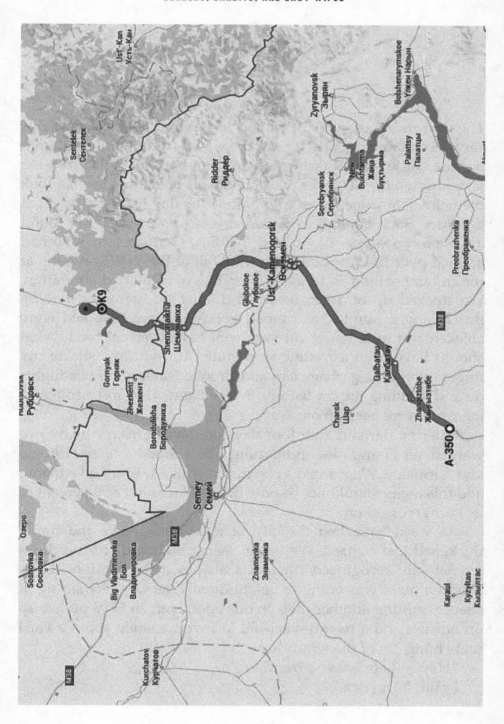

Day 24

The next morning, none of us had lost a limb to a bear, and our car was still there. *It's the simple things.* After our Nutella, a shared banana, and oatmeal (which always got way too cold, way too fast, and which we never really finished) breakfast, Brooke took the helm again since most of the previous day had been spent at a border. Soon enough, civilization was upon us and we found a Costco-type store. We looked like East German kids who had ambled over to West Berlin after the fall of the Wall, gawking at the amount of food and choices after days of culinary dilapidation. We stocked up on fruit, bread, and jams, and tempted fate by purchasing a number of canned goods that we assumed were chicken and tuna but could very well have been cat food. What should have been a routine stop ended up with me slicing my finger open on a garbage can and Brooke leaving the headlights on and draining the car battery. A few Band-Aids and a roll-start later, we were back on our way.

Entering Barnaul after four days on the run from Almaty, we wanted Wi-Fi and air-conditioning. We wanted a taste of home and normalcy. We wanted a restaurant with a waiter and a menu, and this menu should not be only in Russian or have 90 percent of its items crossed off.

As we approached the city of a million people the traffic thickened like custard. We began seeing billboards for products we actually recognized (that was always a tell for how First-World a place was going to be). Suddenly, as we were sitting in silence, putting another mile on our odometer, an SUV pulled up on our left and a twenty-year-old kid with a smile about a yard wide hung out of the window.

"Hey! Where are you from?"

I said, "America."

"Where are you going?"

"Uh, well, Mongolia."

"Mongolia?"

"Yeah."

"You're gonna need a bigger car."

We laughed.

"You're going today?" he asked.

"No, today we just want some lunch, to be honest."

"Come eat with us." He pointed to his friend driving.

"Okay. We want some real food. We've been camping for four days."

"Yes, no problem."

"And Wi-Fi. We need a place with Wi-Fi."

"Of course. Follow us."

They pulled in front and we tailed them without further discussion. I broke the silence with, "You know you're deep in the Mongol Rally when that happens and no one questions anything." It was impossible for us not to think that there was *some* sort of angle to their offer, but if they were taking us to waiter-served food and Wi-Fi, I'd give them hand jobs if they asked.

Barnaul is a proper city with universities, big squares, shopping centers, and all that. The restaurant was on the seventh floor of a nondescript office building we'd never have found on our own. We felt a bit like children who had been raised by wolves, seeing civilization for the first time: scurrying at the sight of elevator doors opening, fixing our gaze on fluorescent lights. The dirt and grime caked on our shins and flip-flop-clad feet were not much different than a homeless person's. Our new friends picked out a sushi place for us that also served pizza. We didn't care about the crazy food combinations — we were in!

One of our hosts, Artur, was studying in Vienna and spoke four languages. His shorter, weightlifter friend, Nik, was studying locally. Nik's English was not as good as Artur's, but it was way better than my Russian. They were so honored to give up their Saturday to host us. We asked them what they would be doing if they weren't with us and they said that they would be kicking it and chasing girls on their day off. Two things that have been verified on the Mongol Rally: everyone in this world kicks it and young men are always chasing girls.

We ate sushi and pizza, and of course had to guzzle the customary vodka shot. For an hour and a half, we talked about life, school, relationships, politics, and why Putin was beloved by so many. Brooke, Greg, and I learned things about each other that only come to light when people who don't know anything about you ask questions.

"Greg, I've known you for sixteen years, I didn't know your parents met in high school."

"No, my dad was twenty-two, coaching high school football. My *mom* was in high school. She was eighteen, and a drum major for the marching band. You know...the person in front swinging the baton around? Yeah...well, my mom saw my dad roll up on his Harley for practice one day and that was that."

"Fucking legend."

Or, "You majored in sports management, Brooke? What did you do with that degree?"

"I used to work for a dirt car racetrack."

"You what?"

"I was their fan experience coordinator."

"Fascinating."

And on and on...Artur and Nik asked us questions we hadn't asked one another in the car because we kind of just learned about each other through diffusion. Greg, Brooke, and I didn't have to do the formal, short-term, get-to-know-you basics. Instead, we knew odd, subtle, long-term shit about each other that only moms and significant others find out.

We practically had to fight Artur and Nik in order to pay the check. Had they somehow paid the tab or even their share, I would have drowned in my own shame and guilt on the spot. Cause of death: inferiority as a human being. My one-third portion of Marco Polover's monetary kindness was the best I could offer right now to keep my moral compass afloat. I was still a newbie in this limitless-kindness-to-strangers thing, so much of a newbie that when our hosts suggested they tour us around the city for a bit, I tried to get us out of there saying that we had to hit the road. But Artur and Nik kept asking us what our real hurry was; surely we had some time for them to show us the home city they were so proud of.

Bluff called.

Like Alexi in Samarkand, this was hospitality I felt uncomfortable accepting because of what it said about me as a person. When I was at home I didn't behave like these, so I didn't want to be shown that people *do* indeed act like this. But how could we turn them down? *Thanks for the generosity and showing us a great place to eat, guys, but we really have to get out of here in the middle of the day to sleep in our tent.*

They became not only our tour guides but also our bodyguards. They yelled at the parking attendant, telling him that our car would stay in the restaurant-only parking lot and nothing would happen to it. We then jumped into Artur's SUV. We crossed the Ob River and admired the Hollywoodish sign that said "Barnaul." We saw the universities, the Lenin Squares, and at a stoplight we even met Artur's mother when she randomly pulled up next to us in her SUV. She asked Artur who the people were in his car. He said that we were his new friends. She shook her head, smiling, and wished us well.

Insane.

As their final gesture of kindness, Artur and Nik drove us to a supermarket so we could pick up some goodies for the road. They even bought us a bottle of vodka as a gift.

College students. On a summer Saturday. We were complete strangers.

I can't.

We exchanged hugs and Instagram handles but we had to be on our way before I was crippled by my lack of inherent selflessness compared to other people in this world. Some people need a transfusion of blood platelets in life, but on the rally people like Annette, Emin, Alexi, Artur, and Nik had provided me with kindness transfusions to up my baseline level of decency.

I'm working on it, folks.

***

While filling up on gasoline on the outskirts of town, we ran into another Mongol Rally team for the first time since Samarkand, eight days earlier. It was Darren and Myles. The resiliency they had to keep moving on was impressive but we could see that they were a fissured partnership. Short-fused and hot-tempered, the finish line was all they sought. The world was taking its toll. I inched out on my vulnerability limb and asked them if they needed help of any sort or if they wanted to (*gulp*) convoy with us. They didn't. They were staying at a lodge a few miles ahead with two other rally teams. We were invited to join them but we wanted to move on as far as possible, so we said goodbye and remained solo in our pursuit for now.

Barnaul was the farthest north we'd get on the entire rally, save for a spot in Holland, but after our four-day northeasterly climb, it was now time to veer southeast, so that we could circumnavigate the Altai Mountains and follow the M52 road to the Mongol border, 450 miles away.

On and on we went through ski resort towns that hugged the Katun River. If I hadn't known where we were, I would have thought it was the Alps. In the late afternoon we were able to secure a camping spot at one of the designated public locations that peppered the riverbanks. We had it all to ourselves, and we couldn't have been happier. Okay, at least I couldn't be happier. My teammates might not be as misanthropic — well, maybe just anti-random human beings — as I was.

We were a bit low on clean clothes so Brooke, channeling her inner Stone Age domesticity, graciously volunteered to wash our laundry in the freezing-cold glacier runoff river. We each took baths in there as well. It's amazing what odors can fester in a limbed nook.

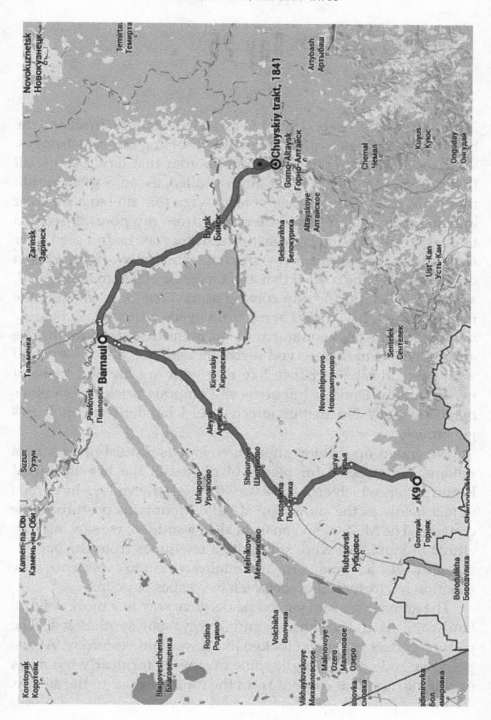

Day 25

It was a particularly good sleep. We had fresh mountain air and the buoyancy that came with knowing that, barring any catastrophes, we were going to reach the Mongol border that day. Despite all that was in our favor, I still almost killed us on a giant uphill mountain pass when my self-control wore thin due to a slow car in front of us. With confidence oozing from my pores, I decided to pass around a blind right-hand turn since we hadn't seen a car in minutes. My optimism was proven statistically wrong when a car came down the road at that exact moment. I had to brake, skid, and swerve as did the guy coming at us. I can only imagine the insults being fairly hurled at me from inside that vehicle. I surely understood the ones coming at me from inside ours. Both Brooke and Greg gave me a deserved verbal thrashing. I can't understand why I would take a chance like that with my life and those of my friends in Donata. Impatience? Pompous prick? Mongolia's magnetic pull? No matter which one, I handed out apologies generously.

We ended up driving amid three joyous Scottish med school ralliers. We stopped for plenty of photos of the heavily rafted Katun River, which etches its way through the valleys hundreds of feet below as the snowcapped Altai Mountains posture in the distance. The M52 snaked on until all of a sudden, we saw our first ethnic Mongol. We were still quite a few miles from the border, but since we had crossed the mountains we got to experience how isolation led to speciation between two tribes of people.

The green grass and jagged peaks gave way to a more delicate landscape as if Kazakhstan and Kyrgyzstan synthesized. The picture-perfect pavement looked like it was laid yesterday. At one point we rode on a straight spine of asphalt for nearly ten miles during our gradual descent from the mountains onto the steppe.

This rivaled the elation I'd had driving from the Turkish border to the outskirts of Istanbul.

It must have been a great joyride for Donata too. Although we were taking her to her death, we had shown her the world and escorted her onto patches of tarmac that she wouldn't have encountered otherwise. On this day, it was 800-thread count Egyptian cotton under her wheels. The only blips on the road were the shadows cast by the power lines that ran parallel to it. Due to our never changing her oil, Donata had developed a bit of a throaty gargle upon acceleration, like the muscle car she always thought she was. Her last ride was a maverick one, far from the civility and aristocracy that was Great Britain.

In what looked like the accidental and forgotten town of Tashanta we filled up on Russian gas one last time. Tashanta is what an abandoned city in America's Old West would look like if the Gold Rush happened in 1949 instead of 1849. I'm guessing some Soviet dissidents were banished here back in the day, and when the Cold War ended those people couldn't be bothered to hoof it back across the Ural Mountains.

We spent our last rubles on whatever unidentified canned goods we had cash for before motoring onward. There was something deviously joyful about dumping all our local currency ten miles from the border. It was our adolescent dare and our commitment to moving east, hoping that this maneuver would impress the travel gods.

The sky was a bright blue igloo amid the endless caramel-tinted fields that rose smoothly into the distant, rounded mountaintops as if the summits were the crests of people's heads pressing up beneath a golden bed sheet we happened to be driving on. Those peaks surrounded us like we were performers in an ethereal stadium.

There it was! The gate that represented the end of the largest country on earth, and the beginning of the ultimate adventure: Mongolia. I couldn't help but think that on this entire voyage we were like Indiana Jones at the end of *Indiana Jones and the Last*

Crusade, having to solve puzzles to get to the Holy Grail, which in our case was Mongolia. I remember a friend who had participated in the rally a few years back telling me, "The entire trip is worth it just for western Mongolia." Now, we were on the last leap-of-faith ride together: Me, Greg, Brooke, and Donata—unified and euphoric.

Our plan was to cross the border, set up camp before the impending sunset, and move on at daybreak. However, when we reached the gate, we noticed two other rally teams parked on our right in a giant dirt field that bled into a boundless stretch of land. The passengers of said vehicles had set up lawn chairs, and were enjoying a beverage and a bite.

"What happened?"

"Border just closed five minutes ago."

"Serious?"

"Yeah, there is no way to get to the other side and through in time, so we have to try in the morning."

And so we did what we so often had to do on the rally, we had to be okay with a whole lot of time to do nothing at all.

Visually, the flat steppe we were on could have been sea level or thereabouts, but then the sun set, and the wind at our six thousand-foot elevation grabbed my balls and gave them a "Hey, how'd ya do?" to remind me of our vertical whereabouts.

Other teams trickled up to the border and joined our little squad, making us the least intimidating twelve-engine car show in history. We took turns defecating over a small hill in the distance, we started a fire, we shared stories and food, and we all reveled in one last border…one last inquisition…one last time when we would have to beg for good graces like feudal serfs.

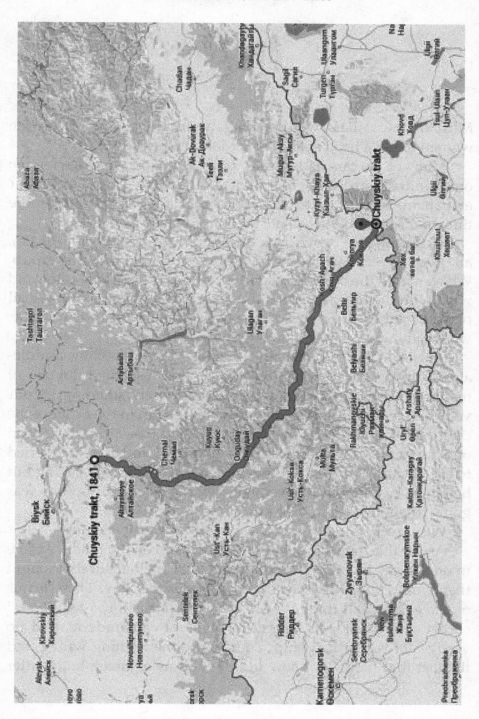

Day 26

Most of the ralliers were stirring when we got up. Everyone wanted to get a head start on the Mongolian wilderness.

A few of the cars had already packed up and were driving the one hundred yards back to the small hut where we had to get our exit stamp from Russia. Our pontoon of a tent took some more time to disassemble so we ate breakfast by our car.

By the time we drove back the hundred yards, it was 8:30 a.m. and we were maybe the seventh or eighth car out of our group. We were told the booth would open at 9 a.m., but 9 a.m. came and went with the breeze and still no one arrived at the booth. We all played football or Frisbee in the street like a bunch of vagrants with nothing on our agenda but doing nothing.

Finally, at 10 a.m. our chain-smoking, Mongol-looking, middle-aged Russian friend with greasy black hair assumed domain of his bureaucratic post. We moved from loosely standing by our vehicles to waiting single file in front of the hut in the order of the cars that parked first. While the line inched forward at the speed of plate tectonics, a Mongolian driver of a van full of trekkers tried to cut ahead. We couldn't understand a word he was saying but he edged his way in like someone who was certain no one was going to punch him in the face.

We agreed as a group that we would not be cut again.

About this time, we could see — upstream on the road we came in on the day before — two Mongol Rally cars that surely thought they would be the first team at the border that day. These teams of three Brits and three Welsh showed up much too happy and cheery with their perfect accents, evident camaraderie, and no vestiges of recent hardship. They had done nothing wrong, but the fact that they were now in line with us eighteen hours after we had arrived was a bit annoying. I was thrilled to give them the update on their agenda for the day.

This was also a continuing social lesson on tribes, about who was in and who was out, about how much bonding had to be done to unite a group, and about when one feels most threatened. The answer to that last point became clear for me on the trip: when my control was at a minimum. This was about the time that a second van of Mongolian travelers showed up and once again a driver tried to cut our line.

Not so fast, shit bird.

One of the members of our group told the driver that he would have to wait his turn. We didn't care how many "just one minute" fingers he put up or how many times he pointed to the twelve passports in his hand. *We wait, you wait, pal.* The guy was intimidated enough to go back to his vehicle and accept his lot in life, or at least his lot that day, which was in the driver's seat, feet on the dashboard, wondering how long this was all going to take.

This worked fine for twenty minutes until he got out of the van and tried to cut the line again, but this time he had to get past me, Greg, and Brooke as we were next in line. He pleaded in a language that we didn't understand, bringing back memories of the drugged-out bandit in Azerbaijan. No one likes to be made someone's bitch in broad daylight in front of a crowd of peers, so the question became, how little did we like being cut? Enough to punch a man in the face in Russia? Of course not, that would be absurd, but we wanted him and our group to think that we might. It was about defending our honor without risking injury or delay.

We did the tough-guy thing when you know you're not going to fight someone and you know he isn't going to fight you, so you physically stand your ground and stare, putting forth a meager verbal berating. Eventually our grimy Mongol friend got his wish to cut the line and set us back another twenty minutes or so since he had twelve passports to process.

The only consolation was that the group approved our lackluster stand.

Finally, it was our turn to get processed. Thank God, someone had told us to check the "Tourist" box on the random form because the Scots behind us hadn't and spent an hour arguing with the guy, eventually paying a bribe instead of driving back 2,700 miles to Moscow to get a new form. I'm not making that up. That's how arbitrarily irrational the border process could be.

With our stamps in hand, we got into our cars and drove to the border gate, where officials were handling only one car at a time. 11 a.m. became 11:30 a.m., which became noon right when we were the next car to go. But for government employees everywhere, a lunch break is a lunch break. The guards filed out of the building, walked past us without even a glance, got in their cars, and left.

We set up camping chairs and embraced the boredom. Some people slept. Some people read. Some people chatted. Some balanced a plastic foosball set on a metal trash can. As composed and Zen as I aspired to be, it was a testy hour of the trip. The supply of patience for the red tape of borders I had in London had dwindled down to a few measly morsels, like a couple of loose nickels tumbling around in a spinning dryer.

Breathe in…breathe out.

The helplessness that comes with lingering at a border with no knowledge of when the purgatory might end is akin to a fish accidentally left behind in a tidal pool. Alone and powerless to swim to safety, it has to wait for the sea to return and connect its escape route. Its freedom is coming at some point, impatience the only thing that will doom its chances.

Before any of us could make another fake statement about what criminal activity we would engage in if we had to continue waiting, the Russian guards returned. We were summoned through the gate, thus keeping our imaginary gangster selves out of trouble. Greg and I were sent upstairs to wait for Brooke, who would come up after Donata was cleared.

We were the first car in the post-lunch crew. All the teams before us had been sent through to Mongolia — or their bodies were in a shallow grave over a nearby hill — so we had no one to talk to or ask about the process. After about ten minutes, Brooke entered and was led into another room, followed by a feisty female guard. Brooke's body language radiated impatience, indicating how well things were going. Moments later she was sent back downstairs while Greg and I were left to ponder our fate.

Brooke came back up a few minutes later and asked us if we ever got a customs form when we entered Kyrgyzstan.

Um, no…

The guard told Brooke that we had to go back to Kyrgyzstan to get one. Kyrgyzstan—that country seven days behind us.

"Go! Go!" she shouted and then shooed Brooke away with a flip of her hand like Brooke was a seagull getting too close to the Pringles.

Well, that's not good.

Some other teams trickled into the waiting area. Half of them had the customs form in hand and half had dicks in hand, like us. This was, of course, a country's way of screwing us good. If we didn't have the form we'd have to pay a bribe…I'm sorry, a *fee*.

Greg and I peered over the windowsill to see how Brooke was getting on. She was talking and gesturing to *every* guard on site and they were all now huddled around her: military, colonels, male, female, *everyone*. Oh, goodness. She had either insulted the entire Red Army, or she was gathering support for our impending release. There wasn't anything money couldn't solve at this point but we wanted to avoid an international incident.

That one salty female guard had it out for Brooke. I don't know why. Maybe she was stationed at this lonesome outpost due to insubordination and had decided to take her frustration out on an American blonde. Whatever it was, she kept accusing Brooke and *ergo*, us, of losing this form and she bet that it was somewhere in the car. She had Brooke remove everything while she jammed her head and grubby paws into every nook, thumbing through all the papers she could find, but never found the form because we never had it.

Brooke, our unwavering border leader, convinced the colonel that we had done everything by the book, that we were not horrible people, and that we really should be going. Twenty hours at a border was long enough.

He agreed.

Brooke told us the good news. She went ahead with the car documents to be processed first, but the female immigration officer (a different one) wasn't going to make it easy for her. Her passport got the spy treatment. There were paper tests, questions, magnifying glasses, and multiple photo-to-face comparisons, which, each time, elicited a barely audible, "Are you fucking serious?" out of Brooke.

Greg and I got stamped and were asked to move on without even a glance at our passports. We were prepared to tranquilize Brooke, lest she raise hell and break everything in sight over this, but she admirably let the drama and unfairness roll off her back, leaving the china shop intact.

We passed through the gate and were bid adieu by the last guard in the complex. We'd had a great time in Russia but it was also an emotionally frigid place. After about twenty kilometers of driving we reached another gate tended by one last Russian guard. On the other side of that fence was a sign that announced "Mongolia." The guard joked with us for a bit. We asked him what life was like in his small hut and what it was like to literally be the last man in Russia. He laughed. We asked him if he'd ever been to Mongolia and he said no.

"But it's right there!" Still, he'd never been; couldn't handle the commute, maybe.

Our passports were handed back to us and we were waved on. Goodbye Russia, hello Mongolia!

When we reached the checkpoint, we went through the song and dance of getting our passports stamped, registering our car and all that, but it was painless because Mongolia, like Kyrgyzstan, didn't require Americans to have a visa to visit.

Then, for the last time, Brooke had to go to the car with one of the inspectors while Greg and I waited inside the customs building, peeking back to see Brooke, in heavy gesture mode. Arrogantly, we thought the worst. We tried to walk towards the car to see if we could help but the guard yelled for us to wait inside.

It turned out that the guard had lived in Seattle for years and spoke perfect English. He was more curious about us than anything. Brooke was handling the situation admirably. She gave us the thumbs up and we were good to go. Last border crossing, last hurdle cleared. For all my teasing about Brooke's flusterability, she got Donata and my drone into every country we entered and we never had to pay a border bribe. Who knows if Greg or I could have done that? I highly doubt it.

***

With no red tape remaining between Ulaanbaatar and us, our smiles lit up like magnesium. It wasn't just an instant of happiness; it was a culmination of joy. There is a difference between the two. Happiness is what takes your breath away; joy is what no one can ever take away from you. Happiness is the moment; joy is the story. Happiness is what is felt; joy is what is earned. We earned this.

Donata's forty-two horses of hope and prayer had traveled more than 8,200 miles and she was now a thousand miles from her destination. We were going to do our damnedest to get her over the Mongol steppe, one tire rotation at a time.

We set off into a place like nothing we had ever seen. The first thing we noticed driving in the dream of western Mongolia was that the rugged landscape holds power over man, not the other way around. Yes, the deserts of Turkmenistan didn't allow a blade of grass to raise its head, and yes, the fields of Kazakhstan hypnotized us by redundancy, but Mongolia offered up nothingness and depth simultaneously. Whether I was staring at a painting, a mountain, or Mars was up for debate. It was as if the scenery had been designed to inspire people to ponder their place on earth.

It was all too perfect, too desolate, and too aesthetic. There wasn't a tree in sight. The mountains in the distance never seemed to get closer, like we were in a Donata-centric view of the universe where points on the horizon stayed in the same spot no matter how far we traveled.

The sun snuck glances through the clouds, deciding if it was okay to come out after a small rainstorm. Our goal for the day was the city of Ulgii (population thirty thousand, about fifty miles from the border), and we were unsure whether we would stay there or camp somewhere beyond.

We felt pretty good about the state of the packed dirt roads and thought that if they remained like this, we'd be in for a great ride. But when the road split between the Northern Route and the Southern Route we took the Southern Route because we'd been told the Northern Route was impassable. There we got a glimpse of the choose-your-own-adventure reality that Mongolia really was. In the open plains, there is no defined path, only places where other cars had flattened the grass until tire tracks claimed eminent domain over any vegetation. If enough cars repeated that line of travel, these tire-wide dirt routes turned into an all-dirt road. Eventually, a driver may choose to abandon one of these routes and start the process all over again in the grass to the left or right.

The result of this endless and haphazard process was revealed to us at that moment. Extending to the summit of the mountain we needed to traverse were a series of overlapping dirt tentacles. Any path would get us there and no two paths were alike, ensuring that our journey was a unique one. These carvings in the earth were like invading armies trying to flank up the side of the mountain. Hannibal had his elephants and we had Donata. We weaved and slipped our way towards the top, switching from one track to another when one became too rough or was submerged under water. The increasing incline created a dread in my gut that Donata might not always be able to handle her shit in this unforgiving and undulating land.

Under some ominous clouds, we saw four guys milling around two identical, Mongol Rally retro MINI Coopers about two hundred yards from the top of the pass. Brooke approached gingerly before stopping parallel to them. Clearly the silverbacks of the entire rally, these two gritty older British men, with deep-lined faces and hard-earned gravelly voices, worked under the hood of one of the MINIs. Their weathered, oil-soaked hands moved about with pit-crew precision. Next to them were two guys in their early twenties, surely their sons or nephews.

We asked the standard, "Do you need any help?" I was hoping they wouldn't call our bluff of sympathy and insight. Okay, I guess that was *my* bluff of sympathy and insight. Clearly, Annette, Emin, Alexi, Artur, and Nik still had their work cut out for me when it came to that giving thing. Fortunately, we were asking mechanics who obviously knew what the hell they were doing and didn't need our input. We were seen as helpful but we didn't have to give anything up. Win-win.

We did need to move, though. The sky was darkening and there was a chill in the air even when the wind wasn't blowing. This was because in Mongolia we were constantly between 3,000 and 9,000 feet elevation. When Brooke tried to depart from our dead stop, she kept spinning the tires and then stalling out. Greg took over, angled the car a little downhill, and got Donata rolling before turning the wheel back uphill. The engine — in first gear — provided enough power to keep us climbing at a constant speed until we hit the pass, torque beating gravity by a nose. When we came around the bend, we saw that the dirt connected with a tarmac road a few hundred yards ahead.

Gers sprinkled the landscape more frequently, and after coming up and over another giant mountain pass, Ulgii and her indiscriminate spread of one- and two-story buildings emerged in the grassy valley below. We erupted into cheers. We were only about fifty miles in from the Mongol border but it was a hell of a win for us. Even if we didn't make it to Ulaanbaatar, we wanted to be able to say that we made it to somewhere in Mongolia. Ulgii was somewhere.

I think what surprised us most was how normal the city was: streets, cars, humans, bars, stores, and concrete or brick structures. Mongols, they're just like us! There were even things called "Nightclubs."

We pulled over when we saw two "hotels" side by side. The neighborhood felt normal enough but it didn't seem like it was the best part of town. We had prepared to camp — for the fifth night in a row — beyond the city, but with the prospects of a warm bed in front of us, we had to investigate. I waited in the car while Greg and Brooke took a closer look.

Suddenly, Myles (yes, Kiwi Myles) drove by with a Mongol man riding shotgun.

Interesting…

We exchanged pleasantries and Myles told me that he and two other rally teams were staying with this man — Manat — and his family. We could join them. We'd have dinner, breakfast, a hot shower, and a bed for the night for much cheaper than the hotel.

Manat's sixteen-word English vocabulary informed us that if we stayed at the hotel, there was a high probability our car would be on blocks come morning, or something like that. He could have been lying but there was no way for us to validate his claim. Yelp hadn't caught on in Ulgii yet.

So with nightfall looming, this lovable, crazy, Mongol man convinced us to spend the night with him. There was some comfort in knowing that rally teams would be together and it would help us create a convoy for the next morning. It was time to stop driving solo.

In Manat's neighborhood at the outskirts of Ulgii, many of the houses had unfinished walls in need of bricks and some had finished walls in need of roofs. Manat's one-story, white plaster house was a complete structure, thankfully, and we spotted two other rally cars. Manat showed us around while he started to drink, heavily. His two daughters and his wife scurried this way and that, preparing beds and food, while Manat didn't do much but laugh and yell the ever-decreasing words of English he had dominion over in his now inebriated state. He kept repeating, "Okay, okay…one moment, one moment." As the night wore on, "One moment" became "moment."

After we had settled in and were assured of our places to sleep, three other rally cars showed up. These happened to be the two teams who joined us late at the Russian border earlier that day, and a car of three Irishmen. I did a quick head count of the now small army of ralliers present and couldn't figure out how seventeen people were going to sleep in this small, one-story abode, so I went in with one of the newly arrived Brits (Scott) while manic Manat showed him the facilities. Scott was in his late twenties, slender, 6-foot 3-inches with the beginnings of a scruffy, ginger beard. He was also armed with an abundance of traditional dry British wit.

Manat tried to pretend that everything was hunky-dory, identifying the same beds that he had pointed out to us earlier, but Scott wasn't a fool. In his classically accented English he said, "Hang on a minute. This doesn't add up." We asked Manat how seventeen people were going to fit in nine beds. I liked Scott. We were best friends now.

Manat repeated, "Yes, yes, yes. Okay, okay, okay."

He walked us around into a new room and pointed at the one bed in the corner, suggesting a solution to our conundrum. Pyramid orgies aside, this bed would not hold eight individuals. Our patience was running thin because the sun was setting, we had already paid Manat, he was hammered, and we were six beds short.

Scott and I tried one more time to explain this to Manat, but then Manat pointed at Scott then pointed outside and then did the index finger in the round, cupped hole of the other hand routine, like a fifteen-year old would tell his friends that he had sex with someone, to which Scott — arms crossed and not amused — replied with, "I have absolutely no idea what that means." Neither did, I but I busted out laughing as Scott kept repeating, "I don't know what you're trying to tell me with that gesture."

Manat kept the motion going, laughing hysterically until he said, "One moment. One moment."

The status of our sleeping arrangements was shrouded in doubt until Manat got one of his daughters to lead us to a house next door that had many more beds. Happy with the math now, we knew we were all safe for our first night in Mongolia.

Paper-thin. Razor-sharp.

***

Most people in this town, including our hosts, showered with buckets of cold water, but our pampered asses were willing to pay to use the town's hot water shower, about a ten-minute walk away. This wasn't exactly a spa experience but as long as hot water was coming out of a spout, the ratty pipes, moldy plastic curtains, dirty floors, and absence of hooks to hang our clothes on didn't matter. It's amazing what lengths we humans will go to avoid having a single cold bead of water trickle down our spines.

Clean, we made our way back to the house, and became this part of town's main attraction. Children's heads poked over walls and through holes, wondering who these strange people were. We shared smiles, high-fives, and gum whenever possible.

When we got back to Manat's, some of the ralliers were playing soccer with local kids, while other people were doing last look-ins of their cars. Before we knew it, dinner was ready. So our band of merry imbeciles and slave-driving drunk of a host hunkered down for an entertaining evening. Half the group went into the kitchen to eat at the main table, and the other half of us huddled together in a small side room.

The food was pretty damn good and we did not go for want. This was, of course, thanks to the efforts of Manat's wife and his two daughters. Manat, on the other hand, took the night by storm, force-feeding us a never-before-experienced sandwich of goodwill, swindling, and sexual harassment. He poured beer, asked for our hard alcohol, and tried to find a way to marry Brooke. He was so drunk that he only had about six words left in his repertoire. He was loud, gregarious, and in no mood to be told what to do even if we could communicate, but he was proud to be our host.

We loved it. In a million years we would have never predicted a night like this. We drank into the wee hours of the morning, in a house hidden from the road, in a city we never knew existed, and in a country we thought we'd never get to see. *What else was going on in the world? Where were we going to be tomorrow? What would happen when we finished? Who cares?* We had tonight.

I had another out-of-body cultural realization at the dinner table, like the one when I shared that waiting room with the locals on the ship in the Caspian Sea. This one solidified for me that everyone in the world wants the same damn thing. Yes, there are different starting points, but we all want to end up a little better than before, we want to be loved by the people we love, we want honest work and a bit of leisure. The rest is ornamental.

The funny thing about being a traveler and exploring a new land is that you're always an outsider and yet you have to connect via the things that make us all insiders as a species: laughter, food, shelter, gasoline, whatever. Travel really does expand your ability to be in the visceral, what's-right-in-front-of-you moment while also balancing the look-how-grand-the-world-is reality. Traveling is about the character stretching, about instantly adapting, about the end of the bell curves of ourselves that we rarely get to reach. St. Augustine may have coined it best with, "The world is a book, and those who do not travel read only one page."

Our beds in the neighboring building never came to fruition. Maybe that wasn't even Manat's property. Since he was stumbling and shouting like a doped up, schizophrenic boxer at this point, chatting about what he had promised us would be like rearranging the deck chairs on the sinking *Titanic*. He had pulled the wool over our eyes. Well played, sir. We were given some pillows and blankets but we had to get our mattress pads and sleeping bags from our cars. No matter. At this stage of the trip the ground felt like home.

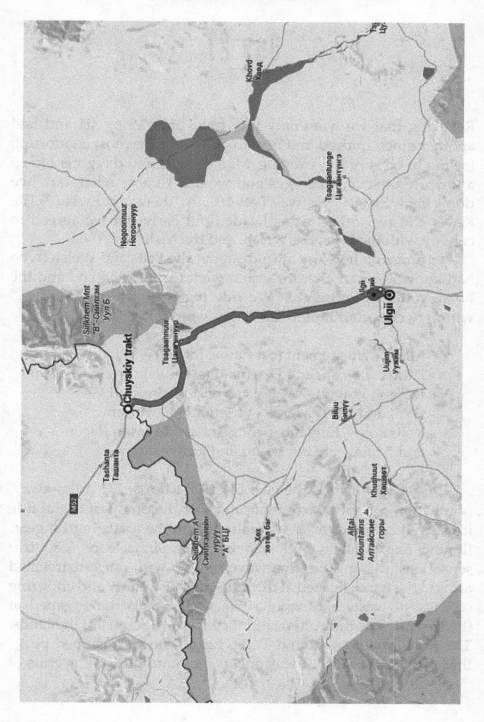

Day 27

Realizing that we were only fifty miles into Mongolia and had another nine hundred and fifty to go wasn't the most comforting feeling but it sure was exciting. Manat's wife and daughter fed us a mixture of scrambled eggs and we don't know what. But "we don't know what" was way better than "there is no what." The Kiwis and two other teams headed out early but we agreed to convoy with the Brits, the Welsh, and the Irish.

It's amazing how my attitude about the Brits and Welsh (who had known one another for years) went from "Fuck you and the horse you rode in on" to "We ride together, we die together," within twenty-four hours. The teams were:

- Micra Management (car name: Jolene) — Ireland: Paddy, Lorcan, and Diarmaid (all guys)
- Dragon Wagon — Wales: Garreth, Vicky, and Will (Will and Vicky were boyfriend and girlfriend)
- Yolo Polo — England: Scott, Anna, and Jason (Jason and Anna were boyfriend and girlfriend)

We set off towards the next big city, Khovd, 135 miles away, population roughly thirty thousand. For the first part of the ride it was red carpet tarmac. We slalomed on the roads in fifth gear, filming one another, and enjoying that pinnacle of road trip sensations: making the sine wave motion with our outstretched arms in the wind. I gazed at the preposterous beauty and enduring serenity of western Mongolia like settlers must have gaped at the treasures of the American Northwest or Scottish Highlands. The crash of colors around Tolbo Lake…the snowcapped peaks that pierced the sky…it was one of the more pleasant eyefuls of

BORDERS, BANDITS, AND BABY WIPES

wilderness I'd ever seen. We were explorers and this was our victory lap. Ulaanbaatar here we...

Bang.

I think it was the Irish leading the way but all we saw from our vantage point was a flurry of brake lights fighting through a cloud of dirt. Bye-bye tarmac. We were able to slow down enough to deal with the one-foot drop between the paved road and the dirt without our undercarriage committing *seppuku*. The delineation between the road and off-road was so exact, violent, and unmarked, I thought we were driving on a colossal Hot Wheels track, and the giant who assembled it forgot to insert a piece.

Needless to say, our rate of travel slowed considerably. If we were too close to the car ahead, the screen of sand kicked up by their tires would blind us. This led to driving in V-formation, which became the common configuration on the steppe.

Not too far ahead on the side of the road we came across a business-savvy man who owned a golden eagle and let us take photos with it for a small fee. *What a regal animal.* We'd seen them patrolling the Mongolian skies from time to time, elegantly and effortlessly maneuvering on their search for an unsuspecting desert gerbil or something. But while birds seem very light and small because they can fly, holding a ten-pound raptor with a seven-foot wingspan on my arm gave me a close-up look at his graspable kitchen knives for feet and nature's version of an ax for a beak. This was a killing machine. I immediately understood why there were no chickens in Mongolia. They wouldn't stand a chance. There are even reports of golden eagles being used in teams to hunt deer, antelope, and wolves.

Wolves, dude.

We navigated ranges and valleys and made our first "river" crossing. We, of course, uttered the, "It's not so bad! Look at us... fucking river crossing!" sentiments, but it wasn't really so much a river as it was the amount of water you had to pass through when a fire hydrant on your street has accidentally leaked. The unbroken treeless vistas magnified the mesmeric fluidity of the place. Nothing ever blocked our view. With a sweep of the eyes, I could trace a continuous path in any direction from our car to mountain peaks miles and miles away.

Somewhere down in that wide valley during a pee break, we met our first Mongol cowboy. He couldn't have been older than eleven, but he rolled up on horseback out of nowhere like Wyatt Earp. He didn't speak English. Then again, he didn't speak or make any facial expressions at all. Someone this cool didn't need to do either. He was way more of a man than I was. We petted his horse, took some photos with him, and went on our way with the complete understanding that he had given us permission to do so, like we'd passed some unspoken wilderness test.

A few minutes later, with mountains painted in the background and long green grass dotting the foreground, we came across twenty wild horses running, well, wild. We dead-man stared in dumbfound admiration, unable to move or think, afraid that we would wake from a dream.

Is any of this real? Where the hell are we?

Our good luck with the off-roading came to a grinding halt when we reached the low point of the valley. Valleys in Mongolia aren't like valleys in the Alps, where the low point is clearly visible; these are wide valleys that stretch to all ends of the horizon so we never really knew where the low point actually was.

But water does.

It was at one of these low points we encountered a muddy bog. Other vehicles had navigated the area in even slipperier conditions because in some sections there was a morass of tire ridges hardening in the afternoon sun. Mud is like clay. Think of how clay can be manipulated when it's wet and how hard it is when it dries into pottery. And then imagine shattering this gracefully curved pot and sticking the shards in the ground and trying to drive over them. This is what it's like to rumble over deep, dried-out tire gullies.

This was no time to get heroic and blaze through the mud like characters on the *Dukes of Hazzard*.

We got out of our cars to assess the options. Every spot in the thicker grass was off limits because it was waterlogged like a Burmese rice paddy, so we had to stay within a 30-yard jungle of mud and hardened tire tracks to find our best path through.

Anna decided that she had had enough of the mostly male posturing about angles, speeds, and ground consistency. She was going to power Yolo Polo through the general vicinity of the road best traveled and it would be prudent to get out of her way. God bless Anna's directness but her efforts ended up with Yolo Polo's front right end submerged in slop. No amount of forward or reverse dislodged her. She looked at us as if to say, "You figure out how to get me out of here yet?" Her adorable smile and laid-back attitude made us less mad at the demon behind the wheel.

We grabbed our shovels and tried to dig the VW out from the front. While navigating around the car, 6-foot-2-inch-tall Diarmaid took one awkward step and sunk down to his knee. Scott casually lent his hand thinking that Diarmaid had lost his balance, but Diarmaid had practically lost a leg and needed a bit more support from Scott. Scott still didn't exactly understand what was going on with Diarmaid, so we had Anna revving the engine, spewing mud everywhere, Will and Greg lifting the front of the car, and Diarmaid leaning on the car with one hand, pleading with Scott to provide some leverage so he could get out from the grips of the vacuum entombing his leg.

Scott, who wouldn't exert one more newton of force in life unless he absolutely had to, gave Diarmaid the leverage he needed to lift his leg out of the mud vice, but when his leg came out it was missing a flip-flop. I almost lost my flip-flop on the Hungarian-Serbian border so I knew his pain. As much as Diarmaid dug to retrieve it, it was clear that the mud had recovered that fumble. It was his price of freedom—that and our incessant laughter.

Oh, and we were no closer to getting Yolo Polo out of the mud.

Luckily, a van filled with Mongols stopped and assessed the situation, using Anna as an example of what not to do. They had a bit more horsepower and strength than our cars and thus were able to power through some seriously spotty parts of the mud bath. After they got through, the passengers agreed to help us.

We attached a tow rope to the back of Yolo Polo so that eight people could pull backwards while everyone else worked at the front of the car to lift its nose out of the mud. I, of course, was on camera duty to get this rescue on film. With teams in place, smiles and nods confirmed mission readiness. We gave a countdown and Anna hit the gas in reverse while everyone else did their job of lifting or pulling. Sure enough, the car came free, but lead-foot "Anna the Hammer" stayed on the gas so long that she almost ran over a Mongolian boy.

Vehicular manslaughter averted we thanked the people we'd almost killed and sent them on their way. We were back to where we'd started thirty minutes ago, not past the bog. For the next ten minutes we created and marked out a path. We had it down to when to turn, when to accelerate, and when to breathe. It was quite the team-building exercise.

Yolo Polo was again the first car to try.

Anna got through the messy bit she'd been stuck in before but soon reached the undulating lattice of dry tire tracks, bouncing her left, right, and every way in between. We howled at her to stay on the gas while we pushed her through until she made it out.

Momentum is a hell of a thing.

Now that the path was confirmed, we were all able to follow suit with the aid of a hand or two pushing on the rear bumper, leveraged by feet submerged in muck. Once through, we took a photo of all the cars covered in mud and parked in every direction, like we were doing a shoot for *Top Gear*.

After nibbling on some snacks for "lunch," the afternoon unwound with us reaching small rivers where we would have to venture up- or downstream to find a better place to cross, all the while being careful to not get caught in the thick mud randomly hidden below the grass at the banks. Locals on the far side of these crossings looked on in amazement at how our tiny-ass cars were navigating their land.

At this point of our Eurasian adventure, we were masters of adaptation. Every choice made along the way had massaged out the knots of our fragility and rigidity. No impediment was too weird and no span was impassable (in our minds, at least). When confronted with a detour, we no longer cared. This whole journey was a detour, a detour from life, from the familiar.

Mongolian driving was a microcosm of the entire rally in a lot of ways. While there were multiple routes *to* Mongolia there was only one passable route (The Southern Route) *through* Mongolia, but when you zoomed in closer, this "route" had multiple variations and choices. In a sense, that's what life is: a series of unique decisions that makes you, *you*. There is no preordained, guaranteed channel to safely navigate the complexities of existence. Your life, and how people describe you when you aren't there, is a collection of the choices you make and the demeanor you use to make them when confronted with something you didn't prepare for. Right then in the grass, dirt, and mud of Mongolia, we were accountable not for the obstructions, but for our decisions around them.

We could see on our map that we needed to traverse a main river before we hit some higher ground on our way into Khovd. The waterways we had bisected up until this point weren't on the map. That was a little disconcerting. Our cars couldn't handle a river much bigger than the ones we'd crossed, so if there was a body of water big enough to be on a map, there better be a bridge.

***

We didn't see the actual river at first. All we saw were two cars stopped in the distance. As we got closer, we realized that those cars were on the far side of a truly flowing river, roughly 60-feet-wide.

There was no bridge.

One of the cars on the other side belonged to "The Skoda Boys," three male British ralliers in their mid-twenties with unmatched optimism and "Fuck-it-ness." They were the kind of guys who could avoid 93 percent of their troubles if they had a little better judgment, patience, or foresight, but the kind of guys who also loved each and every toil that came with calculated ignorance. If you asked them to, they would probably drive blindfolded just to see what would happen. Case in point, they currently had everything out of their teal, 1990s, beat-up Skoda Something-or-Other because an hour earlier, they had tried to plow through the thigh-high river, but flooded the engine (and their car), and had to wait an hour until a Mongol family in a Land Rover Defender spotted them and pulled them out for ten dollars per person.

Luckily for us, the Skoda Boys' failed crossing was all the reason we needed not to try it on our own. We happily agreed to pay the family ten dollars per person to pull our cars across, but since we didn't want to get anything wet, we took everything out and portaged it across the river. We were like a long chain of refugees without the strife, death, and starvation that comes from being an actual refugee.

At its deepest point the water was quite strong and a few of the girls got a larger bath than they bargained for when they were knocked off balance. Once the cars had their insides emptied, the entire family (husband, wife, and child) in the Defender crossed over to the western side of the river. They turned around and placed the truck in front of whatever car was going next, and waited for us to attach the towrope.

The Irish were first. We all looked on wide-eyed and mouths agape as the water went *above* their hood. Jesus. This made it even more ridiculous that the Skoda Boys tried to cross on their own, unless they were planning to skip off the surface of the water like a rounded stone. The "tug truck" process repeated itself in what was one of the more unforgettable moments of the trip. No matter when we got home, we had a story worth telling about the Mongolian back country. Everyone's engines started up fine. The thing that took the most time with the crossing was the Russian nesting-doll game of packing and unpacking our cars. Whoever had fallen in the river changed attire and laid out their wet clothes on top of everything else in their back seats.

We were a five-car convoy now, and barring any freak storms, free to make it to Khovd without any more river crossings. We found a decent spot of road where we could take in the sights, and were back on the...

Bam!

Brooke hit a small, crooked rock cresting above the soil. There were millions of them, but this one punctured our back left tire. We'd traveled over 8,300 miles before our first flat. Not a bad run.

We had one complete spare tire on a rim that we could use and we had an extra tire that we could have mounted by a mechanic in Khovd. The perk about traveling in a convoy is that we didn't have to feel bad about breaking down or causing delay because we knew that it would happen to everyone at some point. At convoy stops, the American football or the soccer ball would come out and everyone would do their thing. It was liberating when "late" had no meaning connected to "arrival."

It took us a while but the tarmac eventually returned and we made it to Khovd—like Ulgii, a proper town on anyone's Mongolia map. We were hoping for a restaurant of sorts, but before we had a chance to take a look around, Jolene (the Irish car) stalled crossing the bridge into town. Out of all the places for a car to break down in Mongolia, entering a town was about the best option.

We rolled Jolene until we ended up in front of a restaurant/karaoke establishment. No one knew what was wrong with the car but we were starving. We might as well make plans on a full stomach. The staff didn't know what to do with the fifteen boisterous foreigners who took up every seat in the place and ordered by pointing at the photos of food that were on the wall since the menus were written in Mongolian.

Outside, the Irish asked some locals for a mechanic. "*Mechanica*" seems to be one of those words that transcend borders like "phone" or "battery." On a blank sheet of paper someone drew directions like a treasure map.

After we ate a tasty meal of noodles and meat, the group split into three: mechanic finding, hotel finding, and staying put at the restaurant (HQ). Greg piggybacked a ride to the mechanic with Yolo Polo so he could mount our spare tire on the rim of the recently changed flat. Our tire mounting set us back a measly ten dollars. And once the mechanics got a look at Jolene, they were eager to fix her with whatever parts they had, like engineers fitting a square peg in a round hole on the *Apollo 13* mission.

It worked. The industriousness of Third-World mechanics was another lesson in ingenuity.

The girls located a hotel that had room for all of us. The Buyant Hotel was a three-story, brick structure that had the exterior charm of an insane asylum. Saying that it was "rough around the edges" would be double entendre since there wasn't a curve within six light-years of this place. It was simple, it was dingy, but after climbing an extremely wide, switch-backed central staircase, we had our own room with three twin beds in it. We wondered if we were cheating the Mongol experience by sleeping in a hotel, but when it's dark outside, you're exhausted, and there's a mattress two feet from you, you say the hell with wilderness.

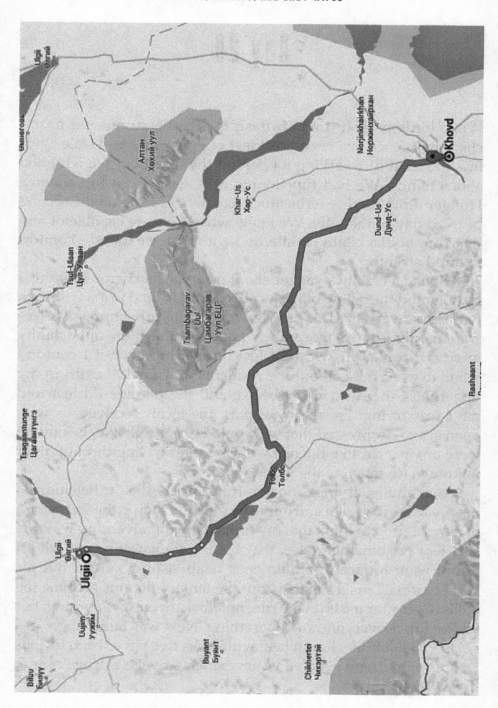

Day 28

While birds pecked through trash that had accumulated near a chain-link fence, we ate a breakfast of tangerines and stale chips in a deserted dirt parking lot behind the hotel, but we felt good about things. We had functioning cars, gas, and a fun convoy. Hunger didn't bother us as much as it would have on the second or third day of the rally. We knew what we were capable of and what our bodies could handle, and with that, we found a comfort in our discomfort.

We had a certain swagger about us at the local grocery store. I didn't mind the ogling of the local population, and in a weird way, felt it was warranted. What we were doing *was* impressive. We were modern-day explorers. My good fortune at the opportunity to *do* a trip like this was not lost on me, but even if I couldn't relate to everything about the residents of Khovd, the dirt in my fingernails, the dust in my beard, and the pounds I'd lost told me I was trying. For the most part, the locals received us with open arms — impressed that we would be on a trek like the one we were on, in a car like the one we were in, traveling through their unknown (to much of the world) town.

As draining, trying, and wit-frazzling as the "exhaustion of new" can be, it's equal and opposite phenomenon is the "addiction of new." I used to think that my propensity for adventure was due to a fear of something else, that I was compensating for what I didn't want to face: commitments, relationships, career. But it's not. "Normal" makes me anxious. Sedentary notions give me the chills. Home for me is on the run, not *from* anyone or anything, but on the run *to* everyone and everything. New was humbling.

I'm a xenophile. I'm in love with cities I've never been to, jobs I've never had, and people I've never met. Travel is a drug I cannot live without.

Thankfully, it looks like there might be some research backing up the propensity to move. For all you fellow nomads, bask in the existence of the "wanderlust gene." From Avi Tuschman's *Our Political Nature*:

> Dopamine, a neurotransmitter found in the brains of a wide variety of animals, serves many different functions. Dopamine is particularly implicated in motivation and gratification. Human beings have at least five subtypes of dopamine receptors in their heads. The fourth kind of dopamine receptor (D4) may shed some light on the dispersal mystery. Geneticists have located the gene that codes for D4 on the short arm of human chromosome 11. But not everyone has the same form of this gene. Individuals with a longer D4 allele have brains that collect dopamine less efficiently (it seems like dopamine does not bind as strongly to their D4 receptors). Consequently, these people tend to take greater risks and seek more novelties in order to get the same dopamine reward as people who live a more sedentary lifestyle. The novelty seekers have a lower tolerance for monotony. So they search for new experiences to alter their mood.
>
> A team of psychologists and an anthropologist from the University of California, Irvine, calculated the allele frequencies for the D4 dopamine receptor gene among thirty-nine populations around the world. They found a very strong correlation (.85) between the novelty-seeking gene and populations that had undertaken long-distance migrations. Sedentary populations, on the other hand, had much lower frequencies of the D4 allele. So the gene determines brain physiology, which in turn motivates dispersal and probably outbreeding.

After we bid adieu to Khovd, the asphalt disappeared and we were on our dirt and grassy road the rest of the way east. At one hundred and ten meters, 9 de Julio Avenue in Buenos Aires is considered the widest road in the world, but the people measuring it have never been to Mongolia to see the ever-expanding braid of tracks meandering together across the land, sometimes two hundred meters between the outer edges. If something was in our way, if the road became a bog or if we didn't like driving where someone else had driven, we turned the wheel slightly and traveled parallel to whatever path we were just on. We could hit 60 mph on good stretches.

Sometimes the shrubbery was a little too thick or the stones a little too big for us to freely etch-a-sketch on the earthly canvas, so what tended to happen was that we would follow the car in front, but as soon as we were on a path that was less than stellar or if we thought our leader wasn't traveling as fast as we wanted, or if we were tired of getting dirt spewed in our face, we would choose a different route when an opening presented itself.

Eventually, every team picked one of the fifteen or so dirt capillaries, hoping their choice was best or at least as good as the others. There was no worse feeling than selecting a route and then seeing one or two other cars in the convoy pass fifty yards to the left on smoother terrain. Sunk costs would be calculated and eventually, we would give up on our shit route, drive across the field to fall in with the other cars that had passed us, much to the silent gloating of the driver who had chosen the best route for that section.

Fall in line, suckers.

This all sounds like a giant joyride at the end of a movie in *The Fast and the Furious* series but this was not the case. Sure, there were sections that felt like packed powder under our tires but our nemesis never allowed that bliss for long.

Stretches of velvet would eventually be infiltrated by washboard ridges of death (RODs) that spread through every stretch of road like the flu. These hardened dirt ripples propagating perpendicular to the direction of travel caused our cars to shudder uncontrollably. This was the maddening reality of driving in Mongolia. At times the rattle was so bad we thought every lug nut, washer, and bolt was unscrewing itself, like a gyrating bed at a cheap motel whose dial automatically turned faster, until we were powerless, waiting for the bed to vibrate itself to shambles.

Duh-duh-Duh-Duh-*Duh-Duh-Duh*...

Sometimes the unabated siege got so bad that coming to a complete stop was the only way to cease the trembling. We'd giggle and gather our scattered wits, hoping that if we went about things slowly and respectfully, we'd find our groove. But the oscillations would be waiting right there for us. It was like hearing a mosquito in your ear at night, rushing to switch on the light, and then finding nothing at all. Maybe you'd killed it? Maybe it left? Then you'd turn the light off and within seconds, the buzz was back in the folds of your ear. During tough stretches—in other words, about one-third of Mongolia—travel was no more than 15 mph. Third gear was considered a good piece of road but second gear saw the most play.

With so many paths and so much earth at our disposal, our solution seemed like it was all around us, but like being stuck on a raft at sea unable to drink the ocean water, these diabolical ridges would find their ways out to even the most far-flung dirt strands of tangled spaghetti where we drove, turning us into real-life bobblehead dolls. This was the battle for pretty much the entire day. Even Donata's shocks received a "Get Well Soon" card from a jackhammer saying, "Damn..."

We would get on the walkie-talkies each team had and theorize about how and why the ridges formed. Was it the wind? Was it the tires? Was it the drying after a rain? Was it aliens?

Whatever it was, it was all-powerful.

That's when Yolo Polo lost their roof rack. I'm not sure what happened but I'm guessing it was between the millionth and billionth rattle that caused it to loosen and break from its hinges. Shoelaces and mallets reassembled the rack but the newly scarred windshield, and the cracks that came with it, was a concern. Because of the sheer amount of dust that encapsulated everything in our car like volcanic ash, the last place we'd want it coming at us while driving in this country was directly into our faces, driving goggles or not.

Patchwork completed, our armada drove on but without the Irish, who had sped ahead since they had a deadline to hit with their flights out of Ulaanbaatar, but we picked up the two MINI Coopers again to put us at a six-car convoy for now.

We had it in our hearts to reach the next river crossing on the map before night fell. The last thing we wanted to do was camp ten minutes west of the river, and then find out that we needed ten hours to cross it the next day. Well, I guess the *last* thing we wanted would be needing to be dredged out of its depths after an overzealous decision to cross based on an "I think it's fine!" assessment made at the river's bank, but you catch my drift.

The roads were deteriorating fast. In some places we encountered thick sand, forcing us to gun it, power slide through, and hope there was packed dirt on the other side to provide the grip. When the thick sand wasn't there, the RODs were vibrating the patience and wherewithal out of our souls.

In the eastern sky we began to see the dark blue, white-dotted blanket dragging west behind the setting sun, but we still did not see the river. We were close to giving up hope when pavement appeared out of nowhere. If there's pavement, there has to be a bridge close by. Before we knew it, there it was. It was a real bridge made out of steel and concrete. Ironically, the river was so low on this day that calling it a stream would have been audacious. Any one of us could cross it by stepping over it, but judging from the size of the riverbed, when the rains came, this place would be Poseidon's playground.

We crossed the bridge and did an off-road U-turn so we could camp for the night on the soft grass on the east side of the river. The eternal sky overwhelmed us with its luminosity like it had been covering up part of herself these past four weeks, and now she wanted to reward us by dropping her robe, making the Milky Way so vast, bright, and dense that it looked more like a brushstroke than a series of pinholes.

It was like nothing I'd ever seen. Truly. I know I've talked about the Turkmen desert sky, but here, when I looked in the distance and wondered what street lamp was on down the road, I realized that it was a star right on the horizon, shining as bright as the ones directly overhead.

You beautiful thing.

We basked in drinks, food, and laughter. We knew that this was a special night but instead of trying to analyze this adventurous lightning in a bottle, we remained present. The significance of it would come to us at random moments, many weeks from now in line at the supermarket, in traffic, on a train, and the corners of our mouths would tilt up and we'd remember how alive and free the sky made us feel that night on the other side of the world.

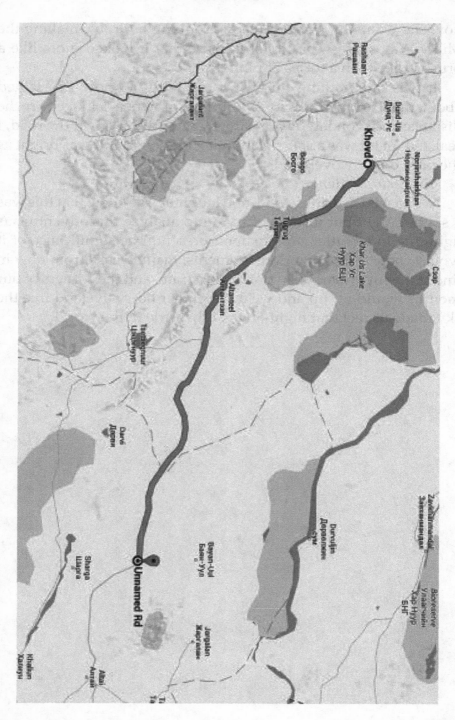

Day 29

We packed our car and watched the guys with the MINIs reassemble tires and axles, and tend to a whole bunch of other ailments, any of which would have crippled us unless we were within fifty feet of a body shop. They told us to head off, hoping to catch up with us a little later.

The goal for the day was to continue eastward but we knew we would be passing through a town called Altai (population roughly fifteen thousand), so gasoline (we had to use our jerry can for the first time all trip) and, possibly, a hearty lunch would be in order. We also hoped to find an internet cafe to book our flights home because barring any catastrophes, we had a decent idea of when we would be in Ulaanbaatar.

As usual, the Skoda Boys sped off like kamikaze pilots into the Mongolian hinterland. We all shook our heads wondering when we'd find their car smoldering in a heap on the side of the road. I felt like a dad who wanted his kids to learn a lesson while at the same time not wanting them to get hurt.

This was one of the more brutal and forsaken stretches of the Mongolian trip. Gone were the large mountains and splendor of colors. In their stead were beige sand and the RODs. Sure enough, as we were all spread out on the web of tracks inching along, we spotted the Skoda boys leaning on their broken-down car, still jovial, as if this were all part of their plan. Our entire convoy stopped. Pretty much all the guys went over to the car and looked under the hood, kibitzing, because this was the XY-chromosome thing to do. Look at, grab hold of, agree with, and feel like a man. I knew I had no idea what was wrong, so not even feigning concern, I took pictures and played football instead.

The guys in the MINI showed up—compressing this convoy accordion—and fixed the car MacGyver-style. Sadly, I can't tell you what was wrong but it had to do with a hose carrying liquid of some sort. Evidently these hoses are paramount in the proper functioning of a car.

Back on the road we had our minds erased by RODs for a few hours until we crept up the slopes towards Altai. Just as a man on horseback passed us at a lazy trot, the roads smoothed out, we sped up, and Altai showed itself at 7,260 feet above sea level. After filling up on gas, the Skoda Boys and the MINIs headed to a mechanic while the rest of us went for a bite to eat.

Following a tasty lunch of pointing at boards, miming orders, and wondering what we were even eating, we found an internet cafe. It was strange to dip a toe into the world we would be returning to in a few days. I couldn't get over seeing "JFK Airport" on the screen when last night we'd been under a shower of stars in the Mongolian desert. It didn't seem right. It felt too abrupt, like I was insulting Mongolia and the experience. While I tried to balance that feeling in my head, I searched the internet for soccer scores and other worldly news, slowly wading back into the river of information. I tried steering clear of email and social media but my curiosity got the better of me. Thoughts of my soon-to-be life back home infiltrated my conscience, and anxiety started to pile up.

And then it happened.

I saw a story on Facebook about a guy I was always a little jealous of as a business coach and entrepreneur. Truth be told, I couldn't stand the guy, not for anything he did or didn't do, but because I thought he was a fraud and a fake. I had no proof of that, of course, it was just a vibe. Anyhow, he'd been recognized for an award in New York City. Instead of being happy for him or healthily indifferent, my thoughts immediately moved to jealousy and anger that if I had been home to apply for the award, I might have won it instead of him. I could have been someone people admired. If only I wasn't here.

Whoa.

What in the hell was I thinking? *If only I wasn't here*…in Mongolia…on a trip of a lifetime? I was dizzy with shame, trying to dissipate these noxious gases wafting in my head. Where did this anger and regret come from?

No one could see the mental miasma swishing and swirling behind my eyes, each person locked into their own screen, digesting the visual drug of an internet connection. But then, like a piece of molten steel after having been forged into shape by many mallet blows, my thoughts were dropped into a bath, coagulating the glowing mess into a sharp spear, which I used to slash through the curtain that was hiding the window to my soul.

I was the fraud. I was the fake.

I was mad that this guy *liked* what he did, while all this time I hadn't ever really enjoyed being a coach, and I'd only just realized it. Having my own business and being my own boss was supposed to be the sexiest thing I could do. It's the envy of everyone who is trying to get out of the so-called rat race, but somehow along the way my bold quest for geographical and financial freedom became a fruitless drive for recognition. Coaching, writing, speaking, doing, and finishing weren't about setting an example, bringing my clients joy, or unlocking their processes anymore; it was about me seeking the approval of the invisible audience to prove to myself that I was enough, that I somehow belonged after years of stunted careers and failed endeavors. And now I was balking at a great opportunity at Omnibuild because it wasn't *sexy* enough for me, the story I told, and the story I imagined other people recounted about me when I wasn't there. Was I, Bassam Tarazi, going to work for a *construction company* and scale back my coaching business?

In that two-bit, pay-by-the-minute internet café at the outskirts of Altai, Mongolia, a mile and a half in the sky, I realized that yes, yes, I was, because I could be part of a team again. I could be valued by the people I worked with, not the strangers I worked in front of. I could be one layer below the principals, who would act like the upper atmosphere of the organization, absorbing the

BASSAM TARAZI

cosmic rays of public perception. They would deal with the kind of outward-facing things I was frankly tired of dealing with at my own company right now, the things that were indirectly making me cold and curt, my faults that were magnified when I met people like Annette, Emin, Alexi, Artur, and Nik. I was supremely proud of what I was able to build with Colipera, the books I wrote, the classes I taught, the people I helped, the discipline that was needed, but I couldn't ignore the fact that I was caught up in hustling to be seen, when all the while what I really wanted was to hustle to disappear.

In an instant, I became happy for that guy in New York, truly happy that he got something he went after, something he enjoyed doing. I shed the skin of comparison and perception, free from the "me" I didn't want to be.

***

Fresh off that burst of spiritual oxygen, I rejoined the group. We stopped off at the only bodega that happened to be open and plundered its water. All of it: large bottles, small bottles, whatever. Some bullies slap books out of peoples' hands and others take all of a city's potable drinking supply.

On a new high and starting to believe that we were going to get to Ulaanbaatar, the three-car convoy—Donata, Yolo Polo, and Dragon Wagon—joked on the walkie-talkies about anything and nothing at all. Oh, how I miss the sultry voice and poetic Welsh accents of Will and his lovely sidekick Vicky.

Our elation was short-lived when our map said that we were supposed to stay east (on the "Southern Route") but east was a dirt road, whereas southeast was tarmac. The route to the southeast veered a bit out of the way but Brooke (who was driving) was quite adamant about staying on the pavement as she saw semitrucks go that route. Semis, it was thought, were in the business of shipping goods and would most likely take the road most traveled. Following them would no doubt be a wise decision.

After a small team meeting, I used my powers of persuasion to have us inexplicably stay on the dirt road with the logic of, "The map says we go east. We could always travel southeast and hook back up with the tarmac if need be."

The point where the main road turned southeast and our route continued east was a complete drop-off that some people in the mountaineering world might describe as a ledge. We dipped down it delicately and saw the remnants of a burnt-out car on the dusty plain off to our left. There was a 100 percent chance that this car came tearing down the main road and didn't realize that the "straight" road was a cliff onto the dirt road. That should have been our warning.

Our route deteriorated like papier-mâché in a fire. For the first time on the entire Mongol Rally, Donata was grounded in deep trail sand that forced me and Greg to get out and push. While we were situating ourselves behind the car and out of Brooke's earshot, Greg asked, "You still think this is the best option?"

I conceded, "Not entirely."

"Ready?" Brooke yelled from inside the car.

I tapped the back side of Donata and said, "Go for it!"

From right behind the muffler, Donata's growling durability rumbled like a low-flying WWII Japanese Zero. *Maybe we should have given her an oil change*...Sand from the spinning tires pelted my shins. Eventually, we extracted Donata from her quagmire, but before getting back in the car I stared off at the truck dust trails five miles south, seriously second-guessing my decision to stay north of them. At this stage, it would have been suicide for us to off-road it to them because the terrain in-between was too unruly. We would have to backtrack thirty minutes to the main road if we were to change our tune.

We convened with the caravan because I did not want to be the sealer of our fates, but Yolo Polo and Dragon Wagon agreed to stay on our course. However, if we were to break down out here, there wouldn't be many, if any, cars passing us. Those plane tickets we'd bought two hours earlier now had an expiration date attached to them.

After another thirty minutes or so, we were off the map completely. Those were some tense times in the car. Brooke had no interest in being this enterprising so close to Ulaanbaatar, especially when there was another perfectly good option that we'd ignored. I kept reiterating that if we continued moving east, it was essentially a good thing. "A good thing until we reach a river we can't cross," Greg chimed in.

Touché, Greg.

There were a few moments when the road had stayed on a slightly northern trajectory for a little too long. Greg looked at his compass and I was looking at the sun through the back left window. I was counting the seconds before either he or I said that we had to turn back, but each time it felt like it was going to happen, the faint dirt or flattened grass road would bend back east again, buying us a few more minutes of grace, or adding a few more minutes of backpedaling in the near future.

At one point an SUV screamed past us. We couldn't stay with him without risking turning our car into a thousand-pound paperweight so we tried to follow his dust trail, but even that became an exercise of false dreams as it vanished in the distance in no time, providing us the same aid as a smoke signal in the fog.

There have been other times in my life where I've been off the beaten path, but I hadn't been off the beaten planet like this. Thanks to the rally, we had a matador's calm about the situation. We had fuel, we had food, we had water, we had our tent, and we had one another. We weren't going to die anytime soon.

Before we lost the sun, I hopped on the walkies and said, "How about here?" pointing out of the window to the small hill on our right. We figured that if we got up and over it we could have a little protection from the wind and from anyone interested in stealing our shit that night. We traveled over some dirt and grass patches and pitched our tents in the "valley" between two ten-foot high hills.

Home for the night.

I took the drone for a spin and got some of the best vantage shots of the whole trip. To see us in an immeasurable stretch of treeless green, picking a spot seemingly no better than any other within one hundred square miles, was extraordinary. It was 7 o'clock and we had nothing to do for thirteen hours, so we ate and we drank a bottle of schnapps that the Brits had gotten in Kazakhstan. We told stories until late in the night, just a jubilant dot on a map sheltered by an umbrella of stars. It was the time of our lives.

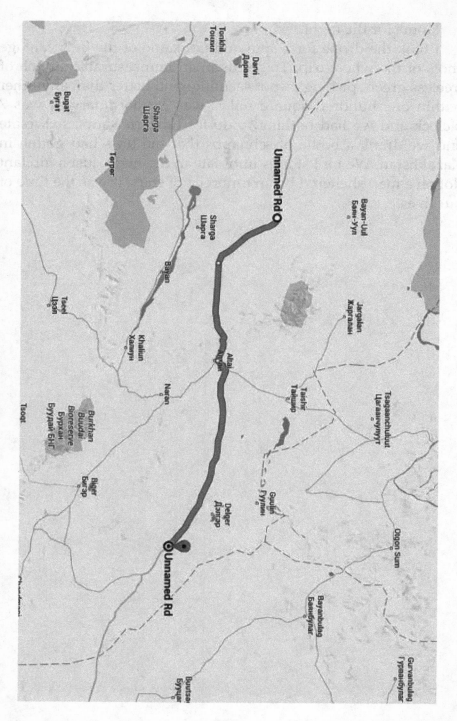

Day 30

Bedraggled hair, long stares, and slow movements meant that our thirtieth day on the road started with a well-earned collective hangover. We ate our breakfasts, packed up shop, and left no trace behind other than our fecal matter buried in the dirt encircling the camp. We continued on our road-to-nowhere route but soon ascertained that we were on what was called the Northern-Southern Route and to our south was the *Southern*-Southern Route. These Abbot-and-Costello themed roads would reconnect somewhere before the town of Bayankhongor. I was relieved that Brooke could now erase my name from her "People to Kill" list.

Bayankhongor was significant because we heard that after this city, it was tarmac, more or less, all the way to Ulaanbaatar. This last bit of deplorable road on the trip did not peter out gracefully. It made its last stand, in its own sick version of the Battle of the Bulge(s). The RODs, these middle fingers of the road, were torturous. There was a moment when we got out of our cars and tried to stomp on them in frustration (to no avail). The only respite was to confirm with other ralliers that the rattling was equally bad for them. None of our cars had functioning shocks anymore.

When the two southern roads connected, we were at the low point of another horizon-reaching valley that we didn't even know we were in. It looked like rain had fallen recently. Some cars had gone through since then, leaving the crisscrossing, negative imprints of tires (like the ones that caused such havoc a few days earlier). It looked like a giant display of dried paint in front of us.

These spiky earth fragments might as well have been land mines. Every time we drove over one, Greg yanked the wheel left, then right, then straight, then left again to try to avoid them. It was futile. We'd hear fingernails scratching the bottom of our car, the tires rising and falling off ridges, tossing us around like the inside of a popcorn machine even as we crawled forward at about 4 mph.

After about thirty minutes of high intensity driving at walking speeds, the more level ground reappeared. Our convoy had made it! No matter what Mongolia threw at us, our Little Cars That Could kept on moving.

Around 2 o'clock, we crossed a finely constructed bridge over a low river. We decided to take a swim and cool off from the summer sun. We parked in the dried riverbed of a gigantic tributary. During the rainy season or after a storm, driving must be an utterly useless means of transportation here.

Thankfully, there was still about a waist-deep flow of water 40-feet-wide at the center of the main river, so we all joyously hopped in as days of dirt, sweat, and grime sloughed from our bodies, hijacked by the water droplets now streaming off our skin.

Next concern? Food. There was a baseline hunger that gripped us at all waking hours, but we were in the now enviable position of being able to eat a good portion of our reserves. I had a rule in London that we couldn't touch the twelve power bars or the giant tub of mixed nuts until we reached Mongolia. Greg and Brooke had wanted me to break that rule many times but I stayed strong (stubborn and idiotic) and we were happily getting into these now.

We also had a few fish/salmon cans left over from that Russian Costco. These were hot because they had been baking in our cargo carrier all day. I knew even before Brooke opened a can that this was going to be a bad idea, but hunger is a hell of a thing. I dipped a bland cracker into the puréed pigswill and reluctantly took a bite, hoping that squinting would smother the disgust that comes with eating warm fish out of a flimsy tin can.

Goddamnit. I honestly feel sick writing this.

I don't know why I had two crackers' worth. I stopped after that but the damage was done. I gagged, burped, and had to spit pretty much the rest of the day. It was the deal I made with the gastro devil to keep me from vomiting. I hate vomiting.

Back in the car, we made it out of the riverbed and lumbered on to Bayankhongor, weaving around each other on the endless dirt roads. From time to time we also had to dodge the roaming sheep and goats that impeded our way, a fact that was of no great concern to any of them. Since we were close to a crossroads city, we began to see more large trucks—half eighteen-wheelers, half dump-truck behemoths. The RODs turned them into a cacophony of clattering metal when they rumbled past.

Coming into Bayankhongor (elevation 6,152 feet, population, roughly twenty-seven thousand) at the end of the day was like a scene out of a movie. From our high vantage point we saw the city in the distance aglow from the sun setting behind us. What did early American settlers feel when they saw the blue of the Pacific Ocean in the distance? I didn't know, but if they could have told me, I'm sure I would have put a dusty arm around them, shot a smile through my thicket of beard, and say, "I know the feeling." Bayankhongor wasn't Ulaanbaatar but that didn't keep us from trying to "smell the ocean breeze," so to speak.

The asphalt returned, but the pavement gods threw one last pothole gauntlet at us, demanding patience even when the city was so close. We made it through, elated, albeit mentally drained. Bayankhongor was a big enough city to have at least one stoplight. That is saying a lot in Mongolia.

Hunger resurged even though the salmon regurgitation was still singing in the back of my throat and front of my mind. However, Yolo Polo was struggling a bit. The car stabbed forward at odd acceleration intervals so we had to make the oft too common choice between food and safety.

At around 7 o'clock the sun was still hanging on for dear life above the mountaintops. We did a little loop-de-loop around the city to see if there were any restaurants open. Most places, as usual, were closed for reasons unbeknownst to us. Establishments in this part of the world don't really cater to the customer, or maybe they do, but for a customer showing up at a very specific hour. It is unnecessary to stay open for the random tourist passing through at odd times looking to shell out a little Mongolian *tugrik*. We noticed a place that had the word "Restaurant" illuminated in English, so we felt good about the prospects of eating there as soon as we tended to the temperamental Yolo Polo.

Where there are cars, there are mechanics. Doctors and mechanics — they're never going out of business. We went to one mechanic but he couldn't help, so he pointed *across the street* to another mechanic. That's right. Even in this tiny town. At this lively shop a heavyset gentleman came out to talk with us. He didn't speak English, though. Scott kept asking us, "What is 'lurching' in Mongolian?" The conversation became a game of charades once the hood was opened.

After about thirty minutes, the Yolo Polo was fixed — thanks again to desert resourcefulness. We were about to hop back into our cars when suddenly, on the horizon, like a cockroach that wouldn't die, we saw the Skoda Boys ricocheting into town. How the hell that car was still operating is beyond me, but the guys saw us, pulled into the lot, and got out as if we had all previously agreed to meet here for happy hour.

The Skoda Boys didn't do anything wrong, but it was their naive optimism that bothered me, the "everything-will-work-out" attitude. Sadly, the delusional optimists are always happier in life, and us realists are left to deal with the harsh truths of, well, reality. But I was hungry, so let's take it easy on my existential self.

With all cars functioning at least temporarily, we headed back to the restaurant we had seen earlier. The eatery was part of a two-story hotel that was in the midst of a major renovation. Once we navigated through scaffolding, paint cans, and tile work, we learned that there were rooms available if we wanted them. As usual, we were the only people in the place. The owner and waitress spoke enough English for us all to communicate on a basic level. Our waitress gave us the rundown of what was or wasn't on the menu. We ended up ordering eleven of one thing and one of another to keep prep and cooking time to a minimum.

The lone depressing fact was that on Mondays, by law, they were not allowed to serve beer. Police did random checks in restaurants and fined the establishment if people were drinking.

Gosh, that's terrible news. We'll have twelve beers, please.

Seriously.

Seeing a quick profit, she obliged our request. We guzzled our suds safe from persecution, and everyone was a winner. There may be no better buzz than the one-beer drunk of a famished man.

While waiting for our food, we studied the map and realized that if the roads were all tarmac tomorrow as we had been told, this could be our last night in the wild. The Skoda Boys wanted to stay in the hotel but the nine of us had so much fun camping that we wanted to recreate that joy one more time. Unfortunately, we were now tipsy, nightfall was coming, and it was going to be God knows when until we received our dinner.

Fine, fuck it, we'll stay here and have a real bed.

Mongolia does that to you. One minute, you think you're a modern-day Lewis and Clark, and the next minute, someone is cooking your dinner and you're sleeping in a hotel bed. Realizing that the only thing we needed to do to ensure a comfortable roof over our heads was to say, "Yes," the decision was easy. There was no sense in paddling upstream in a sinking canoe. We'll make the most of our last night if this is what it was.

Someone noticed that there was free Wi-Fi that worked in the rocky entrance and construction staging area to the hotel, but this network wasn't ready to handle twelve Westerners trying to Skype, Instagram, email, and all that. We all kept refreshing the network on our phones, hoping to kick off the friend right next to us who was talking to their mother, or trying to confirm flights home. There was no honor in the actions of the Wi-Fi-deprived.

It might have been better if there had been no Wi-Fi whatsoever but it was fun to hear the ping and ding of relevance. Oh we fickle beasts, unable to separate from the mother tit of validation and connection. Thankfully, we all understood the magnitude of this possibly being our last night on the road, so we checked what we needed to for a few minutes before we convened in one of our hotel rooms, sitting around telling stories and joyously drinking cans of cold Borgio beer we had managed to buy.

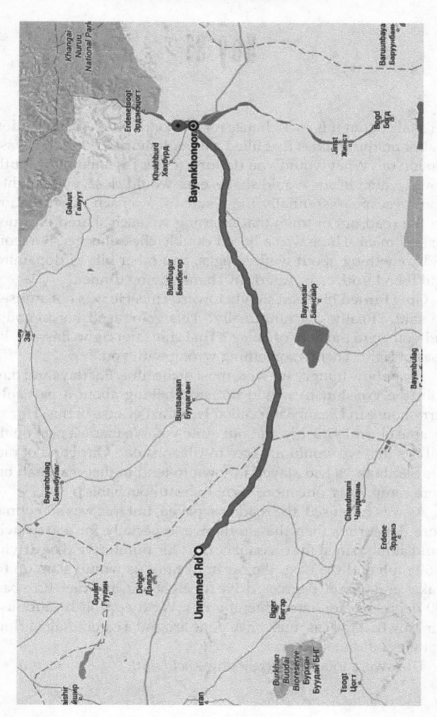

Day 31

Let's talk about this curry house for a second. Much of the random chatter on the walkies that filled a monotonous driving day was a version of "What would you do for a (enter food item)?" Mouths would water, heads would shake, eyes would close, and laughter would escape—essentially the results of stomach masturbation. On the road out of town that morning we each shared our most desired meal. There was a bacon double cheeseburger. Someone said something about waffles, eggs, and other bits of dopamine. And then I said, "An American Thanksgiving dinner."

Greg turned his head slowly towards me. He was not amused. He said, "Really? Fucking really? This game isn't hard enough and you go to the holy of holies? That shit's not right, Bassam. It's just not right. There's something wrong with you."

That's how hungry we were most of the time. For days and days Will (the Welshman) would not stop talking about a particular curry house in Ulaanbaatar called Hazara. Because of this, Hazara became our rallying cry, but not quite yet. We made a pact on the walkies that we would not race to Ulaanbaatar. Our band of nine (the Skoda Boys had stayed in town to tend to their car) had one more camp in us, one more night to be untouchable.

As was promised, the road was paved, but this was sometimes more dangerous than the alternative, especially for a crew who could almost smell the coconut curry. One minute we'd be driving at 60 mph and the next, the car in front of us would slam on the brakes and turn 90 degrees, drive for eight feet, and then turn back 180 degrees before straightening out. We'd approach cautiously thinking that the car must have gone around a camouflaged rhino that we couldn't see yet.

They were totally overreacting—*holy shit!*

And then we'd see the Sarlacc from *Return of the Jedi*, right there in the middle of the road — a gaping maw waiting to swallow our car.

Upon encountering grave obstacles, the rule was for the lead car to turn on its hazards and warn the drivers following them. This was fine in theory but if I had just mashed our whole front end in a pothole, so much shit was going on that I first had to make sure I had control of the car before engaging in pothole protocol. In this situation, the cars behind us could definitely see our distress so the hazards weren't needed.

Every now and then, we'd luckily miss a pothole because we happened to be on the right part of the road, so braking and swerving weren't necessary. That's when we would use our hazards. At that point, riding second kind of sucked. If you weren't actually paying attention to the lead car's exact line but then saw its hazards, you'd slam on the brakes to avoid the torpedo that was somewhere out in front aiming to turn your hull into the *Lusitania*.

At one point Yolo Polo was leading and we were second. After cresting a hill, I saw a pothole created by a wrecking ball dropped from a plane or some other violent act of gravity. Yolo Polo didn't have a chance. Her right wheels hit the depression. It was as if a bomb had gone off. Dirt from the car and gravel from the crater scattered everywhere. Spinal columns surely rearranged. A hubcap rolled parallel to Yolo Polo for a second, while all of us in Donata assumed that an actual tire had come undone, because a snapped axle and a tire saying, "Okay, fuck this shit. I'm done," was 100 percent plausible.

Greg theoretically had enough time to move, but when in that position, your arms were so frozen that the only defense against the sinkhole was a clenching of the teeth, a recoiling of the butthole, a widening of the lips, an emitting of *"eeeeeeeeee,"* and waiting for the explosion.

Somehow, we missed it.

Dragon Wagon saw the blinding brake lights in time, avoiding disaster as well. We all pulled over to the side of the road a few hundred feet ahead of Yolo Polo and looked back as cars screeched and swerved around the gorge. This was the most dangerous thing I've seen on a road, especially cresting the top of a hill, where speeds were between 60 to 75 mph. How Donata didn't break up into a thousand pieces on this trip was beyond me, but I do think it was due to our general mind-set of driving 5 or 10 mph slower than we could have.

Limbs, wheels, and underwear intact, we kept on, eventually passing through another town, large enough to have a main strip. We picked up some snacks and a bottle of Chinggis Vodka. This was the most badass looking vodka I'd ever seen. It had a demonic-looking Genghis Khan on the label, for God's sake.

We navigated the taunting roads and even began seeing, sprinkled in the brush, resorts catering to Westerners and offering horseback riding tours, spas, stays in *gers*, and other modern adventure luxuries. Mammoth coach buses charged towards us taking up three-quarters of the slim road, emerging from Ulaanbaatar to provide tourists with a chance to see the "real" Mongolia. Of course, we laughed at these powder-puff pioneers, these plastic explorers riding in their cattle vans (buses) or bitch cars (4x4s), who would go home and tell their friends that they knew the wilderness. We joked about conversations we could have with them.

"Oh, you're from London, that's great. How'd you get here?"

"We flew via Dubai. It's such a long flight but it's worth it. How about you?"

"Oh, we came from London too."

"Via?"

"Tires."

I was offended that they were where we were since they weren't doing what we were doing. This is, of course, egomaniacal and ridiculous but it was a testament to the strength of the bond we had as teammates, as convoy partners, as ralliers. We were fighting tooth-and-nail to be travelers, not tourists. It was our social proof. The presence of outsiders tainted our metaphorical victory lap now that we were so close to Ulaanbaatar. I didn't want to see their roller bags, their cameras, their clean shaves, their stupid safari hats with the chin straps, their excess sunscreen not rubbed in on their necks, their T-shirts tucked into their cargo hiking pants. None of it.

We drove on looking for a desolate patch of earth, free from anyone who did not know what it was like to cross Central Asian borders by car. Around 7 o'clock we located a field as good as any. We pushed a half mile or so into the grass and then stopped, with nary a tree to provide cover. (In fact, we hadn't seen more than five trees in the entire length of Mongolia.) There were small hills and some undulating mountains in the deep distance, but other than that, we were in open land that stretched as far as the eye could see. It was another jewel of pure nowhere in the country's vast stockpile of it.

Before we made dinner and set up camp I wanted to be rid of the image of those throngs hermetically sealed in their tour buses. I knew it wasn't about them personally or the diluted experience I wanted them to have in comparison to ours. It was as if I were a Native American preparing for a holy ceremony and suddenly noticed a Spanish galleon approaching offshore. Those tourists signaled that my Mongol Rally dream was coming to an end and soon we would be boarding the same kind of plane they flew on to get here. That spooked me. As much as I was ready for the finish line, I wasn't ready for it to be over.

I contemplated an act of defiance in the face of the bright white coach bus imprinted in my memory. I needed to shake our Mongol Rally snow globe one last time so I could frolic in that alternate universe, shielded from the realities on the other side of the glass.

In order to reset my vagabond self a final time, I slid a toilet paper roll over the handle of the camping shovel, placed it on my shoulder and walked with it over a small hill. I made sure I was out of sight of our convoy and the road before stepping out of my flip-flops, stripping completely naked and digging a hole to defecate in. Squatting bare-assed and looking over what seemed like all of Mongolia was one of the most liberating moments of my life. I giggled. I cried. I was in touch with both my inner animal and my soft human shell. Oddly, the view and the moment brought back the childhood memory of my dad telling me that the house I lived in was not mine, I was a guest for the time being. That's how I now felt about my place on the planet. I am a guest on this earth for the time being, trying to live a life worthy of the gift. I am not special. Nothing is "mine." But hot damn, I do have some stories to tell.

Back at camp, we took lots of group photos. We were euphoric in the knowledge that Ulaanbaatar was only one hundred and fifty miles away. We donned our hoodies, sat around the portable table the Brits had brought, ate our pasta dinners, and drank vodka and wine from our goblets of happiness. The only thing on our agenda was to enjoy one another's company one last, technology-free, uninterrupted time. It was a five-hour meal, marinated in a sense of accomplishment. The food was bland, we were dirty, our accommodations were as simple as they could be, but I laughed harder than I had in a long time and I talked about things that I never talked about, because these conversations had been unearthed, unwrapped, and unwound over a month on the road. That's what travel does. It exposes us like never before. When we peel away the facade, we find out how fragile we all are. Adventure reminds us we are all delicately connected with the earth and to everyone that calls it home.

Our last night living like latter-day barbarians in the unbounded frontier had to end at some point, but it wasn't rushed. With faces sore from laughter and blood infused with booze, the stars saluted us one more time. Goodnight, moon. Goodnight, Mongolia. Goodnight, rally.

God...that night was magical. I think about it often, maybe more than I should. It's a moment that was earned, but whose place on our map was never planned. Life moves on, and I can't live in the Mongolian outback forever, but I can keep certain memories and I can hope that those moments push my needle a few notches towards where I want to be: a little kinder, a little more selfless, a little more aligned. A little more Gandhi and a little less Ayn Rand. Maybe the potholes shook the sediment at the bottom of my being, but whatever it was, I was different than I had been thirty-one days ago. Way different? Hard to say, but this felt like a molded ball of clay change, not just an elongated rubber band that would snap back once I got home. When I began the rally I was running dangerously close to giving too much of a shit what random people thought about me, my business, and my place in the world. And now, the less I had to connect with people who weren't physically there, the more I connected with people who actually were. The less I worried what other people thought, the more I was able to think about what I wanted. Life isn't my Instagram photos, Twitter updates, or blog posts; it's what happens in between them. The only thing that ends up mattering in life are the people directly in front of my face and the eighteen or so people who really give a shit about me.

The rest is chasing ghosts.

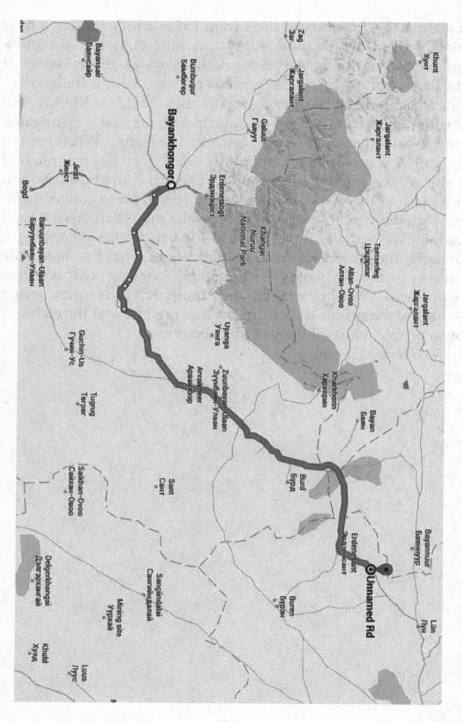

Day 32

We awoke in a haze, Chinggis Vodka seeping from our pores. Being good citizens of the planet, we packed all our garbage from the previous night. A few miles down the road we saw a trash can at the outcropping of three random buildings in the middle of nowhere. What started as dumping our waste turned into us getting rid of the things that we no longer needed: chairs, mats, broken thingamajigs, whatever. After we had filled the trash can we continued piling tchotchkes next to it. Before we knew it, men, women, and a really shady 6-foot 3-inch guy with a cowboy hat, trench coat, and an eyepatch came out of the buildings to claim their new treasures.

The natives were overjoyed with the camping chairs, utensils, and the rest. What they would do with a U.S.-pronged tent fan is beyond me but it was a hot commodity. And as is the custom in this part of the world, if you want to say thanks for something, you offer vodka. No matter if it is 9 a.m. and we had been guzzling the same damn swill nine hours earlier. "No" was not an acceptable answer, so we all assumed the position and threw back a giant swig of Chinggis Vodka. Jason, who was driving Yolo Polo, said to me, "Mate, I'm half in the bag now because of that."

Tipsy, we bid goodbye to our Mongolian friends. All of this seemed somewhat normal now. The road changes your baseline of wow. We had one more stop, though, one last adventure before we hit the city center. *Lonely Planet* had mentioned an old military installation in the middle of nowhere where one could drive tanks, fire guns, and launch rocket-propelled grenades. It sounded like a scene from a Japanese reality television show.

We had loose directions to our West Point-style amusement park, but we didn't know exactly what we were looking for and we didn't know if it was advertised in any way. Instead of guessing,

Jason and Scott asked around at the first market we passed. After a minute, Scott bolted towards us like gunfire had broken out. I'm not sure what this says about Scott since he left Jason in the store by himself, and I don't know what it says about the rest of us who remained glued to our seats hoping that we wouldn't be called to defensive action this close to Ulaanbaatar.

It turns out that Scott wasn't running from danger, he was running from generosity. He and Jason had gotten the directions they needed, but the owners of the store also wanted to share good cheer and offer up these two foreigners some liquid gratitude. Solo now, Jason had to drink what was, in his words, "a glass of vodka." When he got back to the car, his glazed eyes and unprovoked grin told us that he should cede control of the wheel for the rest of the day.

Intoxicating hospitality behind us, we had our directions, although like the gas crater in Turkmenistan, nothing was clear. We had kind-of-sort-ofs, more-or-lesses, and swinging arms for road crossings. When we reached a turnoff that was within the gestured facts and distances ascertained earlier, we found ourselves back on an untended dirt road leading to a mountain pass. Specifically, the kind of terrain we swore off once we reached Bayankhongor.

Now in another valley, and after forty-five minutes (!) of encouraging Donata to be a mountain goat, we reached some kind of military installation. That giant field of freewheeling tanks firing rounds into the mountainside was nowhere to be seen.

We asked a Mongolian soldier in full military attire where we could fire guns and drive tanks and he looked at us like we had just insulted his mother. He informed us in perfect English that this kind of thing was not allowed under any circumstances whatsoever.

This didn't seem like a negotiation.

We must have been high on Mongol Rallyness.

Tails between our legs, we headed back to the main road, worried we might break down in the searing heat without a tank story to show for it. Miraculously, we reached the apex of the canyon wall, apologized to a frustrated Donata, and crept back down to the main highway. Next stop: Ulaanbaatar.

***

Traffic thickened even though a lane had been added in our direction of travel. Suddenly, the smoggy veil surrounding the city center revealed itself over the horizon like an approaching ship.

We're actually going to make it!

We had heard that it can take an hour or two to get anywhere within the sprawling city, which houses half of the Mongolian population (1.4 million out of the 2.8 million), but before we could marvel at finishing this crazy odyssey, we saw a giant sign for the Mongol Rally Graveyard.

Huh? We're here already?

It was as if someone screamed "Surprise!" before the guest of honor had a chance to walk through the door. We actually drove past the sign and had to U-turn to enter the holding area where Donata's journey would officially end. I was disoriented—a soldier knocked off my feet by a nearby blast, tinnitus ringing in my ears. Everything moved in slow motion.

Wait...we did it?

Immediately, my thoughts went to Donata. Her tires were making some of the last rotations that they ever would. It was like walking a pet cow through the gates of an abattoir. She had no idea what was happening. Inside the walled-in scrapyard, we became reacquainted with some cars we had seen along the way, happy that those teams had made it through. Who knew how many stories those dirt-blasted relics could tell?

We took a bunch of photos with one another and our cars on the finish-line stage that The Adventurists had made, but it wasn't very ceremonial. There was no parade, no applause, no TV interviews, no ticker tape, and no key to the city. It was two

Mongol Rally volunteers telling the nine of us the formalities for transferring the titles of our vehicles.

Jesus Christ, man! Have some respect. Donata's body isn't even cold yet.

The closest we came to being anointed was when two Mongolian women dressed in traditional garb came out of the central tent and presented us with a cup of warm, fermented mare's milk. That was the only homage we received.

Here, here, Marco Polover.

It all made sense, though. We hadn't done anything globally vital over the previous thirty-two days. This journey was personal, and so was the celebration.

We were directed to Donata's final parking place

Wheels stopped. Ignition off. E-brake engaged. Fourteen million tire rotations, 9,126 miles. Thirty-two days. Nineteen countries. Mission complete.

We unloaded the chocolate-stained everything and dust-covered whatnots from Donata. To be honest, saying goodbye to this car was an emotional experience. She was our conduit of conversation between cultures. She brought us to human histories and lifestyles that shattered our warped definitions of "normal" or "typical," while simultaneously displaying the world at such an intimate level that the lines between "us" and "them" will forever be blurred. She taught us that all anyone wants to hear is "Cool" and "Thanks" and "I love you."

Our beloved had crossed a third of the Earth on thirteen-inch wheels, overloaded by four hundred pounds, propelled by 42 horsepower. We never gave her an oil change and all she had to say about it was to be a little hoarse when we asked her to go—her plastic rims, her funky smell, and the empty bags of chips and extra water bottles rolling around on her floor. Greg and Brooke got to keep the license plates and I removed the mud-spattered silver plastic "D" emblem from the front of the Daihatsu. Donata. Dignitary. Divinity.

It now hangs framed on a wall in my home.

The volunteers arranged a van and hotel booking for us, and without time to prepare, we found ourselves in a strange vehicle in bumper-to-bumper traffic. Familiar names and sights passed by our overstimulated gazes: Skyscrapers, Levi's, McDonald's, business suits, electronic stores, hospitals, taxis, and everyday life. It was unsettling to be finished. We were separated from our car, knowing that what we went through over the past month had become memory. No longer *on* the Mongol Rally and not yet back in the States, we were stuck in an experiential no-man's-land.

Ulaanbaatar, the "home" I had been so obsessed with reaching for weeks and months on end, felt like a halfway house. It was as fitting a time as any for a Hemingway quote: "It is good to have an end to a journey toward; but it is the journey that matters, in the end." The road was home. Donata was home. Tasting that *laghman* soup was home. A passport stamp was home. Being pulled over by the cops was home. The tyrannical heat was home. Annette, Emin, Alexi, Artur, and Nik were home. Even Ishmael was home. Ulaanbaatar was only the destination.

Paper-thin. Razor-sharp.

***

Our hotel was functional. It reminded me of the one in Almaty, Kazakhstan. Greg and I shared a room while Brooke had her own. The shower I took caused me to audibly exhale in joy. Warm water, soap, shampoo, and masturbation...*yes*.

After a meetup at the Mongol Rally HQ to officially put our names on the finishers' wall and get our certificates of completion, we made our way to Hazara for curry. It was fine dining by any standard, really. Like a kid who had missed Christmas for five years in a row, I thought Will was going to pass out in anticipation. We ordered like kings but ate like birds. Our stomachs had shrunk so much on the trip (I had lost seventeen pounds) that we were full after the appetizers. When the main dishes arrived we took photos of the impossible abundance. An hour later, Will sat unable to move and barely able to breathe. He had yet to taste my curry, so cupped in a spoon at the end of my outstretched arm I presented him with one of the last bites, both out of thanks and out of my own state of glut. He said that there was no way on earth he could. I said, "For a week you've been talking about this place, making us salivate, making us yearn, and now you're going to sit here and turn down a gulp of the sweet nectar?"

His pleading eyes gave way to concession. He put the spoonful of rice and chicken in his mouth, moaned at the flavor, moaned at being stuffed, and moaned because dinner and everything else were over.

We mingled at a bar with other ralliers who had finished, but I didn't want to talk to any of them. Their stories weren't ours. My story and my immediate family were Brooke and Greg. Scott, Anna, Jason, Will, Garreth, and Vicky were my extended family. We did, however, see friendly faces that we didn't expect. Jorge and Ozvaldo, the Spanish friends who had been turned away at the Uzbek border because of the misdated visa, had arrived in Ulaanbaatar the day we did! I couldn't believe my eyes.

We walked around the city for a bit, but everyone was in a daze. It was the first night in almost five weeks when we didn't have a purposeful tomorrow. I don't think anyone really knew what was happening or what we were supposed to be feeling. When we returned to the hotel, the finality of it all was shocking. The nine of us stood around in the foyer staring at each other, circling the drain and delaying the inevitable.

Greg and I were booked on a 6 a.m. flight to San Francisco and were the first of the group to break the spell. We had to say goodbye to the adventure. We had to say goodbye to our Mongolian convoy. We had to say goodbye to Brooke—our teammate, our sister, and our companion across the Earth. I didn't hug her—I enveloped her. As long as I didn't let go, I could fend off the finale. As long as I clung to her, we were still Marco Polover, we were still wide-eyed in London, unsure of the experiences about to unfold, the ones that eventually and undeniably changed us forever.

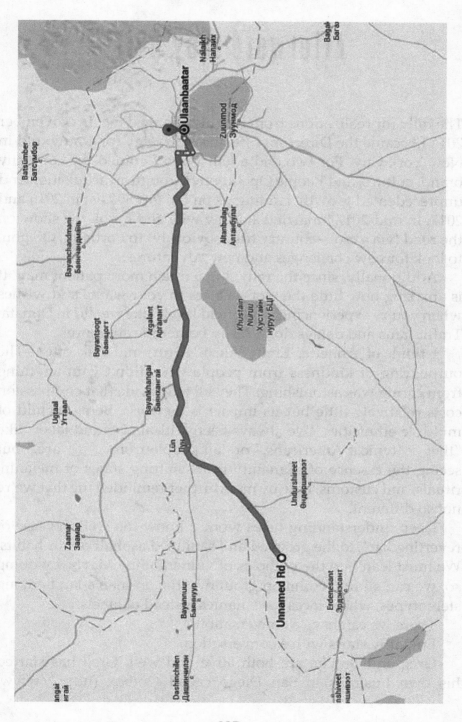

Afterword (Day 991)

The rally (or realizations from it) truly changed me. In November 2014 I became the Director of Business Strategy for Omnibuild in New York City. For two and a half years I guided the company brand, culture, and People Operations through an acquisition and unprecedented growth, landing us on the *Inc. 500* list in 2016 and 2017. In mid-2017 I married and my wife and I took the show on the road (via a cross-country trip, obviously) to Portland, Oregon, to look for new challenges and new adventures.

Additionally, since the rally, I'm a much more patient man. It is amazing how little the world caters to your wants and wishes when you're experiencing it on "field level" like we did in Donata. Traffic jams and delays don't really bother me anymore.

I think of Annette, Emin, Alexi, Artur, and Nik often. The outpouring of kindness from people who didn't gain anything from caring was astonishing. They all taught me that compassion costs relatively little but its impact is meteoric. Being a child of multiple ethnicities, I've always been critical of grand labels like "they," "typical Americans," or "all people from _____ are," but seeing the essence of humanity in its shifting states of melanin, rituals, and customs, mile by mile, further reminded me that we're not so different.

Deep understanding takes work. I know too well the ease of reverting back to the grooved and sanitized asphalt of our habits. We must lean into the potholes of vulnerability. Maybe by doing so, we can all find common ground in the no-man's-land among stereotypes, where faces have names instead of labels.

There we can have a conversation.

Empathy starts with a conversation.

Greg and Brooke are both alive and well. Greg has started his own business in San Diego called Ootbox (http://www.

thinkootbox.com/) and Brooke is now Tony Robbins's personal assistant. Flying around with rich people does have its perks, it seems.

I'm still traveling as much as I can, whenever I can, engaging with the planet at its most unforgiving or its most nourishing. I've reached all seven continents and have touched seventy-two countries. If my heavyweight dreams come true, this curiosity will take me into outer space one day. Views from the drone were a start but I would give anything to see the Earth with my own eyes from beyond the Earth. NASA, Elon Musk, heads up, I'm coming with you to Mars. Hold a spot for me.

Whatever our reasons for travel and no matter how many miles from home we venture, all our journeys are worthwhile. Trips are temporary, but exploration is a mind-set. Being interested is our duty. Being interesting is our choice. Don't let the biggest thing on your bucket list be the number of its uncrossed items.

We have but one chance to check out the planet that cradles us. So go out, go forth, go once more into the breach, and do something your seventy-five-year-old self will thank you for. Because when we're old and gray, we'll smile fondly about the stories we have to tell, and those around us will smile because we're the one telling them.

I hope to see you somewhere out on the open road, straddling the paper-thin but razor-sharp divide between passports and borders, between curiosity and understanding, between strangers and friends, between us and them.

The Entire Journey

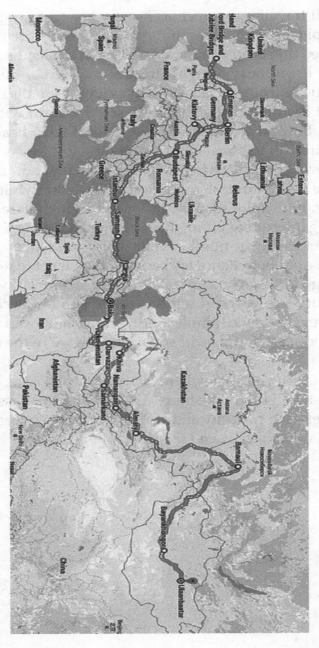

Acknowledgments

Like a good acceptance speech, I could thank individual friends and family members until the music comes on, but I'll keep this laser-focused. If it hadn't been for two people in particular, this book would have been a shell of its current self, a broken jukebox replaying the same five songs. With their help, I added color, depth, and whole new genres of literary "music." I'll never be able to thank them enough, so this will have to do for now.

Antonio Neves (www.theantonioneves.com) is a dear friend and confidant who read an early version of the book and unapologetically and directly said to me over the phone, "It's good, but it's not great. I want you to make this great. You know you're a good writer, now let's try to make you a great writer. I challenge you to hire an editor, hire a pro who will dissect your work from a vantage point you've never been to." I followed his orders, thankfully.

This leads me to Alice Peck, my editor (alicepeckeditorial.com). I didn't know it was possible for so much red ink to fit on a page. Alice not only dismantled my words, sentences, and punctuation but she helped weave the pace and arc of what you just read. Each time I submitted a new draft, I thought I was finally done, but undoubtedly, Alice would challenge me to be better, write smoother, go further. At some points I cried looking at her crimson strewn notes, because I didn't think I could hack through the verbal weeds one more time. I wanted it to end. But Alice wouldn't let me. She gently pushed until we got to where we needed to be. If you enjoyed this book at all, it is because Alice was riding shotgun with me through the literary journey of rough draft to final manuscript.

And thanks to the Post Hill Press team of Anthony Ziccardi, Michael Wilson, Debra Englander, Devon Brown, Billie Brownell, Alana Mills, and Sarah Heneghan.

About the Author

American born Bassam Tarazi is half Palestinian and half Dutch. He is the founder of Colipera, a motivational blog, and an author, speaker, and international traveler. A wanderer at heart, Tarazi co-founded the Nomading Film Festival, has traveled to 7 continents and 72 countries, and is always looking for his next adventure. When he's not traveling or consulting, he's enjoying time with his wife in Portland, OR. Connect with him at bassam.com.